BETRAYAL ON MT. PARNASSUS

BETRAYAL ON MOUNT PARNASSUS

by
William E. Drake

Philosophical Library
New York

All of the characters presented in this novel are fictitious. Any resemblance to any person, living or dead, is coincidental.

This is not a "left" or "right" book. The basic roots of its meaning and value are of the essence of our cultural heritage.

Library of Congress Cataloging in Publication Data

Drake, William E. (William Earle)
  Betrayal on Mount Parnassus.

  I. Title.
PS3507.R414B4 1983   813'.54   82-24582
ISBN 0-8022-2416-4

Copyright, 1983, by Philosophical Library, Inc.
200 West 57th Street, New York, N.Y. 10019.

All rights reserved.

Manufactured in the United States of America.

DEDICATION

To my former graduate students whose faith and confidence in me as a teacher was a source of inspiration in writing this book.

AFFIRMATION

"There is no absolute knowledge. And those who claim it, whether they are scientists or dogmatists, open tho door to tragedy. All information is imperfect. We have to treat it with humility." - Bronowski, J., *The Ascent of Man*, Boston, Little, Brown and Company, 1973, pages 436-437.

President A. Bartlett Giamatti, Yale University, Connecticut, speaking to the graduating class, June, 1981:

What concerns me most today is the way we have disconnected ideas from power in America and created for ourselves thoughtful citizens who disdain politics and politicians when more than ever we need to value politics and what politicians do....

Christopher Booker, Author of *The Seventies* (Penguin, London), writing in the *Daily Telegraph of London* (Nov. 1, 1980), had this to say about a faltering America:

> From the very beginning it was believed that the New World across the Atlantic was going to be the place which would compensate for the imperfections of our own oppressive, poor, unjust societies .... America was the place of freedom ... more than any other country on earth, the way forward for the human race .... We suddenly no longer have faith in that as a way forward for the human race. We know that a complete rethink is required, a complete change of perspective on what man and life is all about.

On June 18, 1940, Walter Lippmann, while speaking before his classmates at their thirtieth reunion dinner, Cambridge, Massachusetts, spoke of a condition which he saw prevailing in the United States, but which seems to be even more true today:

> We here in America may soon be the last stronghold of our civilization. Organized mechanized evil has been turned lose in the world because of our lazy, self-indulgent materialism, the amiable lackadaisical, footless, confused complacency of those most responsible for the welfare of our country.

TABLE OF CONTENTS

Preface XIII

I. The College Professor as a Thing 1

II. A Program of Free Public Education 41

III. Higher Education in a Free Society 85

IV. The Rape of Science as a Way of Life............. 125

V. The Politics of Power in a Free Society............ 165

VI. Leadership in the Culture Process 201

VII. Commercialized Athletics: A Cancer in the Body Politic of the University....................... 237

VIII. Epilogue..................................... 273

Addenda 309

PREFACE

Our nation is in deep trouble because of the schizophrenic nature of the culture in which we live. On the one hand, because of advancements in the area of the physical sciences, we place men on the moon and send instruments millions of miles, which take close-up pictures of the planets Mars and Saturn; whereas, on the other hand, in terms of our meaning and value frame of reference, we confine ourselves to the mental and religious outlook which dominated the western world all during the period of the Middle Ages. In this respect, we fail to understand that our world of culture is vertical as well as horizontal, and that it occupies both space and time. Because of our ignorance of history, we are ignorant of the fact that the naturalistic tendencies of the ancient Greeks were lost in the wake of the rise of Neo-Plantonism, which dominated the Western world after the passing of the Periclean Age of Socrates, Plato, and Aristotle. In terms of a meaning and value frame of reference, those who provide the thoughts and knowledge of our physical world, we call physical scientists; whereas those who provide the thoughts and beliefs of our world of human relations occupy the pulpits of the hundreds of churches in our cities and counties throughout our country.

The complexity of the problem which we now face calls for a quality of mind in the field of human relations, which we do not have anywhere in the world. We continue to utilize the products of the mind of the physicist, but WE REJECT THE INTELLECTUAL NATURE OF THE SCIENTIFIC MIND. Note how a leading spokesman, in the field of religious thought, speaks of talking to a 900-feet-tall Jesus, and, in return, receives more than $5,000,000 in gifts from a believing public. At the same time, others of a similar mind (politicians), exploit an ignorant public of millions of dollars in their lust for power.

Because of the nature of our free society, if we are going to cope with the demands of our present-day human relations, the meaning and value frame of reference in our state universities must become culture centered, and not continue to be academically neutral. Church schools, in keeping with their allegiance to a traditional theological dogma, will continue to be fundamentally different. Since meaning and value are a derivative of culture, our continuing reliance upon the Christian-Jewish cultural pattern has created a situation where life in an urbanized society has been reduced to a fruitless search for those things which give satisfaction only at the animal level of existence. Also, it must be kept in mind that the core of Christian theology is escapist and otherworldly, and centers primarily on a doctrine of personal salvation. The effect of this type of indoctrination, in so far as the growth of the creative mind is concerned, has been deadly and tragic.

It was during the period of the seventeenth century that there was an agreement between the Christian Church leadership and the physical scientists that each would confine themselves to their own area of operation and significance. The physical scientists would delve only into those matters concerning the physical world, while the leaders of the Christian faith would limit their doctrinal claims to matters social and spiritual. While this division of thought and action laid the groundwork for the Industrial revolution, it, at the same time, stifled the growth and evolution of the human mind. As a result, the intellectual world of Western culture was divided into two realms of thought and action which, in time, produced our schizophrenic culture.

Out of this schizophrenic culture, beginning with the eighteenth century, there have come three major revolts against Orthodox Christianity; (a) that revolt involved in the thinking of those who laid the ground work for the American Revolution; (b) that revolt which brought about the rise of Marxist Communism; and (c) that revolt which led to the rise of Adolph Hilter and Benito Mussolini, Philosophical Nihilism.

Leaders of the American Revolution, who sought to restore a unified sense of cultural reality, held that the ethics of the Christian Faith could only be achieved by adopting a scientific approach to man's social and spiritual nature as well as to his physical world. As Deists and Free Masons, both Benjamin Franklin and Thomas Jefferson sought to substitute the idea of a search for God in Nature for the Christian medieval God of miracles and mystical reality. To achieve their end and purpose, they promoted the establishment of a state university which, all during the nineteenth century, was attacked by Orthodox Christians as an atheistic and godless institution. It was a betrayal of their hopes and faith, by those who have been responsible for the operation of these state universities, that has led to our growing sense of cultural and economic chaos in the Western world. While the colleges of education in our state universities lay claim to promoting a science of education, in truth, they promote only a scientific method in the teaching of the subject matters of the college of arts and sciences.

The failure of the Western world to follow through with the basic conceptions of reality held by the leaders of the American Revolution has had much to do with the rising power of communism and the establishment of a theology of science in the U.S.S.R. If the scientific approach to a resolution of the problems of the human race could not be achieved by democratic methods (witness what happened in the nation of Chile when President Allende was murdered), then such would be achieved by revolutionary and dogmatic means. The ethical principles, implicit in the Jewish Christian tradition, would be achieved by centralized authority exercised through the instrument of the Communist Party. So said Nikolai Lenin, with the overthrowing of the brutal Czarist Romanov Family. The Communist Party had rejected the religion of Orthodox Christianity, but, in doing so, had replaced the scientific humanism of Jefferson, Franklin, and Paine with a mechanistic, materialist frame of reference on the nature of reality.

The Western world, with its continuing schizophrenic culture, has not only spawned the new theology of Communism, but, with the coming of the twentieth century, has given rise to a third revolt against Orthodox Christianity, which is bent on wiping out all the ethical gains made in the last 2000 years. This revolt has been identified as PHILOSOPHICAL NIHILISM. While the organized political form of Nihilism, known as Nazism or Fascism, was put down by the military power of the Allied Nations, it has survived in guerrilla form to wreak violence and terror throughout the western world.

In Philosophical Nihilism, the politics of power and power alone define the nature of truth, goodness, and beauty. "War is to man what maternity is to woman," said Mussolini. To Adolph Hitler, Christianity was a feminine breed, weak and sissy, the kind of religion that divided the German people. He would unify his people by returning them to the Pagan Gods of Siegfried and Thor, to the warrior soldier and a unified God State. In essence, the physical sciences, which, in the mind of those who led the American Revolution, held out so much hope for the betterment of mankind, had now become a means for the destruction of the human race, a SCIENCE OF DEATH. Instead of doing away with the four horsemen of the Apocalypse, the sorrows and tragedies of war, hunger, famine, and disease, the physical sciences had been turned into an instrument of death. The United States, having failed to provide a quality leadership for the world, was now selling these weapons of death around the world, hoping to use them as a means of stopping the spread of Communism. Unfortunately, there seems to be no leadership in our Nation, or around the world, which can explain the nature of this new world to us, men or women with a vision that projects us into the progressive free world of the future.

A democratic philosophy of education should be at the heart of the public school program, from the kindergarten through the graduate school of the state university. In a fundamental sense, we are not talking about a subject taught on the periphery of the program at any grade-school level, or in the university. What is needed is a commitment, on the part of all school administrators and teachers, to a meaning and value frame of reference consistent with the purpose and aspirations of our Revolutionary Fathers. Such a commitment should include an analysis of the three most significant areas which make up the substance of the cultural conflicts found throughout the world of today, and the differences arising from these conflicts. These areas have been classified as (a) the nature of the universe, (b) the nature of man, and (c) the nature of social reality.

Since the beginning of historical man, three patterns concerning the origin of mind are clearly apparent in the evolution of a meaning and value frame of reference: (a) the Man-God Relation; (b) the Man-Object Relation; and (c) the Man-Man Relation. Today, we as a people are still dominated mentally by the medieval Man-God Relation, but we actually worship at the shrine of the golden calf. In so far as a frame of reference is concerned, we have no cultural Man-Man Relation that is grounded in the physical, biological, and social sciences, though we constantly mouth the words Democracy and Freedom.

We now turn to the substantive nature of this novel. This is the story of a man who from early adolescence began to wrestle with the problem of meaning and value in his life, and whether or not our culture was truly democratic in our everyday human relations. The contradiction which was most glaringly evident to him in those early years of his life was not so much a matter of knowledge, as it was of how cultural practices affected him personally. If Jesus really loved him, as they said he did, and if every growing child had an equal opportunity to be successful in life, why was life so hard on him?

If God really loved Jesus, why did He have him crucified? Why was it said that if a child died, God had taken the little one away to punish the parent for wrongdoing?

Because his father had left him an orphan when he was only two years of age, it was necessary for Ron Jervis, at the age of thirteen years, to go to work to take care of his mother and himself. At first, it was during the summer months in a furniture factory, and then, during his last three years in high school, in a Greek Restaurant. All of this was necessary in order for him to continue his education. Going to school in the morning hours, and working from twelve noon until ten o'clock at night, during the weekdays from Monday through Friday, and then sixteen hours a day on Saturdays and Sundays, was a hardship to which he thought no young boy should be subjected.

It was while taking courses in Biology and American History that the intellectual challenge to a growing mind presented itself. How could so many people believe that what was nothing more than primitive Jewish culture was the word of God? How could a virgin girl give birth to a baby boy? Why did the leaders of the Christian Church order the death of those early scientists Bruno and Servetus, and persecute other scientists such as Copernicus and Galileo? Jesus was a noble character, but why did they turn him into a God? If the *Bible* was correct in holding that we should seek the truth for the truth would make us free, why were Christians so opposed to the advancement of knowledge? If Christians were so supportive of the idea of peace in the world, why were they involved in so many wars? Why have Christians been so adamant in opposing Charles Darwin's THE ORIGIN OF SPECIES when there was so much evidence to support his conclusions? It must be that Christians base their beliefs on a culture that prevailed more than 2000 years ago, and accept only that knowledge which tends to support their beliefs. As for Ron Jervis, he would seek knowledge first, and then base whatever he believed in that knowledge.

Now what could Ron Jervis believe about the history of his country, about the founding of the Government of the United

States, about the Declaration of Independence? What did the men who founded this Nation believe about the nature of God, about the nature of man, and on what grounds? Ron Jervis noted with special interest that there was no statute for religious freedom in any one of the original thirteen colonies during the entire colonial period from 1607 to 1776, and that a statute for religious freedom was first proposed by Thomas Jefferson for Virginia in 1779. If the people of the United States really believed in what was written in the Declaration of Independence, and in the First Amendment of the Constitution of the United States, then somewhere along the line we had betrayed the Fathers of our Country with our present practices.

It was during his college years, at one of our state universities, that Ron Jervis first began to see in clearer light what had happened since the American Revolution that had led to a betrayal of the aspirations and hopes of those who had founded this Nation. Definitely there had been a failure to provide the leadership necessary for the development of a society of free men and women. That failure he believed could be traced primarily to the public school system and to the state universities. In his mind and in his efforts, Jefferson had combined The Statute for Religious Freedom in Virginia, and the founding of the University of Virginia, with the Declaration of Independence. If we were to have a free nation, we muct have the leadership which only the state university could provide. In his research, while a graduate student, Ron had learned that the first of the state universities, the Universtiy of North Carolina, was a child of the American Revolution, and that, at the time of its origin, it was thought of as THE SUN OF SCIENCE. Here was to be educated the leadership that would promote the new way of life in the new world. The state university was to be held responsible for providing leadership for the offices of government, local, state, and national.

Why the title of this biographical novel + BETRAYAL ON MT. PARNASSUS? Since ancient times Parnassus has been the name of the mountain on Phocis which lies near the Gulf of Corinth. Here, on the southern slope of this mountain, is the site of Castalia where the people of ancient Greece constructed their temple to the Delphic God Apollo. As the son of Zeus, Apollo came to represent, in the minds of the people, not only the God of Light and Purity, but the God of Ethical Character, of spiritual light, the source of all progress, intellectual, social, and political. What better and more appropriate title could be given to this novel, whose primary concern is how those who were responsible for the operation of the state university have betrayed those who were the fathers of its creation. In all of these respects we will leave it to the reader to determine why those who founded the state university adopted the shield of Apollo to symbolize their purpose in founding the new institution.

The following premises are of the essence on which this biographical novel was based and developed,

1. We have contributed and continue to contribute to the mess in which our world finds itself, and largely because of the lack of quality leadership in our government — local, state, and national.

2. Throughout the twentieth century we have operated as a Nation without any meaning and value frame of reference, which, as of today, is best pointed up in our various forms of commercialized entertainment.

3. Those who were primarily responsible for founding our Nation (Adams, Franklin, and Jefferson) were deeply aware of the challenge which freedom (in the scientific sense) presented to the Western world.

4. The human tragedies in which dogma in any form limits the development of the human mind are at the heart of the failure of government in the Western world for the past two thousand years.

5. By limiting the scientific movement to the development of the physical sciences we have created a schizophrenic culture in all the nations of the Western world.

6. To free the mind of man from the chains of dogma and to

provide for a unifying cultural pattern based upon philosophical naturalism ... mandatory if our Nation was to provide the leadership necessary for a free society.

(7). To achieve this new type of mind and leadership, the state university, as a child of the American Revolution, was brought into being.

(8). Failure to bring into reality the hopes of our Revolutionary Fathers produced the second major modern revolt against religious domatism, that of the dogma of scientific communism.

(9). The failure of Protestant Capitalism and U.S.S.R. Communism has led to a 20th century form of philosophical nihilism, namely Nazism, and Fascism, and the various forms of terrorist activities in today's world.

(10). Religious dogmas would continue to prevail in our country, but no longer in the halls of government by mandate of the First Amendment to the Federal Constitution.

(11). Now, with the nuclear bomb in the hands of a medieval mind, we are confronted with the possibility of an international holocaust.

(12). Failure of the state university to provide a quality leadership in our several professions, and especially in that of teaching, is a prime reason for the pronounced anti-intellectualism in our political life.

(13). Our simplified definition of DEMOCRACY AS MAJORITY RULE has contributed greatly to the cultivation of the adolescent mind in our adult population.

(14). Failure of the state university to give priority to a socially functional, scientific liberal education that is humanistic has been a dominant factor in the now pervasive concept that the individual is only a cog in a machine.

(15). It was the development of the biological sciences, following the publication of Darwin's ORIGIN OF SPECIES, that brought into meaningful significance the thinking of our Revolutionary Fathers.

(16). Whatever our problems may be (personal, domestic, or foreign) the scientific, creative, artistic mind will never run out on the human race.

As a final word, each chapter in this book spells out the way in which the state university has failed to carry out the mandate of its founders. The reasons for this failure are a significant part of each chapter.

William E. Drake
Austin, Texas

BETRAYAL ON MT. PARNASSUS

CHAPTER I

THE COLLEGE PROFESSOR AS A THING

It was one of those usual get-togethers that college professors hold in the early spring, along with their wives, in order to establish a more understanding relation with each other. In this particular occasion, Ron Jervis and his wife were visiting in the home of Jim Thomas, a well-liked and friendly man, who had served for many years as a Professor of French in this midwestern state university. There was the usual round of cocktails for the dozen or more people present, and, as Ron drank his scotch and soda, Jim Thomas approached him in the following manner.

"Well, Ron," said Jim Thomas, "now that you have been promoted to a full professorship, you will no longer need to concern yourself or get involved in all of these matters of a national or social nature. You can draw your salary, enjoy yourself, and take it easy."

It had taken Ron Jervis fourteen years of teaching in four state universities to achieve the level of a full professorship, and most of the time at a salary of less than $3000 a year, for this was during the period of the Great Depression of 1929. How could he, whose life had been so much involved in the problems of the General Welfare of his country, throw away the very nature of his being and become a person that he was not? So he replied to Jim Thomas in a very positive manner.

"No, Jim, while I fully understand your position, and that of many of our friends, I can no more disassociate myself from the human and personal problems that have bugged me most of my life, than I could take off this very day and land on the barren wastelands of the moon."

"Yes, Ron," said Jim, "I can appreciate what you are saying, but we must draw a clear cut line as professors between what we teach in the classroom and our personal beliefs. Our job is limited to the teaching of the facts and letting the student do his own thinking. We have no business injecting our beliefs into the jungle of social conflicts that exist in the outside world. Such involvement is not only bad in theory, but would interfere with the financial support of this university, by the state legislature, as well as by private donors."

"Well, Jim," said Ron, "I can see the possibility of jeopardizing the financial support of this university by taking a radical stand, such as that of the Communist on social and political policy, but I cannot agree with you that the only responsibility that I have as a professor is to teach a mass of facts. Facts to have meaning must be taught in some kind of relationship. The point of view which you express could be justified only if it were true that man is a rational animal by his nature. This point of view was held by the leaders of the American Revolution, but, ever since the publication of Charles Darwin's THE ORIGIN OF SPECIES, this assumption has been contradicted by scientific evidence."

"What you have to say, Ron, is all very intersting," said Jim Thomas, "and may be true, but, if I were to agree with you about man not being a rational animal by his nature, I would still feel responsible to teach the facts to my students if they are to learn the French Language. As to what use he or she makes of his or her knowledge of French is none of my business. In this respect, I am sure that the great majority of my colleagues in the college of Arts and Sciences agree with me."

"Of what you are saying, Jim," said Ron, "I am well aware, but it may be that the very point of view which you are expressing has something to do with the Board of Regents idea that college professors are as interchangeable as common bricks, hired hands, if you please, to be fired as common laborers were always fired until they organized themselves into a union. How is it possible for us to teach as free professionals if we are always under the threat of being discarded because we are no longer suited to the master's purpose? It so happens Jim that I take very seriously the meaning of the title PROFESSOR."

At this point, and before Jim could make a reply to Ron Jervis, his wife approaced them, and, seeing both Ron and her husband engaged in serious conversation, commented in a frivolous manner, "You fellows, this is no place or time for academic discussion. What about, I do not know, but I do know that both of you need to get into the swing of things, and not separate yourselves from the rest of the party."

Following these remarks, Jim and Ron acquiesed to the pressure of Jim's wife, and moved over to where several members of the party were engaged in a free-for-all about a report on the conduct of one of Ron's college associates. The professor in question, although having a wife and seven children, had been caught under a bridge, near the campus, in a compromising position with one of the female faculty members. The matter was supposed to have been kept quiet by the police authorities, but, like other matters on the campus, it was too titillating to be kept quiet. On this particular occasion, it was one of the female members of the Mathematics Department that had brought the matter up.

"Ron Jervis, as I recall," said Miss Jackson, "Professor Sterling offices with you. Since he is one of the stooges of the administration, it is my guess that his free-lancing conduct will be ignored, but not .... my female associate. She will be pressured to resign her position and will do so quietly. Talk about justice, nothing could be farther from the truth. When are we going to be treated as equals regardless of sex?"

"Miss Jackson," replied Ron Jervis, "I agree with all that you have said. Our entire culture is filled with discrimination and hypocrisy. We like to utter beautiful words about freedom and democracy, but when it comes down to real cases, such as the one you have mentioned, vested interests take over. Professor Sterling, as I know him, is a decent man, but he does have a weakness for young women. Because of the charges which have been levied against him by other members of your sex, I have been moved out of his office. Also, a glass window has been placed in the door leading into his office. It is because of his attitude toward the Negro race problem that I am under the most severe criticism."

"I suppose that you would say, Professor Jervis," said Miss Jackson, "that this is another example of our blatant hypocrisy about freedom and democracy, but I don't see it that way. Black people would much prefer to have their own university; and, in this respect, the state has done well by them. Since I am a native of the South, I see no reason why a black student should have the right to attend this universtiy."

At this point, all of those in attendance at the party joined in the discussion. Most of them tended to play down opinions on the matter of Negro students attending the university, and favored letting the university administration handle the problem. They would assert their right to teach according to their professional privileges, but, in so far as speaking out in public on controversial social issues, they would keep quiet. As for Ron Jervis, that would be impossible. For him the matter was not one to be resolved by academic discussion. The concepts of freedom and equality were so much a part of his being that it was impossible for him to conduct himself in a hypocritical manner. What was important, however, was that he not make a fool of himself. Progress, either for himself or his country, would not come from his making a fool of himself, or acting like a fanatic. The means, that is his conduct, should correlate with the ends which he sought. Thus he would always try to act with wisdom and forethought, and not give the administration a chance to fire him. As for the party, the discussion of the evening now shifted to that which was trivial in nature, especially as the cocktails began to have their effect upon the brain. When the time came for the group to break up, everyone was in a jovial mood. The party had indeed been a happy occasion for all of those present.

Ron Jervis, since the days of his youth, had held firmly to the belief that the Bill of Rights of the Federal Constitution guaranteed every citizen equality of education opportunity, and it was this belief that got him into trouble with the university administration. The issue, over the right of black students to attend the university, was soon to come up before the United States Supreme Court, and, while Ron Jervis was deliberately taking sides, he was doing so quietly and with good pragmatic sense. The occasion which brought the issue to a head in his case was his agreement to speak on the subject of "Equal Educational Opportunity for the Negro in the Southern States." The meeting was to be held on a Sunday afternoon, and was open to the public. Fortunately or unfortunately for Ron Jervis, he had come down with a case of the flu in the morning before the meeting, and had found it necessary to get a graduate student to take his place. This, however, did not keep the Secretary of the Board of Regents from calling him at his home about what he was going to say.

"Professor Jervis," inquired Jesse Rowan, "I understand that you are to speak on the subject 'The Higher Education of the Negro in the South' this afternoon. Since I will not find it possible to attend the meeting, I am curious as to what you intend to say."

"Well, Mr Rowan," replied Ron Jervis, "since this is a free country, I did not hesitate to speak on the subject when I was asked to do so. I find it difficult to understand why you, or any member of the Board should be opposed to members of the faculty speaking out on this or any other subject of interest to the people of this state. What I had intended to say, if I had not come down with the flu, and was forced to have a graduate student take my place, was that, in my judgment, we, in forbidding Black students to enter this university, were not only violating the purpose for which the state university was created, but that this separation policy is in conflict with the Bill of Rights of the Constitution of the United States."

"What you are saying, Professor Jervis, may be well and true," replied Jesse Rowan, "but the people of this state have mandated through their Constitution that Black students not be admitted to this University, and it is the obligation of the Board of Regents to carry out that mandate. As a university professor you have no right to take a contrary position, since, when you speak out in public, anyone hearing you will think that you are speaking for the university administration."

"Under no condition," replied Ron Jervis, "would I attempt to speak for the university administration. I do have the right, however, to speak as a free citizen on any subject of public interest, and will continue to do so, but always with discretion."

"That may be well and good," replied Jesse Rowan, "but you must remember that you are the hired hand of this administration, and that as such, you are as interchangeable as a brick."

At this point the conversation broke off, but this was not the end of the matter for, on the very next day, Ron received a letter from his Dean stating that the Board of Regents would not tolerate any interference on the part of any faculty member with board policy, and especially on the issue of the Black race. At this point Ron Jervis sat down and addressed the following letter to his Dean.

Dear Dean Winters:

It must be that you have been talking to Secretary Rowan about my point of view on the subject of the right of Black students attending this university, else you would not have taken the time to write me a three-page letter on the subject. May I say, and say very positively, that I have no intention of interfering with the Board's policy on this or any other matter. I do hold, however, that, as a free citizen, I have the right to express an opinion on this or any other matter of general public interest.

Speaking quite frankly, I find it hard to understand why the university administration is so dogmatic on this issue, when the substance of this controversy is not whether the university is to admit Black Students, but whether or not the Constitution of this state is to be changed. You know, as well as I do, that in due time the issue will be resolved by a decision of the Supreme Court of the United States. If you deem it necessary to discuss this matter further, I will be most happy to have a conference with you.

                                              Cordially
                                              Ron Jervis

Dean Theodore Winters was a reasonably mature, well-educated man. He had received his doctorate from Columbia University, and, while he had majored in the field of Educational Psychology, he had, at the same time, devoted himself to a study of the Philosophy of John Dewey. It was he, more than any one else, who was responsible for Ron Jervis's coming to the University. He had been especially impressed by Ron's graduate adviser telling him that Ron "would not burn his buildings down." They had gotten along well up to this time, but Ron had observed that the Dean had a weakness to bend when pressure was put on him by the President of the University or the Board of Regents. On this particular occasion, after receiving Ron's letter, he had called him in for a conference. Ron had accepted the offer immediately, and so, on the following day found himself sitting in the Dean's office.

"Ron," said Dean Winters, "you know that when I brought you here I was of the opinion that you were a young man of great promise, and I still believe so, even to the point of recommending you for the Deanship when I retire, which will be in the not too distant future. Now, I don't want to get at cross purposes with the administration, for we are bound to lose out if you do."

"Dean Winters," replied Ron Jervis, "I want you to know, as I have said on previous occasions, how much I appreciate your interest in my welfare. My true nature, as you must know by now, is a firm commitment to the democratic concept of individual freedom; and, in keeping with this basic concept, I try to treat others with the respect that is due them. What puzzles me about your letter is that you seem to have succumbed to a mess of distorted propaganda handed out by the Secretary of the Board of Regents. Believe me, I have no desire to stick my neck out, and get my head chopped off in a power struggle; but how can this state University live up to its responsibility if it violates the central purpose for which it was created?"

"Ron," said Dean, "I fully agree with you in principle, but the University is under terrific political pressure. Now that the issue of the admission of Black students here is up before the United States Supreme Court, the administration will not tolerate any interference with its present policy."

"Speaking quite frankly, Dean Winters," said Ron Jervis, "I cannot see how an open public discussion on the problem of 'Higher Education of the Negro in the South' can be interpreted as interference with the policy of the Board of Regents. As a matter of fact, Secretary Rowan called me last Sunday morning, before the meeting was to be held in the afternoon, to find out what I had planned to say. I informed him, at that time, that I was sick in bed with the flu and would not be able to speak. I told him, however, that what was to be discussed was, in no way, to be an attack on the Board of Regents policy, but rather a discussion of the issues with which all of us should be concerned."

"Are you saying, Ron," asked the Dean, "that you did not even get to attend the meeting? That is not the way it was presented to me. It would seem that what we have here is that a man, in a major position of authority in this University has completely misrepresented the facts of a situation in order to undermine the character of a member of this faculty. What we have here is a man who thinks of the university as nothing more than buildings and grounds, an institutional structure without flesh or feeling."

"Yes, Dean Winters," said Ron Jervis. "That is precisely my point, for how else could he say, as he has said in a number of occasions, that college professors are as interchangeable as bricks."

"Ron, tell me," said the Dean, "why does Rowan think as he does? He seems to deal only in the role of power, and, in this case, is acting solely as a stooge of the Board of Regents. Has the man no moral compuction and no intellectual integrity? There must be a reason for his acts."

"To be honest with you, Dean Winters," replied Ron Jervis, "Rowan reflects the non-thinking mind that is so much a characteristic of the great majority of the people of our country. He is not an educated man, either in terms of mind growth or in terms of academic studies. That a man, who is not even a college graduate, should have the power over this faculty that he does is one thing that falls into the category of power politics. One of the chief reasons for the failure of the state university to provide the leadership mandated by its origin is definitely due to the influence which certain individuals like Rowan have had on our state legislature. If the state universities did not provide the leadership necessary for a society of free men and women the end result would be a brainwashing of the minds of the people. And this is precisely what has happened, for there are few among us who understand the difference between INDIVIDUALISM AND INDIVIDUALITY."

"I see, Ron," said Dean Winters, "that you are familiar with the analysis that John Dewey made on the difference between individualism and individuality. There is no doubt in my mind that our people have been brainwashed into believing that the concept of INDIVIDUALISM, which refers to a free economy, means the same thing as the concept of INDIVIDUALITY, which refers to the right to grow in quality of mind and body. There is a problem here, however, and that is how we define the nature of mind. Many modern psychologists define the mind in matrerialistic-mechanistic terms, a concept directly opposite to both the Christian and the scientific-humanistic point of view. This is exactly what I find in Rowan's attitude toward the college professor."

"Yes, Dean Winters," said Ron Jervis, "that is all too true.

This assumption that the individual is nothing more than a cog in a machine is a direct contradiction of the thinking of our Revolutionary Fathers. It is true that much of the present day research on the nature of the human mind refutes the eighteenth century concept of the rational man, but such research has not undermined the concept of those who founded our state university in respect to a search for God in nature, or a growing understanding of the nature of REALITY. Instead of separating religion and science into two separate categories, what the founders of this Nation sought was to bring the two poles of thought into one common whole. By doing so, they laid the basis for an evolution in our understanding of the nature of man as a social being, a concept which in itself is both a humanistic and vital life force. This is what I understand to be the essence of their concept of a free people in a free society. But what has happened to us is that we now think of freedom as the right to be ignorant; to believe in any form of dogmatic religion that we choose; and, moreover, the right to achieve great wealth at the expense of our fellow man."

"Ron," said Dean Winters, "I can see that you are not too happy about what is going on in our present day culture; and, especially so, with the failure of the state university to provide the kind of intellectual leadership for our professions which could effectively counteract the dogma of the past, as well as the ignorance of the present. Nowhere is this need more evident than in teacher education, which, as you know, is not really education but teacher training."

Ron Jervis had been in the Dean's office for more than two hours, and, since it was past four o'clock in the afternoon, he expressed his appreciation to the Dean for hearing his side of the controversy and the confidence which he had expressed in what he had to say. In departing, however, he knew in his heart that the issue concerning the Negro student and the University was by no means settled. Finally, the issue came to a head for Ron Jervis when one of his graduate students, Robert Combs, decided that he wanted to write his dissertation on the subject of *The Education of the Negro in the State of Montreal.*

While Ron Jervis was aware of the storm which would be

created by allowing Robert Combs to go ahead with his expressed desire to write his dissertation on the subject of the education of the Black man, he had no desire to interfere with the student's interest and determination. The end result was that, after the Graduate Dean had approved the student's project, the four additional men, who were appointed to serve on the student's graduate committee, were sure to give him trouble. The four men included Professor Sterling, the associate Dean of the College, a Professor of Psychology, and a Professor of Curriculum and Instruction. When Ron Jervis received notice of these appointments, he knew that both he and his student were in for a real struggle.

It is important to note that in his research Robert Combs found much that was to be expected, in how the Black student had been discriminated against over a period of years, by the so-called educational leadership in the State of Montreal. In the segregated schools, for every nine dollars spent on the white child, only one dollar was spent on the black. Many of the teachers in those schools attended by Black children could not pass the seventh grade examination for graduation from the elementary school. School buildings, for the Black students, were in a more rundown condition. There was a poverty of good equipment in the classrooms and on the playgrounds.

The chapter in Robert Comb's dissertation that created the most turmoil was in the administration of the black schools, and the way in which the state funds were being distributed. The accumulated evidence was a major indictment of the State Superintendent of Schools and the State Board of Education. Ron Jervis had checked the facts, as they were presented by Mr. Combs, to make sure that the documentary evidence supported what the student had said about the state officials, and had found that the student's conclusions were correct in all respects. Yet, he was extremely skeptical that the members of Robert Combs' dissertation committee would approve the dissertation, and he so informed the student. Mr. Combs insisted on keeping the dissertation as he had written it, and his adviser deferred to his wishes.

At the time of the oral examination of the student, Robert

Combs was confronted with major opposition by two members of his committee. Both Professor Sterling and the Associate Dean of the College of Education attacked the young student for what they called his brazen attitude in criticizing the State Superintendent of Schools and the State Board of Education. They demanded that the entire chapter on the administration of the black schools be rewritten, and that certain paragraphs in the chapter be deleted from the dissertation. Young Combs refused to make the deletions stating that everything in his dissertation was fully supported by documentary evidence. He was thereupon told that his dissertation would never be approved by his committee unless the requested changes were made. The meeting adjourned at this point.

In a conference held in his office on the following day, Professor Jervis further explained to the graduate student the nature of the situation. He either had to make the changes in his dissertation, as recommended by his committee, or he would fail to get his degree. The situation was extremely critical for Mr. Combs because his job in the fall depended upon his getting his doctorate.

"Bob," said Professor Jervis, "ordinarily I would not advise a student to make the changes in his dissertation recommended by the committee. This is especially so when the recommended changes involved the principle of scholarly research. In your case, however, an additional factor is involved which concerns your future career. In no case, however, would I ever advise a student to distort the facts so as to conform to the prejudices of a member of the faculty. In your case, I would advise that you go ahead and delete the material which two members of your committee find objectionable. By doing so, you can get your degree. In the meantime, you can submit the material to an outstanding national Negro magazine, and accomplish a much more satisfying purpose."

"Professor Jervis," replied Mr. Combs, "I appreciate what you have said, and all that you have done on my behalf, but I have never compromised on what I considered an important issue, and I do not expect to do so now. If it is necessary for me to do without the degree, so be it."

"Bob," replied Professor Jervis, "under no condition would I ever advise a graduate student to violate a truth principle. I do not believe that I am doing so now. My job as a graduate professor is to advise the student who comes under my supervision according to what I believe is his best interest and that of the nation. What I am now suggesting is that you give up, only for the time being, what you know to be true about the education of the Negro in this state, and that you have such material, as deleted from your dissertation, published in a national magazine. In doing so, you will not only receive your degree, but will have your efforts read far more widely than they would ever be if left in your dissertation. Give my suggestion much thought during the coming months, and, if you change your mind, it will still not be too late to receive your degree."

At this time the young man left the Professor's office to get ready to fill a teaching position for a six week's summer session. Some four weeks had passed before Ron Jervis heard from him, and this time it was by letter.

Dear Professor Jervis;

Although I have been quite busy with my teaching, it has not kept me from thinking about what I should do about the dissertation. During this period of time I have come to the conclusion that I can delete the material as you suggested without sacrificing my principles relating to the matter of honest research. Please see to it that all the details concerning the completion of my degree are in order. I will be seeing you just as soon as I finish my six weeks of teaching.

You will be pleased to learn that two chapters of the dissertation have been accepted for publication by a well-known national magazine, the editor of which has commended me for the quality of the chapter which the committee requested that I delete.

I can now rest in peace believing that my efforts were not in vain.

It is with much sadness that I inform you that my beloved wife has taken ill with the deadly disease infantile paralysis, and is not expected to live. Were it not for her encouragement and confidence in me, I do not think that I would have had the strength and desire to continue my professional career. She is such a beautiful person, beautiful in mind and body, that I will not know what to do with myself should I lose her. But I need not tell you all these things for you know her quite well.

Your student
Robert Combs

Unfortunately for Robert Combs, his beautiful wife died before he finished his six weeks of summer teaching, and he was left to himself to finish his degree. In so far as the issue of Robert Combs and his dissertation was concerned, the matter was settled, but settled at a price which demonstrated how the state university was failing to live up to the dreams and hopes of those who were responsible for its origin.

It was not on the matter of race alone that the betrayal of those who founded the state university was being exemplified. Nor was this betrayal solely a matter of administrative policy. The university faculty, as has been shown, gave little evidence of operating from a meaning and value frame of reference consistent with the aspirations of free men and women. This condition was further demonstrated in the case of a young girl graduate student who came to Ron Jervis's office one morning seeking admission to his graduate program. After she was admitted by Professor Jervis's secretary, Ron asked the young lady how he could be of help to her.

"Professor Jervis, my name is Iris Clayton," said the young lady. "I have come to you because you have been highly recommended to me as a professor who would be helpful in solving my problem."

"Miss Clayton, I will be most happy to help you, if there is justification for my doing so," said Professor Jervis. "But first you must tell me what is bothering you, and how I can possibly be of help."

Iris Clayton had come out of the lowest level of poverty in the state of Montreal. In spite of that fact she had, by working at a number of menial tasks, been able to continue her high school education, even to the point of graduating as the valedictorian of her class. It was during her high school years that she made up her mind that she was not only going to graduate from the state university, but that she was going to continue on through the doctorate degree. Let it be said, at this point, that it was her eleventh-grade high school English teacher who contributed most to her desire to go to the University and, in the belief of Miss Clayton, that she could attain a level of excellence equal to that of any of her teachers. It was this kind of background that Iris Clayton brought to Ron Jervis's office that morning to get him to help her in the pursuit of the doctorate.

"Professor Jervis, I know that you will be skeptical of what I am about to say," said Miss Clayton. "What I am telling you, however, is true in every respect, as you can determine by checking up on everything I say. I came to this Graduate School more than a year ago with the hope of completing a doctorate in the Department of English. Up until recently, I thought that everyting was going well. My grades were excellent, all A's, of which I am very proud. I have completed the Master's Degree in the English Department, and hoped to continue the doctorate in the same department. When I went to Professor Logan last week, to get him to act as my graduate adviser, he not only told me that it was impossible for him to so serve, but that it had been determined that I could not pursue the degree in his department. When I asked him why not, he was reluctant to respond. Finally, he said that the faculty of his department had turned me down because they were convinced that I would not be a good representative of the University."

"Miss Clayton," replied Professor Jervis, "I find it difficult to understand, not only how they could come to such a conclusion, but why they thought they had a right to do so."

"My understanding, Professor Jervis," replied Miss Clayton, "is that the Dean of Women has it in for me because of where I live, and because I do not wear the kind of clothes of which she approves. Because she does not approve of the kind of person I am, she made it her personal obligation to go to Professor Logan to see to it that the Faculty of the Department of English turned me down."

"Well, Miss Clayton," said Professor Jervis, "if your grades are as you say they are, and if you are truly interested in the pursuit of the doctorate in this Department, I shall be happy to serve as your adviser. In the meantime, I shall make a check on all of these details with Professor Logan, and, following his report, I will let you know what my decision will be. Call my secretary tomorrow morning, and she will let you know what your next step is to be."

"My thanks and deepest appreciation for your consideration, Professor Jervis," replied Miss Clayton. "You are one of the few professors on this campus who places the student above the institution. I want you to know that, if you take me on, you will not be disappointed in my accomplishments. For many years I have lived with only a dream, and that dream has been to receive my doctorate from this University. I do not have the money to live where the Dean of Women insists that I live. Also, the same holds true for my clothes. Actually, I hardly have enough left to buy my food, and to pay for the minimum necessities of life. I am sure that the Dean has come to the conclusion that, because of all of this, I have turned into a prostitute and am not worthy of the doctorate from this institution. How I live, however, is a matter of necessity and not of choice. Thank you once again for your kindness. I will call your secretary tomorrow morning to get your decision on my case."

Following these remarks, Iris Clayton departed from Professor Jervis's office, and, as she did so, Ron Jervis turned to his secretary and blurted out, in a forceful and upset manner, his true feelings about what he had just heard.

"Miss Stallings," said Professor Jervis, "there is nothing that disturbs me more than to find out that the members of my profession have succumbed to administrative pressure of this kind. How can a member of this faculty substitute the assumed welfare of this institution for the welfare of a conscientious student such as Miss Clayton? Why would the members of the English Department think that this state university was established if not for the benefit of those who seek a higher level of learning? To tell a highly intellectual student such as Miss Clayton, who is willing to sacrifice as much as this girl has, to attain a level of education comparable to that of the best of the academic world, that she is not worthy of being a doctoral graduate, is an outright betrayal of the hopes and dreams of the founders of this institution. Call Professor Logan and seek an appointment with him for this afternoon if possible. I must find out all that I can about this matter."

It was possible for Professor Logan to see Ron Jervis that afternoon at 3 p.m. It was at this time that Ron proceeded to discuss the matter of the qualifications of Iris Clayton.

"Professor Logan," said Professor Jervis, "this morning one of your graduate students came to see me about the prospect of pursuing the doctorate in my Department, and for me to serve as her adviser. Miss Clayton tells me that she did her Master's Degree under your supervision, and that is why I am here. I need to know from you, before agreeing to serve as her adviser, just why Miss Clayton was turned down by your Department. What kind of a promise for intellectual success can we count on from Miss Clayton? She seems to think that your Department turned her down for reasons other than academic."

"Professor Jervis, I will be strictly honest with you about Miss Clayton," replied Professor Logan. "Miss Clayton has no intellectual weakness so far as I am concerned. As to her work in this Department, she made a grade of A in all of her Master's Degree courses. I would have been happy to continue as her adviser for the doctorate, but the other members of the English Department voted against her. Why? The Dean of Women, Miss Rogers, has charged that she is not a fit person to receive the degree from this institution, and we saw no reason to go against her will. On this basic assumption we turned Miss Clayton down. I might add that on this decision the Graduate Dean concurs."

"Speaking quite frankly, Professor Logan," replied Professor Jervis, "I find it extremely difficult to go along with you, and the members of your Department, on this matter. If the Dean of Women wants to bring charges against Miss Clayton, then let her do so, I will be glad to hear them in an open-minded way, but, if she is unable to back them up, then, in all probability, we will have a court case on our hands. Such a court case would indeed do this University far more harm, in the minds of many people, than in allowing this young lady to complete her degree."

"I agree with you, Professor Jervis," said Professor Logan. "I am sure that Dean Rogers will not press charges against Miss Clayton, however, for she has already told me that she did not want to create a stink for the University."

"That being the case," replied Professor Jervis, "I will proceed immediately with the matter of serving as the graduate adviser of Miss Clayton. You know, what I am seeing more and more around here is a betrayal of the purpose for which the state university was established. Miss Clayton's case is of particular significance in this respect. Here is a young lady who has the brains and the determination to contribute to the intellectual life of this country. Here are those who are ready to tear her down, people who are in positions of authority to make the correct decisions. What action has been taken here is not because Miss Clayton is incapable of living up to the intellectual demands placed upon her, but because of some misguided whims of a moralizing Dean."

"More power to you, Professor Jervis," replied Professor Logan. "I wish I had the guts to stand up and speak out as you do."

When the Dean of the Graduate School received the application form of the doctorate, as filled out by Iris Clayton and signed by Professor Jervis, he called Ron Jervis by phone and inquired as to whether or not he had talked to Professor

Logan about the complaint which the Dean of Women had levied against Miss Clayton. Professor Jervis responded that he had talked to Professor Logan about the matter, and that he would like to discuss the question in greater detail with the Dean concerning the reasons for his action.

"You must know, Dean Grant," said Professor Jervis, "that I am very positive in my requirements for the doctorate, and especially with those who major under my supervision. Now, with reference to Miss Clayton, Professor Logan tells me that she is an excellent student, in so far as her grades are concerned, and that the only reason why she was turned down by the English Department was that the Dean of Women had questioned her character and her fitness for the degree. The truth of the matter is that Dean Rogers did not approve of her living quarters and the way she dressed. Now, as I told Professor Logan, it is not in the realm of my prerogative to question the character of my students, but, if Dean Rogers wants to bring charges against Miss Clayton, let her do so, and we will have a hearing on her case. My understanding is that she refuses to do so. Thus, I am left with no other alternative than to accept Miss Clayton as a candidate for the doctorate."

Ron Jervis, having stated his case, now waited for the reaction of his Graduate Dean. He knew Dean Grant to be a fair-minded man, and one who was willing to bend over backwards when the student lived up to his or her responsibility. Dean Grant was a man with a deep sense of justice, and not prone to wilt under subjective judgment. As a well-known chemist, with a national reputation, he responded to Ron Jervis with a high level of objectivity.

"Professor Jervis," said Dean Grant, "I can fully understand the position you have taken on Miss Clayton's case, and I admire you for it. Nevertheless, I must warn you that you must be prepared to face a lot of backfire every step along the way in supporting Miss Clayton for the doctorate. As you know, Dean Rogers carries a lot of weight with the Board of Regents, and you may become the brunt of it."

"Dean Grant," replied Professor Jervis, "for the sake of a principle, and for what I chose to believe is the reason for the existence of this university, I am willing to make any necessary personal sacrifice for Miss Clayton's cause. Miss Clayton comes from the depths of poverty in this state, and yet she was valedictorian of her high school class. She has a desire to achieve the highest academic level that this University provides, and is willing to make any sacrifice necessary to achieve that level. In so far as I can help her, I will not only benefit my country and humanity in general, but this University and its reason for existence."

Following these words, Ron Jervis shook the hand of his Graduate Dean and walked out of his office. In truth, he never seemed to have felt better in all of his life, and he was in high spirits when he sat down at his desk to finish up the obligations of the day.

While Ron Jervis was quite pleased with his discussion with Dean Grant, he knew that his conflict with the university administration would continue, for his conception of the function of a state university was very much at odds with those who sat in the seat of power. What did develop, however, was something that was much beyond his control, and something that he did not anticipate. His first awareness of what was common gossip came from his closest friend in the College of Education, namely Profesor Frank Ruffner. When the gossip reached him, Dr. Ruffner was so upset that he made a personal visit to Ron Jervis's office to discuss the matter with him.

"Ron," said Frank Ruffner, "I have just heard about a matter of such great importance that I considered it imperative for me to see you, and to get your side of the story. It is being rumored, and I got it from a very responsible person, that you and one of your female graduates are having an affair of the body. Now, I am not a prude, and certainly not one of those who always keeps his pecker in his pants, but getting involved with a female student is one of the quickest ways of being thrown out of this University that I can think of."

"Frank," replied Ron Jervis, "I can guess who the graduate student is alleged to be and, while I have no evidence to support my conviction, I can surmise as to who has initiated this gossip. Also, I might add that it is one thing for adolescent boys to brag about getting a piece of free ass, but another for such boys to talk about a college professor having that kind of relation with one of his female graduate students. It is a travesty on our culture, and on our educational system, that college boys continue to look upon a young woman as a thing rather than a loveable human being to be respected for her own personal worth. Iris Clayton is the one you are talking about, Frank, is she not?"

"Yes, Ron," said Frank Ruffner, "and it puzzles me no end as to who or why anyone would start such a lie. I know of the differences that you have had with some of the professors in this University, and with Jesse Rowan, but I can not believe that any of these men would indulge in such a contemptable, rotten act."

"Frank," said Ron Jervis, "I think that you are very correct when you say that you do not think that any one of the men that you have mentioned would indulge in such damnable tactics. No, my own judgment is that this gossip was initiated by the Dean of Women of this University. She has it in for Iris Clayton and saw to it that the English Department turned her down on the doctorate. She even went to Dean Grant to get him to stop me from acting as her adviser for the degree. I shall take this matter up with her, and, if she does not admit to her lying gossip, I shall go to the President about it."

"Ron Jervis," replied Frank Ruffner, "I admire you for your guts in this matter. You have displayed a great deal of courage in dealing with this issue, and especially that part which deals with the rights of students. These young people, regardless of their race, sex, class, or nationality, should be treated as equals in a free society. All of which brings into full focus the role of a state university. I am sure that there are a goodly number of professors in this institution who agree with us but do not have the guts, or the inclination, to involve themselves in a matter of this kind. I am interested, Ron, in how you became so deeply involved in the 'cause celebre' of the state university."

"It's a long story, Frank," replied Ron Jervis, "but I can point out some of the things that literally drove me in the direction of a major concern for the state university's role in our free society. What we have here, in my case, is a combination of experience, social thought, and graduate research. As a young boy, I had to go out on my own at the age of thirteen years. At that time, I was fortunate enough to have a high school principal who, in spite of the objection of the school superintendent, let me go to school in the morning hours, so that I could work in a restaurant in the afternoon and evening on weekdays, and sixteen hours a day on Saturdays and Sundays. This I did for a period of three years, missing only four days with the flu during the entire period. After graduating from high school, I went to the state university on a freshman scholarship, and, with a few dollars that I had saved, was able to make my way, even though I was supporting my mother at the same time. While the state university that I attended met its responsibility to me, in so far as support is concerned, having to struggle, as I did, made a deep impression on me, especially as to the injustices of an economic system that deprived a young person of his or her natural right to get a full and complete education. To see me AS A THING, rather than as a growing young boy with great aspirations, was both brutal and inhumane."

"Well, Ron," said Frank Ruffner," I can see that you feel very deeply what you have just said, but you must admit that the experience had a lasting effect for good on you."

"Yes, Frank, that is very true," said Ron Jervis, "but the experience could have made me a revolutionist, and would have done so had it not been for the fact that I was able to grow in social intelligence, and to understand that the problem was no one person's fault, but a problem of the evolution of the human mind. It was in a course in American History that I gained my first insight into what the American Revolution was all about. In essence, the problem boiled down to the nature of Reality, of the universe as well as of the individual. People were not to be thought of as THINGS on the one hand, and as spiritual beings on the other, but as individuals created free and equal in the sight of the law. The overall environmental conditions which prevailed at that time had to be changed —

economic, political, social and religious. But how changed? The answer was to be found in the role of government and education."

"Ron," said Frank Ruffner, "I get the impression that you think that we have grossly distorted the concept of free and equal, so much so as to make it conform to our traditional, vested cultural interests."

"Frank, that is exactly what we have done," said Ron Jervis." In doing so, we have not only betrayed our forefathers, but are in the process of losing what freedom we have attained as a result of their efforts. Instead of the development of a free mind, which the founders of our Nation saw necessary to the development of a free society, we have interpreted the concept of freedom to mean the right to be ignorant and dogmatic, to accumulate wealth and power, and to be a religious bigot. We readily tolerate economic exploitation as a right of the individual, and even the right to be a criminal, if you don't get caught. On the matter of being equal, we have substituted the concept of equality of identity for that of equality of individuality. Any stupid ass should know that individuals are not equal in terms of heredity or environment, nor is such necessary or desirable. What is necessary is that we should be equal in the sight of the law. What this distorted concept of democracy has done to us is to promote an anti- intellectualism, which has so pervaded our entire history that it has warped our minds and made us incapable of dealing effectively with our crucial economic and social problems."

"Ron," said Frank Ruffner, "I can see that you have devoted considerable time and thought to the problems that lie at the heart of the welfare of our nation; but where do you find justification for holding that the state university has a unique responsibility in this struggle for the freedom of the individual?"

"Frank," said Ron, "I was not aware of the relationship between the American State University and the American Revolution until I got into the graduate school, and began my research in the field of higher education. It was at that time that I learned how the Free Masons not only took the leadership in promoting the American Revolution, but how they took the initiative in promoting the establishment of the state university. It was their conviction that if we were to have a free Nation it could be achieved only by promoting a new kind of leadership, and that such leadership could be brought into reality by establishing a new kind of higher institution of learning. The first of such institutions was founded in 1789, through the initiative of one of our revolutionary fathers, William R. Davie, and in the state of North Carolina. Interestingly enough this state university was referred to at the time as THE SUN OF SCIENCE, thus giving expression to the underlying concept that freedom of knowledge was the essential ingredient for promoting a free individual in a free society."

"You amaze me, Ron Jervis," said Frank Ruffner, "at the knowledge which you bring to bear on this subject. I, and I am sure that most of the members of this faculty, have no knowledge of the origin of this state university, or just why it was created. When I came into your office, I was concerned about your future well-being, but I can now see that the problem involving Iris Clayton is much bigger than I had thought. I now know that you are fully capable of handling this situation. Let me know how you come out with Dean Rogers. I do not know of anyone that I would like to see take her on than you."

After Frank Ruffner left Ron Jervis's office, Ron knew that he had no choice but to seek an appointment with the Dean of Women, and he proceeded to do so immediately. By way of a call on the phone, he made an appointment with the Dean on the afternoon of the following day. Yet the problem was further aggravated when he walked into his home that afternoon and was confronted by a wife who had heard about him and his graduate student from one of the wives of a member of the College of Education Faculty.

"Ron Jervis," said Helen, "I have never interfered with your teaching or with your relations to your students up until now, but what I hear about you and this Iris Clayton is something about which I need a clearer explanation."

"Helen," sad Ron, "all that you have heard about Iris Clayton, and my conduct, is the biggest pack of lies to which I have ever been exposed. I first heard about this scandal this afternoon from Frank Ruffner, but the level that it has taken on is unbelievable. I think I know who started these lies, and I have already made arrangements to see her tomorrow afternoon, at which time I expect to clear up the entire matter. If I cannot get a satisfactory response from this woman, then I shall take the matter up with President Middlebrook. Also, there is the possibility of a court suit."

"You speak of a woman, Ron," replied Helen. "Just who are you talking about?"

"It's a long story, Helen," said Ron Jervis, "but, to begin with your question, the woman to whom I referred is the Dean of Women of this University. She has taken upon herself the right to destroy Iris Clayton, first by getting the English Department to turn her down on the doctorate, and then, when I accepted her application, she went to the Dean of the Graduate School to get him to talk to me about my accepting her as a graduate student. When that failed, I am sure that she started this scandal about my relation with the girl. Why this woman is so down on this poor girl, I know not, but I am sure going to find out."

"From your past record, Ron Jervis," said Helen, "I must assume that Iris Clayton is a very intelligent student, else you would not have accepted her as a candidate for the doctorate. On the other hand, is it possible that this girl has so much sex appeal that the poor man could not resist the temptation?"

"Helen, knowing me as you do," said Ron, "there are several aspects about this dirty situation that need to be clarified. First, I thoroughly investigated Miss Clayton's record before accepting her as a graduate student. Although she came from a very poor family in this state, she was valedictorian of her high school graduating class. She was a Phi Beta Kappa undergraduate of this University, and made all A's on her Master's Degree in English. My understanding is that Miss Clayton does not live in an apartment approved by the Dean of Women, and for this reason the Dean thinks that she is a prostitute. Also, the Dean says that she is dirty, and does not wear the right kind of clothes. Whether or not all of this is true, I know not, but I do know what it is to be poor, and what it is not to have enough food to keep the body warm and healthy. So I have much sympathy for this woman. Also, more than anything else, it is a responsibility of a state university to treat every student, and I do mean every student, as a human being and not an object or a THING. As for myself, I shall do everything possible to help these students develop their God-given talents to the highest possible level. That is all that I have to say for the present. Let us drop the matter at this point, Helen, for it in no way concerns you personally. You must know that it upsets me no end to see my attempt to treat a student with decency and kindness scandalized."

By this time, Ron Jervis had been subjected to all that he could take on the matter of Iris Clayton. That damn bitch of a Dean, who does she think she is anyway? He would settle the matter once and for all on the following afternoon or know the reason why. When a Dean of Women proceeds to destroy the character of a student who really cares about her educational career, then it is time for someone to call her cards, and he was the one to do it. He slept fretfully that night, and was not in the best of moods when he attended his classes the next morning. Some of his students had undoubtedly heard the gossip about him and Miss Clayton, but nothing was said about it. When he walked into Dean Rogers's office that afternoon, it was clearly apparent that she knew why he was there.

"Dean Rogers," said Professor Jervis, "I am sure that you know why I am here. It is my understanding, both from Professor Logan and Dean Grant, that you do not consider Iris Clayton a suitable candidate for the doctorate from this University; and that you have gone out of your way to see to it that she does not get the degree. In all of this I have kept quiet up until now; but, since you, in an underhanded way, have sought to scandalize both Miss Clayton and myself, I am here to tell you that, if you do not publicly apologize to both Miss Clayton and myself, I am ready to proceed with court action against you. Before proceeding with court action, however, I will take the matter up with the President of this University, so that he will fully understand my reasons for so acting."

The response of Dean Rogers to Professor Jervis's remarks was one of complete dismay. Never before had she been confronted with a challenge of this kind. In some way or other she would like to have gotten around the issue, but the door had been closed on her, and there was no way out.

"Professor Jervis," said Dean Rogers, "I do not deny going to Professor Logan and to Dean Grant concerning the possibility of Miss Clayton's taking the doctorate at this University. I have done my best to see to it that she does not get the degree because I consider her unfit for such recognition and achievement. When my actions failed, I concluded that, knowing Miss Clayton as I did, there must be some kind of an illicit relation between you two, and I so informed a number of my friends. How this matter got out among the students I know not."

"Dean Rogers," said Professor Jervis, "I am more than shocked at your blatant remarks. That you should hate Miss Clayton so much that you would deliberately destroy your own integrity is unbelievable. Also, in doing so, you have set out to defame my character in the process. Frankly, you do not show any evidence whatsoever that you understand why this University was established, or its relation to the American Revolution. You will no longer be able to treat students AS THINGS if I have anything to do with it. Miss Clayton was a challenge to you, and you failed her completely. You put material things first in evaluating this student, rather than quality of individuality. Do you have any facts to support your conclusions about the character of Miss Clayton? Did you know that this student came out of the depths of poverty to get to this institution, and with great sacrifice? Did you know that in spite of all her poverty, this student was valedictorian of her high school graduation class, and that she financed her own way in order to be able to come to this University? For this, our Revolutionary Fathers would have been proud of her.

Miss Clayton is a Phi Beta Kappa student from this University, and now seeks to achieve the doctorate from her Alma Mater. Can you not now see to it that your first obligation is to this student, and not to something composed of buildings and mechanical gadgets?"

"Professor Jervis," said Dean Rogers, "you have not fully convinced me that you are right about Miss Clayton, but I will admit that I was wrong in dragging you into this messy situation. Such being the case, I will publicly apologize to you, and to Miss Clayton, for my remarks. Also, I will see Miss Clayton about the possibility of getting her a part-time job, assisting me in my work with the female graduate students. If she works out, as you think she will, I will be the first to admit that I was wrong about her. On the other hand, if I find her to be nothing more than I have believed her to be, I shall expect you to respond accordingly."

Ron Jervis saw no reason for continuing the discussion beyond this point, as he had already achieved more than he had anticipated. Dean Rogers's willingness to provide Miss Clayton with a part-time job was a real bonanza for her. So, as he departed from the Dean's office, he concluded that the issue involving him in some sexual misconduct had turned out to be a victory for his student.

In due time, Iris Clayton completed the degree which she had so vigorously sought, and with high honors. The work which Dean Rogers had provided her made it possible for her not only to pay her current expenses, but to eat and dress and live in more desirable quarters. Because of her poverty, however, it was not possible for her to provide her professor a copy of her dissertation until some years after her departure into private life.

While Dean Winters, on more than one occasion, had spoken to Ron Jervis about the possibility of his taking over the deanship of the College Of Education, Ron Jervis knew that, in the light of the way that he had challenged the administration on a number of occasions, such would not happen. How all of this was to turn out, however, was more than he had anticipated.

It was while Ron Jervis was on a leave of absence for one year, serving as a special employee of the War Department, and more specifically as an Army University Professor in the European Theater of Operations at the end of World War II, that, due to a breakdown in his health, Dean Winters had been forced to resign from the Deanship of the College of Education. The grounds for the man who was to take the Dean's place had been laid by Professor Sterling, the Associate Dean of the College, and the Secretary of the Board of Regents. It will be recalled that each of these men had been involved in a controversy with Ron Jervis in one form or another. Knowing that Dean Winters had desired that Ron follow him as Dean of the College, these three men had set about to controvert his wishes. This they succeeded in doing by promoting the idea that Ron Jervis was a Communist at heart, and that his appointment would work against the financial support of the University. In this respect, they were eminently successful, for, in a letter received by Ron while he was still overseas, he was informed that Associate Dean Lauren D. Hardbutt had been appointed as Dean of the College of Education.

What kind of a man was this Dean Hardbutt? It had been demonstrated to Ron Jervis that, on the basis of the position he had taken on Bob Combs oral examination, by conniving with Professor Sterling, he had a very limited knowledge of the role of a state university in a free society. Also, Associate Dean Hardbutt had demonstrated at that time that he was not fit, personally or otherwise, to be Dean of any college. Young students in the Laboratory School of the College had given him the nick name COLD FISH because of the way in which he related to them. What kind of a Dean would he make? Ron Jervis was soon to find out for, before he returned home from his assignment, he had received a letter from his wife, Helen, wherein she stated that the Dean had informed her that her husband was needed back home immediately if he expected to hold on to his job.

Life for Ron Jervis under Dean Hardbutt was at best an unpleasant experience. While the Dean could do nothing about Ron's status as a full professor, he could hurt him by denying him any salary increases, and by making life miserable for him when the opportunity was available. Although Ron Jervis had returned from Europe as early as June of the year of the Dean's appointment, Hardbutt had refused to put him back on the university payroll until September. All of which resulted in a loss in salary to Ron in the amount of $1200. Now, more than at any time in his years at the University, it became evident that the underlying philosophies of the two men were at opposite ends of the spectrum. This was made glaringly apparent when Hardbutt called Professors Jervis and Ruffner into his office on the issue of student grades. After the men were seated, the Dean opened up the discussion with a comment on the reason for his action.

"Professors Ruffner and Jervis," said the Dean, "you are no doubt wondering why I have called you into this office. I can assure you that it is on a matter of great significance to me and to the College of Education. You and I are being sued by a graduate student, named Clay Bellows, for failing him on his course work during the past semester. His suit is based on the charge of personal discrimination; but, since I have never had the man in class, the suit is directed primarily at you two men. I have been examining the grades which you have been turning out, and I do not like what I see. Also, I am disturbed by the number of protests which are coming to me about your grades. I must say that you are much too strict in your grading, especially in the number of F's that you are handing out. Who do you think gives you the right of a dictator? Can't you see that you are driving students away from this College, and that your grading will have an influence on the members of the Legislature?"

Since Frank Ruffner was the senior professor involved in the charge of handing out far too many bad grades, Ron Jervis withheld comment to give his friend a chance to make the first response. The reply to the charge was not long in coming.

"Dean Hardbutt," replied Professor Ruffner, "I am stunned

by the fact that you would attack my system of grading students in such a vicious manner. Such comments which you have just made are those of a politician rather than an educator. Your interests are not those of a good teacher, whose first concern is that of the welfare of this country, but rather those which are related to money, and the enslavement of the professor to an institution of lands and buildings. My grades are a result of my best efforts and judgment as a true professional, a commitment to the idea of quality leadership, which teachers must provide if this Nation is to survive as a free society. To deal with students as THINGS to be manipulated according to one's personal interest, and to treat professors as if they were no more than hired hands, is the reason why John Dewey, that great scholar and teacher, took upon himself the responsibility of organizing the American Association of University Professors."

Ron Jervis was jubilant over the way that Frank Ruffner had responded to Dean Hardbutt, for he could not have done a better job, linguistically or otherwise. His reply to the Dean was brief and to the point.

"Dean Hardbutt, Professor Ruffner's comments are so precise and to the point that I can add little to what he just said. I do wish to say, however, that I for one will continue to live up to my professional responsibilities, regardless of what you say. My commitment has been and will continue to be one of both intellectual and moral accountability to the people of this Nation, and to a society of free men and women."

Because of the way in which Professors Ruffner and Jervis responded to his remarks, Dean Hardbutt found it difficult to say anything further. He knew of no way in which he could handle Frank Ruffner, for he was too well known, and had far too many friends on the university faculty who would support him on any and all issues. As for Professor Jervis, that was a different matter. There was no way in which he could downgrade him professionally, for he was too well known nationally as a man of integrity and high scholarship. He had the power, however, to keep him from getting any salary raises;

and, in this respect, he would have the support of the President and the Board of Regents. Now that he was the Dean, Ron Jervis would find out who had the power over him, and over the faculty of the College. It was in this mood that Hardbutt made his final comment.

"Well, gentlemen," said the Dean, "I hope that you will take what I have said in the spirit that it was given. I do want you to know that I had nothing but the best interests of the students and the University at heart when I referred to the way you fellows grade your students. I must say that I commend you for the concern which you express for this great country of ours, and for the welfare of the profession of teaching. If you have nothing more to say, the meeting will stand adjourned, for I know that you are just as busy as I am."

At this point, the two men departed from Dean Hardbutt's office. No sooner had they gotten out of the sight and hearing of the dean, than Ron Jervis found it necessary to speak out on what they had just experienced.

"You know, Frank," said Ron, "I do not trust that man. He is neither personally nor professionally qualified to serve as Dean of this College. As a senior professor in this University he cannot touch you, your salary, or otherwise. Also, he cannot hurt me professionally, but he can keep my salary down and deliberately harass me in a number of ways. Yet, in the final analysis, he can only hurt the College by doing so. By now, he has discovered, of a certainty, that there are some people that cannot be bought, no matter how high the price."

"Ron," said Frank Ruffner, "as I have previously expressed to you, I respect and admire you for standing up to this conniving man. You know, as well as I do, that he got to be Dean instead of you by intrigue and duplicity. He is deeply jealous of both of us, and will do anything he can to make both of us unhappy. But in the end he will fail. I will be parting from you at this point, since I must go by my office to pick up some materials before I return home."

As for Ron Jervis, he knew that Dean Hardbutt would take his jealousy and anger out on him in a number of ways: and it was not long before he took the first step. It had been the policy of Dean Winters, at the beginning of each fall semester, to call a meeting of the departmental chairmen to discuss the use of the college funds. Hardbutt had determined to follow the same policy, but with one exception. He would make the final decision before the meeting, and then inform the heads of the Departments as to how the money would be spent. Thus, when the meeting was held, he informed those present as to what would be done about the Budget. Ron immediately noticed that every department except his had been given some consideration for the coming year. When the Dean concluded his remarks, and asked for comments concerning his action, not a single comment came from any of the Chairmen until Ron spoke out.

"Dean Hardbutt," said Professor Jervis, "I find myself opposed to the action that you have just taken, largely because it has been aimed at me personally; and, in so doing, you have grossly discriminated against my Department. Also, as a result, you have done great harm to the education of the students in this College. Please see to it that my position on this matter is duly noted."

Apart from Frank Ruffner, Ron was convinced that there was little support for his position among the other chairmen. There was no doubt in his mind about where Professor Sterling stood, for he was clearly involved in the intrigue that had led to Hardbutt being apointed Dean of the College. As for the other six chairmen, five had shown little evidence of genuine concern with the problem of the teacher in the American culture, or of the obligation of the College of Education to provide a quality leadership for our public schools. They catered to the Dean, as did Southern slaves to the plantation master, hoping to get a few of the crumbs as they dropped from the table.

During the period of the next ten years, following the appointment of Hardbutt as Dean of the College of Education, Ron Jervis continued to fill his position as Professor of the Intellectual Foundations of Education. He did so in a manner consistent with the needs of his students, and with the continuing conviction that the state university had a primary role in providing a quality leadership for our culture. At the same time, Dean Hardbutt continued his policy of interference with Ron Jervis's efforts by denying him any salary increases, while granting others, as the budget permitted. At another one of these meetings of the departmental chairmen, Ron continued his vigorous protests against the Dean's policy of discrimination, and especially with reference to his salary.

"Dean Hardbutt," said Professor Jervis, "it has been quite evident over a period of years that you have been following a policy of discrimination against me by refusing me a salary increase. In so acting, I repeat, you are not only hurting me, but the College of Education and this University. May I ask you, do you so act because you choose to think of college professors AS THINGS WHICH ARE AS INTERCHANGEABLE AS BRICKS? Do you think of your position as some tool to be applied without concern for your fellow man or the welfare of this Nation? Are you not by such action engaged in the gross pattern of anti-intellectualism which is so pervasive in our culture? I must add, in this respect, that your position runs in direct contradiction to the aspirations of the founders of this Nation."

There was a brief period of silence before Dean Hardbutt spoke up in an aggressive, but clearly upset manner. His response was that of a man who was having great difficulty in justifying his action.

"Professor Jervis," said Dean Hardbutt, "A former President of this University once remarked, when confronted by a similar challenge, that no college professor is competent to determine what his salary should be."

"Yes, my dear Dean," replied Professor Jervis, "but that only raises the question as to who is competent. Are you by such a statement implying that you are acting in the role of God Almighty, and saying that you are right? Surely, there are better ways of making correct decisions."

The Dean had nothing more to say following Ron Jervis's

remarks. In Ron's mind there was no question that the policy being followed by his Dean was both stupid and unfair. Had Frank Ruffner not told him, on more than one occasion, that he was the only real scholar in the College of Education? Also, he, Frank Ruffner, and Professor Chambers were the only ones who had received national recognition by being invited to serve abroad along with the armed forces. From time to time, Ron had been invited to teach at other state universities, such as the University of Illinois, Michigan State University, the University of North Carolina, and Auburn University. He had served on various national committees, as well as being Executive Secretary of his national association. No such national recognition had ever been received by Dean Hardbutt. For this reason, and others, he was extremely jealous of Ron Jervis's professional recognition. But why should such men as Dean Hardbutt, a man of obvious professional limitations, be placed in positions of power over those who were much their superior? Why had the culture pattern of this country developed in such a way as to defeat the very purposes for which the United States had been founded? Was it because of the fact that the concept of Freedom had been reduced to the level of the thirteen-year-old mind? Did not majority political rule, as practiced both in holding office and voting, contribute to the mediocrity of those who held political office? Certainly there was a marked tendency toward a breakdown in ethical and intellectual respnsibility. Such politics of power can be described as fascistic and unworthy of the name of democracy.

It was at a time when Ron Jervis's relation with Dean Hardbutt was at its lowest ebb that the opportunity presented itself for him to accept a more challenging position at another state university. The opportunity had come about as a result of Ron's having taught during a summer session at this particular institution, and his having become acquainted with a number of the faculty, especially the Chairman of the Department of his area of specialization. When one of the senior members of the Department resigned to return to his home state, Ron Jervis was offered the chance to fill the vacancy at a significantly higher salary than he was at present receiving. The need for a change for Ron was not only a matter of money, but of compatibility and professional fredom.

There were, as might be expected, good reasons for Ron Jervis to hesitate in accepting a change of positions. He had, despite the way he had been treated by his Dean, become so well established, after more than fifteen years of tenure, that it meant a loss of daily association with many friends. Also, why should this bastard of a man be able to gloat over having been able to get rid of him? Finally, a new man had come into the Presidency of the University who was a personal friend, and it was possible that, in due time, a change for the better would take place. He would go over and have a conference with his new President before making any final decision. He so notified his secretary of his decision, and an appointment was made for him on the following Monday afternoon at 3 p.m.

Professor Jack Knight had been President of the University just two years when Ron Jervis walked into his office that afternoon in the summer of 1954. He was one of the men that Ron had met on his first visit to the University, and, of all places, at a poker game. Since he was a Professor of History and a friend of Frank Ruffner, the men had come to know each other in a personal, as well as a professional way. As Ron shook his hand that afternoon, and then proceeded to sit down next to his desk, President Knight was the first to speak.

"Well, Professor Jervis," said President Knight, "I have noticed that you have a tendency to get into the hair of your Dean, but, knowing him as I do, I understand why. I do not always agree with your methods, but I do agree with you in principle. Your position as to why the state university was established is fully justified by historical evidence. Unfortunately, that evidence has been covered up by vested interests in religion, politics, and economics for more than one hundred years. Our tragedy is that the concept of individuality in our culture has been separated from the natural self as it has been during the past two thousand years of Western culture. Even more to the point, the concept of individuality held by our Revolutionary Fathers, the men who founded this

Nation, has been lost in our capitalistic concept of laissez-faire individualism. Note how these men of God preach a doctrine of spiritualistic individualism, when our everyday practice boils down to a money-grabbing dogma in which the individual is treated as if he were nothing more than a part of a technological machine. By the way, if you do not know of my action concerning Secretary Rowan, I am happy to inform you that before I accepted this position, I insisted that Rowan be retired when he reaches the age of 65 years. On that basis, he will be retired this coming August 15. Thank God he will no longer be around to gossip about me or the members of this faculty."

"President Knight," said Ron Jervis, "I have long respected you, and especially your contribution to the field of American History. I greatly fear that, now that you have become President of this University, the country has lost a good historian. You were right in getting rid of Secretary Rowan, for he has served as nothing more than a spy for the Board of Regents. There is the continuing problem, however, as to how much influence the President of a state university can have in the operation of the institution."

"In personal relations, Ron," said the President, "his influence can go a long way, but on the basic cultural issues, such as race, religion, politics, and economics, his hands are tied because of the need for financial support from the state legislature. That I have learned the hard way during the past two years. Freedom does not exist in a vacuum, but in the cultural pattern of human relations."

"All of which," replied Ron Jervis, "brings me to the reason why I am here, and why the matter is urgent. I have been offered a full professorship in a sister state university at a considerably higher salary than I am now being paid. Your presidency is one of the reasons why I am reluctant to accept this attractive offer. On the other hand, I find myself so much at odds with Dean Hardbutt that I no longer wish to continue under his administration. He has not only denied me justifiable salary increases, but has deliberately sought to belittle me with my graduate students."

"Ron," replied President Knight, "I know the institution to which you are referring, for the President has written me about you and your work here. Personally, if you do make the change, you will be trading a Dean who is a COLD FISH for a President of a similar nature. You, however, would not be working closely with him, as you must with your Dean. As to salary, we are not at this time able to match in any way the salary that has been offered you, although I very much wish that we could do so. We could squeeze some money from our budget, but I would not want to insult you with so small an amount. Also, the institution which you are considering has a much better retirement system than we have. If you do accept this offer, and I can fully understand why you might do so, I have no reason to doubt that you will be eminently successful in your new position."

Ron Jervis, now that the reason for his appointment had been accomplished, had one more hurdle to cross before making a final decision as to whether or not he continued in his present position. He would talk to his wife, Helen, that very night about their future prospects, and what actions had to be taken if they decided to make the change.

That night, in his discussion with Helen about the possibility of a move to a new appointment, there was no doubt about where she stood on the matter. Helen replied without hesitation that she favored the move. As a well trained secondary science teacher, she had been denied a teaching position in this small western town because her husband was a professor in the University. Since the place to which they would be going was a large city, the opportunity for her employment would be assured. It was the freeze on Ron's salary by Dean Hardbutt, along with the failure of Helen to secure employment, that had created a pattern of conflict in the home, so much so that Helen consistently blamed Ron for her not having the money to buy her personal life necessities. Ron had, up to now, kept silent on how Dean Hardbutt had discriminated against him on his salary, but now it was out in the open. This was enough to cause Helen to determine that, in so far as she was concerned, there was no longer any doubt about their moving. Ron's resignation from his present position was called for, and the quicker he took such action the better.

"Ron Jervis," said Helen, "why did you not tell me about the trouble that you were having with Dean Hardbutt? As your wife I had the right to know, especially since all of this discrimination was having such a devastating effect on our budget."

"Helen," replied Ron, "I did not want to worry you about something that I could not change except by resignation, and that was unthinkable until now. Better to grin and bear it than to place an extra load on your shoulders. Now that I know where you stand on this matter of moving, I shall arrange to see Dean Hardbutt tomorrow and turn in my resignation."

The time for Professor Jervis to see Dean Hardbutt had arrived. It was just one day after Ron and his wife Helen had made the final decision to move on to what they hoped would be a more productive and satisfying life. It was ten a.m. when Ron Jervis walked into the Dean's office. In his hand he carried a letter of resignation which was to take effect August 31, 1955. It was the Dean who spoke first after Professor Jervis had been seated.

"Well, Professor Jervis," asked the Dean, "what can I do for you?"

"Dean Hardbutt," replied Ron Jervis, "on a number of occasions you have made the remark that every man has his price. Well, Dean, here is one man that refutes your argument. To prove that such is the case, here is my resignation, effective August 31, 1955. I am sorry that it had to come to this, I could have been happy during the years I have been here, except for the fact that we have very different ways of interpreting the role of the teacher in our culture. Since we are so diametrically opposed in our thinking, I find it impossible to continue working with you. Therefore, I hope that you will accept my resignation gracefully."

"Professor Jervis," replied the Dean, "I too had hoped that we could in some way find a solution to our differences, but I now see that such was impossible. I have learned from Professor Ruffner of your offer from a sister state university. My best wishes go with you. Now that we understand each other, and your resignation has been accepted, I must bid you good day. I am extremely busy with a problem which affects one of your graduate students."

It was the last conferenc that Professor Jervis was to have with Dean Hardbutt. He knew in his mind that this cynical, unethical, and hypocritical man was insincere in all that he did and said. In so far as his graduate students were concerned, Ron knew that he would be blamed by the Dean for running out on them, when the exact opposite was the truth. What bothered Ron Jervis most in connection with his resignation was the extent to which the pattern of public school administration would continue to follow that laid down by Dean Hardbutt. What a contrast there was between what the Dean represented and what the founders of this Nation visualized for the future. What did all of this pattern of authority hold out for the role of the state university in the American culture?

CHAPTER II

A PROGRAM OF FREE PUBLIC EDUCATION

Before leaving to take up his responsibilities in the new professorship, Ron Jervis had a long talk with his friend Frank Ruffner. As a final gesture, Ron and his wife invited him and his wife over for dinner and an evening of conversation. After the dinner was over, and they had moved to the living room, Frank Ruffner turned to his friend with a comment that warmed Ron Jervis's heart.

"Ron," said Frank Ruffner, "you and I have been friends for many years and, while I personally regret your leaving this campus, I glory in your spunk. I feel sure that you will never regret making the change, and can only say that I wish we were going with you."

"Frank," replied Ron Jervis, "I want you to know that I deeply appreciate the support you have given me over the years. Had Winters continued to be Dean of the College of

Education, and had our friend Jack Knight been the President of the University, I know that I would have continued my tenure here. But Hardbutt's administrative policy, and his negative attitude toward me, has made staying here no longer possible. I know how much he has made things unpleasant for you, but he can't hurt you and your family as he has hurt me and my family. Placing such men as Hardbutt and Rowan in positions of administrative authority in a state university is a betrayal of everything for which this institution was established. President Knight so expressed himself the other day at the time of our conference. It is regrettable, however, that, in a number of these issues, even Jack Knight is unable to make a positive contribution. In this connection, Frank, where do you think the possibility for making a change for the common good should or could begin?"

"Ron, I, as you," said Frank Ruffner, "have wrestled with this problem for many years and, I must say, see no simple answer to your question. Of course, there is always the response that you begin at whatever point that you can. I do feel that the key to our problem is to be found in the way that our public schools are being operated. Since the power and control over the public school system is vested in the state legislature, we must somehow or other bring about a change in the way our representatives view the public education program."

"Frank," said Ron Jervis, "I believe that you have put your finger on the core of our problem as to why our public schools have been a failure in promoting the kind of educational program that is necessary for a society of free people. I consider this situation as another example of what I have called BETRAYAL ON MOUNT PARNASSUS. Scheming, conniving, and corrupt politicians are, in fact, running our public schools. There is an aggressive anti-intellectual attitude expressed in their mode of operation. This anti-intellectual attitude runs throughout the entire history of the public schools system. Our public schools have failed us because they are operated solely as a political institution, rather than being scientifically social centered. There is, however, in this respect, a great difference between the origin of the public school and the state university."

"Ron Jervis," replied Frank Ruffner, "are you saying that the differences in the operation of the two systems have made, or should have made, a difference in the effect that each has had on our culture?"

"Precisely so," said Ron Jervis. "You see, Frank, the state university has an entirely different origin from that of the public school. Rooted in the American Revolution, the role of the state university was to provide a new kind of leadership for the Nation. Since the eight colonial colleges had the distinct purpose of providing ministers of God for the Protestant Churches, there was a need for a new type of higher institution of learning which would provide a different kind of education for a different kind of mind. Such leadership had to be free from the dogmas of the past, and to operate solely on the basis of the creative, scientific, humanistic, and naturalistic point of view. This way of looking at life was in direct contradiction to that of Medieval Orthodox Christianity. There was inherent in this way of looking at life a belief that through the advancement of knowledge the great problems that had plagued mankind for so many centuries could be solved. In the case of the public schools, however, they grew out of the era of Jacksonian Democracy. The state university is rooted in the intellectual tradition of John Locke and Thomas Jefferson; whereas the public school system is rooted in the tradition of Jean-Jacques Rousseau, where no distinction was made between the idea of equality before the law and the idea of equality of identity. Since the Constitution of the United States holds that all powers not vested in the federal government are delegated to the states, the control of public schools is a state operation. It should be remembered, however, that since the state legislatures created the state universities, they hold power over them because of their need for financial support."

"What you are saying, Ron Jervis," commented Frank Ruffner, "is that, by constitutional authority, public schools are a state responsibility, and that the local operation of a public school is by delegation."

"Yes, Frank," replied Ron, "and I think that the real reason why the public schools have operated at such a low level is a result of the power which vested interests have exerted over the local school boards. In this respect, teachers have been at the mercy of the politics of power. It is worthwhile to contrast this practice with the thinking of Thomas Jefferson, who held that it was the obligation of the state to defend the teacher in the exercise of his or her responsibility, and not try to define it. I would be interested in hearing from you about what the problems have been which have kept the public schools from performing at a level acceptable to Jefferson, Franklin and Paine."

"Ron," said Frank Ruffner, "in my opinion the basic problems of the public school always seem to go back to the lack of adequate financial support for a quality-type teacher. This is the place where we come into the picture. Notice how Dean Hardbutt operates at the level of the local politician. Why is he so critical of the way in which we grade our students? The answer is to be found in the fact that he thinks in terms of numbers when it comes to financing the College of Education. He is fearful that with our tough grading we will cause the enrollment to fall. You know as well as I do that upwards of half of the students in our college do not belong there. Can you really justify the sacrificing of quality performance for any amount of Dollars? You cannot do so if you have a creative purpose in mind and are willing to make the necessary sacrifice to achieve it."

"You know, Frank," said Ron Jervis, "a good example of what goes on in our public schools is illustrated by an experience which I had during my first year of teaching at this university. Dean Winters had given me the assignment of visiting a number of public elementary schools in the surrounding county area so as to get my feet wet in the operation of the educational system. On one particular occasion, as I drove up to the school building, the first grade students were singing a song that I had learned in church during my childhood — WHEN THE ROLL IS CALLED UP YONDER I'LL BE THERE. Now, contrast such an otherwordly purpose with the real needs of those children to grow in freedom of mind and body. The pitiful part of this experience is that the teacher was subjecting these children to the medieval dogma of Protestant Christianity, an outlook on life that was diametrically opposed to what our Revolutionary Fathers sought for our people."

Frank Ruffner looked at Ron Jervis in an unbelievable manner before he responded. "You are not kidding me, are you, Ron Jervis? I knew that medieval religious thought continued to prevail in our public schools, but that it could be so blatantly and stupidly taught in the first grade is hard for me to accept."

"No, I am not kidding, Frank," replied Ron Jervis. "What I have just told you is the truth, so help me. Along the same line, a number of years back, when I was a school administrator, a teacher showed me a letter which she had received from a school administrator in which he said that he liked her qualifications except that she had identified herself as a Methodist, whereas the people of his community had insisted that he hire a Baptist. Frank, I could give you an endless number of similar cases on how medieval Christian thought, supported by the power of local politicians, dominates the action of our classroom teachers."

"Ron," replied Frank Ruffner, "it could hardly be different when you consider how the mind of man is formed, and how we have failed to provide a quality of leadership in our teachers, which would give us the organized power to offset the power of those who dominate the teaching of the local church. Here is where the state university has failed, failed to provide teachers whose mental frame of reference is consistent with the minds of those who wrote the Declaration of Independence, and the Bill of Rights of the Federal Constitution. You are aware of the fact, as Bertrand Russell expressed it in his book on THE REVOLT AGAINST THE AGE OF REASON, that the nineteenth century in this country was a reaction against the enlightenment of the eighteenth century. That revolt is being demonstrated daily in the public schools of this Nation."

"Yes, very much so, Frank," responded Ron Jervis. "The history of public education in the United States is not a history of the growing free mind. To a large extent, the opposite is true. For example, look at how teachers in our public schools enthusiastically sing Christmas songs which are a basis for the support of the dogma of the Christian faith, songs such as BORN THE KING OF ANGELS — Christ the Lord — Glory to the New Born King — Christ Is Born in Bethelehem — Veiled in Flesh the God Head See — Hail the Incarnate Deity — Let Earth Receive Her King — Remember Christ Our Savior Was Born on Christmas Day — Round Yon Virgin Mother and Child — HOLY INFANT SO TENDER AND MILD. In this respect, the mind of the teacher is only a reflection of the mind of the local community.

"At no time, during more than a century and a half, have the teachers and the administrators of our public schools provided the necessary leadership to offset the influence of those who occupy the pulpits of our local churches. What is not too well known is that the Protestant church leadership, in the early part of the nineteenth century, supported the estabishment of public schools in order to keep the Catholics from getting tax money for the support of their schools. It was their belief, and they were generally correct, that they could control the public schools, and keep them in line with their particular dogma. The only exception up to now is where the Catholic population controls the election of the local school board."

At this point Mrs. Ruffner, who had been listening intently at what the two men were saying, broke into the conversation.

"Gentlemen," she said, "from what I hear you two men saying, I would have to conclude that both of you are dyed-in-the-wool atheists. Over a period of years I have found myself at odds with Frank because of his attitude toward the Christian Church. As a music teacher and supervisor, I have always found that the music of the church had a positive influence upon my students. Also, where can you find a more positive ethical basis for mankind than that which is identified with Christian doctrine?"

"Ron," replied Frank Ruffner, "what I have tried to point out to this wife of mine is that I have not, and I am sure that you have not, made any attack upon the Christian ethic. A distinction, however, must be made between Christian dogma and Christian ethics, a distinction made by those who were the backbone of the American Revolution, and by Adam Smith, the creator of free capitalistic thought. The real issue, as they saw it, was how to bring the ethics of Christianity into social reality. As for me, it is the Christian Dogma that is the bulwark which negates the possibility of our ever bringing the Christian ethic into our social operations. Scientific knowledge is needed here, and the roadblock to such knowledge is Christian Orthodoxy."

"I agree with you completely, Frank," said Ron Jervis. "It is the priesthood of the Christian church that has opposed every step in the progress of modern thought since the days of Peter Abeelard, first in the physical sciences, and now in the development of the biological sciences. What we have here is two different frames of reference as to the nature of man and the universe. The men who founded this Nation, and who were responsible for the establishment of the state university, had no doubt as to where they stood. The First Amendment to the Constitution of the United States leaves no doubt as to where they stood on this matter. Why have those of the priesthood been so adamant in their opposition to the state university and to the public school? The answer is very clear. It is because their frame of reference as to the nature of man is rooted in the dogma of medieval Christianity. This dogma is openly contrary to the enlightenment of eighteenth century thought. The establishment of the state university and the public school was a threat to their power, a power they have held for the past two thousand years of Western civilization. If you, Mrs. Ruffner, think that all those who reject the idea of a personal God are atheists, the same would hold for Benjamin Franklin, Thomas Jefferson, and Thomas Paine. Instead of belief in a personal God, these men sought for an understanding of the reality of God in nature. Their's was a rational, intellectually warranted concept of the nature of man and his universe, against the mystical intuitive Christian dogma of the Colonial Mind."

"Professor Jervis," said Mrs. Ruffner, "I do not understand all that you are saying, but what about this business of Protestants supporting the establishment of public schools in order to keep the Catholics from getting any tax money for their schools?"

"That is a matter of historical record, Gertrude," replied Ron Jervis. "As I see it now, there was no way of avoiding the issue. At first, the only person available for teaching in the public school was the Protestant minister. This was true all during the Colonial Period where the pattern of Protestant thought existed without opposition. During the early part of the nineteenth century, however, the situation had changed, so much so that the Protestant monopoly was being challenged by the increasing Catholic population. Even with the establishment of the state normal schools, the women who came out of these schools were as Protestant as their ancestors. The Catholic fathers, while establishing their parochial schools, continued their attack upon the public schools on the grounds of their Protestantism. Of recent date, however, with the Protestants losing control over the public schools, the public school has come under the attack of both Protestant and Catholic. In some respects this attack is justified, not because of the loss of Protestant control, but because these public schools no longer operate from any kind of an intellectual or moral frame of reference. Political expediency, dominated by the pressures of an urban society, has taken over. It must be admitted that, and here I repeat myself, there has been a failure of the state universities to provide the leadership necessary for an ethical basis on which our public schools should operate."

"Professor Jervis," said Gertrude Ruffner, "I wish you would comment on what you consider teachers should be doing to fill the ethical and intellectual vacuum that exists in our public schools."

"Well, Gertrude," replied Ron Jervis, "it is not so much a matter of teaching a subject as it is the kind of mind from which the teacher operates in the classroom. Assuming that the state university had done its job, there should be no controversy over the acceptance of the Christian ethic. What would be different, however, would be an understanding of the historical basis for the origin of these ethical concepts. The cultural pattern of the world in which they evolved is important at this point. For example, the period of the last two thousand years or more has brought about three structures of thought (a) the Man-God relation, (b) the Man-Object relation, and (c) the Man-Man relation. Now, how do you relate the one to the other? The quality-mind teacher would have a pattern of thought in which each of these three structures had developed into a unified purpose. After all, underlying the Man-God relation structure is the problem of the reality of life, of creation. With such an insight, the quality-mind teacher would substitute our advancing knowledge in the fields of the biological and the physical sciences on the reality of life for the Christian dogmatic concepts.

"Also, there is the problem of freedom in our society, which is equally as critical an issue as that of Christian dogma. As of now our concept of freedom has no positive meaningful reference. As Eric Fromm has said in his ESCAPE FROM FREEDOM, 'Man would be free to act according to his own will, if he knew what he wanted, thought, and felt.' But he does not know! Thus, man, in believing that he could escape from external authority, has created a crisis in our legal system. Self-will is no substitute for intelligence. Freedom is not the right to be either ignorant or dogmatic. In the final analysis, the quality mind teacher would know that freedom of knowledge, not freedom from knowledge, is imperative in a free society. In short, there is no substitute, if we are to have a quality mind teacher, for a solid grounding in social philosophy and scientific thought. Participation in the artistic, creative, scientific role in life, not conformity, should be the order of our day."

It was at this point that Helen injected her two cents' worth into the discussion. "Don't you two gentlemen think that it is high time for us to get away from this complex and controversial issue concerning the quality of our public schools, and turn to matters of a more immediate and personal interest? Since this is probably the last time that we shall be meeting together, I would hope that we could get down to earth at least for a few minutes..."

"Helen," said Gertrude Ruffner, "tell us about your new home and some of your expectations for the future. I know that you have not been too happy here, especially in the last few years, with the way that Hardbutt has deprived your husband of the salary increases to which he was entitled. The fact that the local school board would not assign you to a teaching position, because of your being the mother of a young child, has created an additional hardship for your family. I know that you must look forward to your new life in that large Capitol City."

"Gertrude," replied Helen, "I know that Frank must have discussed with you some of the difficulties that he and Ron have had with Dean Hardbutt, but you have no idea how these difficulties have affected our family life. Not being able to get a teaching position in this town made it necessary for me to take a number of odd jobs to have the necessary change in my pocket for personal effects. At one time, I even threatened to leave Ron, and you will remember that I did go back home in the eastern part of the country for a period of more than a month. Also, Ron did not tell me of his difficulties with Dean Hardbutt until the matter of his leaving for this new job came up. We were happy here as long as Winters was Dean of the College of Education, but, ever since Ron came back from Europe, after his service with the War Department had come to an end, I have not been at peace with either Ron or myself. The opportunity to leave this place, and to start life over again, is the best thing that has happened to us since Ron received his doctorate."

"Yes, Helen," replied Gertrude, "I can understand why you are so excited about the opportunity to live among oil barons and cowboys. They tell me that you are going to live in a kind of oasis, a cultural center in a desert of backward people. Frank tells me that not only will Ron be getting a considerable increase in salary, but that you should have no difficulty in fulfilling your heart's desire, that of returning to the classroom. But what about your arrangements for moving, and where do you expect to live?"

"Gertrude," said Helen, "when the possibility of Ron's making a change in his teaching position came up, Ron informed Dean Hazwell, the man who will be his new boss, that the expense of moving would be in the neighborhood of $1,000, and that we just did not have that much cash on hand. Dean Hazwell responded immediately by saying that the administration had adequate funds to cover the cost of our moving regardless of the expense. Can you imagine Dean Hardbutt doing such a thing for either Frank or Ron? Well, that gracious reply was enough for us to make the final decision for a change in location.

"Now on the matter of where we shall be living, we are most happy that such a decision has already been made. On our trip to look over the prospects of our taking the new position, I, while Ron was talking to the university administration, visited around the city with a real estate agent. Fortunately, I was able to find just what Ron and I agreed was the perfect home for us. The house, located in a new area of development in the City, is to be completed by the time we arrive with our furniture in late August."

"This Dean Hazwell," asked Frank Ruffner, "what kind of a person is he? He has already indicated that he is very much interested in getting you on his faculty, else he would never have offered to pay for your moving. At any rate he could not be any worse than Hardbutt."

"Frank," replied Ron Jervis, "while my knowledge of the nature of the man is not what I would like for it to have been,

I do know that he has a strong Presbyterian background, and is very ambitious in promoting his cause with the University Board of Regents, both personally and for the College of Education. Also, he is much interested in promoting the Intellectual Foundations of Education, which is very much the opposite of the point of view of Dean Hardbutt. This Presbyterian allegiance of his does give me some concern, but I can respect his orthodox mind if he can respect my Dewey Pragmatism. Also, the College of Education, of which he is Dean, is organized along departmental lines in such a way as to see to it that the Dean does not have the kind of personal power over the faculty as does Dean Hardbutt. As for the overall picture, I do not find that any of our state universities is any more true to the faith of those who founded the state university than the university to which I am going. The basic problem which I will have there is much the same as it has been here, but the specific conditions will be different."

Since the hour was getting late, and since both of the men had an early morning class session, they dropped the discussion at this point. Soon Frank Ruffner and his wife were on their way; but before leaving these good friends expressed to both Helen and Ron their best wishes for a happy life in their new environment. After they had departed, Ron turned to Helen with a comment on the conversation of the evening.

"You know, Helen," said Ron, "I am sure that you noticed a certain amount of friction between Gertrude and Frank. I have known for some time that all was not well between the two of them, which is the reason for Gertrude's outburst against the two of us on the matter of atheism. In a way, I was surprised when you told me that she had accepted your invitation to visit with us tonight. During the past year Frank tells me that she has been in the habit of turning down all the invitations she has received from her friends. I am sure that her actions have contributed more than a little to Frank's having an interest in one of his female graduate students."

"Ron Jervis," said Helen, "how did you come to find out about Frank's new love life? I would have expected that from

Professor Sterling, but not from Frank Ruffner."

"I think that you are being too hard on Frank, Helen," said Ron, "the lady in question is a very fine school teacher, a woman in her thirties, and certainly not one to engage in hanky-panky."

"You speak as if you know the woman, Ron Jervis," said Helen. "Maybe you have a girl friend hidden somewhere in the closet, say, maybe, that Clayton gal."

"Now Helen," said Ron, "if I thought you were serious in what you have just said, I would reply in a hostile manner. I know the woman in question, having had her in class, and having observed her while she was teaching in a public school near this city. Also, If Gertrude will not make the effort to socialize with Frank, why should he not seek the company of a girl friend? If such an association should blossom into a love affair, it is not difficult to see that the break between Frank and Gertrude would be of her own making."

"Well Ron," said Helen, "I can see that we could never agree on this issue. I will agree with you that Gertrude is helping to create a bad situation. I hope, however, that I am never forced to face a similar situation for, if so, I could no longer live with you."

"Helen," said Ron, "what is fair for the goose is fair for the gander. Now let us get to bed, for we have quite a bit of work ahead of us on the tomorrow."

Now, the days for Ron Jervis and his wife were to pass in rapid succession. Yet, there was still much work to be done. There was the problem of Ron's completing his summer session work. Also, there was the problem of closing up their house, and getting the movers to take care of their furniture. One matter did come up that Ron did not expect, a matter involving the leaving of those graduate students who were studying under Ron's supervision. Ron had been informed that Dean Hardbutt was telling them he was responsible for creating the situation, that he was totally to blame for leaving them high and dry. This lying on the part of the Dean, Ron was determined to counteract in every way possible. As a result, he arranged for a meeting with his students as soon as he could get in touch with them. On the Friday afternoon after the rumor, Ron Jervis made the following Statement:

"It has come to my attention that Dean Hardbutt has been saying that I was running out on my responsibility to you. Nothing could be farther from the truth. While it is true that I will be receiving a much higher salary than I am now receiving, that is not the main reason for my departure. Ever since Dean Hardbutt became Dean of this College he has opposed me, not only personally, but what I stand for professionally. To be honest with you, I put up with his discrimination until a better professional offer came my way. Dean Hardbutt's conduct and his political maneuvers have been of such a character that I have lost respect for him personally, as well as for his ability to administer this College justly and with honor. You must know of the differences that I have had with him over the rights of such students as Robert Combs and Iris Clayton. The problem here is that the Dean sees his role in terms of power politics, not in terms of a commitment to the principles of those who were responsible for the founding of this Nation."

"Professor Jervis," responded student John Gray, "is that the reason why you have put so much stress on quality in our education effort? You are convinced that Dean Hardbutt is more interested in numbers than he is in quality performance. I have heard that the Dean is very critical of you and Professor Ruffner because of the number of low grades you have given your students."

"You are right, John," said Professor Jervis. "We have been called into the Dean's office on several occasions for our grading policies."

"There is a real problem here for the graduate student," spoke up Sam Potts. "You must know that if we did as you have advised us to do, we would not last the year out on our first job, and then what would happen to us?"

"I will admit, Sam," said Professor Jervis, "that what I hold as the role of the teacher in our culture is not popular with our public school administrators. On the other hand, unless the public school teacher is willing to assume the role of leadership in our society, there is no future for the free man and woman. I do not think that I am asking more of you than I have been willing to assume for myself. To achieve the purpose which I think that we should seek, it may well be necessary that we organize into a teacher's union. If the state legislature will not defend the teacher in the exercise of his or her responsibility, then we have no other choice than to organize to defend ourselves. Benjamin Franklin said it very well, 'We either stick together or we hang separately.' "

Student John Gray now spoke up again. "If I understand you, Professor Jervis, you are saying that the low status of the public school teacher is traceable to the failure of the state universities to require a high quality of performance before the student is certified as a teacher. This issue seems to be at the root of your conflict with the Dean. Along with the need for a more selective program for going into teaching, what changes would you make in the teacher education curriculum?"

"John," replied Professor Jervis, "you have put your finger on the most significant aspect of my problem with the Dean. What we have in this College, true of most of our teacher education schools and colleges in this country, is a program dominated by the concept of subject matter specialization, on the one hand, and teaching methodology on the other. Since this subject matter content is taught without any ethical or intellectual frame of reference, and with no relation to the culture in which we operate, there is no choice but to assume that the individual is born with an ethical and rational sense. This idea was believed in the eighteenth century, but, as you well know, is without merit in our present-day thinking. The Marxist understands this problem quite well. Also, the rationale for freedom in our lives does not exist in a vacuum. What is grossly needed is a cultural outlook in which freedom is taught and intellectually acquired. Our public schools have no meaning and value frame of reference which serves as a core of thought in the mind of the teacher and the school administrator. If those who are responsible for the operation of our public schools do not give voice to a quality free mind, then the students coming out of these schools cannot be expected to do so."

Emma Leigh, another graduate student, spoke up. "Professor Jervis, what you have just said about a meaning and value frame of reference clears up a number of problems for me, especially that of a free mind in a free society. The people who are coming out of our public schools and universities, instead of being enlightened, are little more than cultural robots. In this connection, I have heard that Dean Hardbutt has criticized both you and Professor Ruffner for your stand on the homosexual issue in this university."

"Miss Leigh," said Professor Jervis, "all of what you have just said is very true. As you must know, I have served on the University Conduct Committee for the past ten years. About four years ago, the issue of homosexuals on this campus, for both faculty and students, became a pressing issue before our Committee. The President of this University, along with all of the Deans, began to press those of us who were on the Committee to do something before the state politicians took advantage of the situation. The issue was so pressing that the Chairman of the Committee divided us into two sub-groups, of one of which I was made Chairman. Because of the fact that this state had a two-year prison term waiting for a proven homosexual, we chose to place the responsibility for such a decision on the medical profession. This was necessary to avoid any court suit against the University. Although we devoted many hours in dealing with the crisis, we got little thanks from the university administration for our efforts. Actually, we were criticized for our decisions after the crisis had passed and the heat was taken off the administration."

"But why were you so hard on those who were held to be homosexuals?" asked Miss Leigh. "Was it just because they were declared to be guilty of such, or had they committed some crime that could not be classified in a different manner?"

"Miss Leigh," replied Professor Jervis, "where the medical profession determined that the individual was a homosexual we were left with no other choice than that of expulsion because of the law. There were a few cases where the individual was involved with the sexual abuse of young boys, and, in such instances, we were tough on the guilty party. Insofar as my opinion is concerned, I would hold that the homosexual has the same rights and privileges as any other individual. What we have in dealing with the homosexual is another example of the way in which we discriminate against minorities, a violation of the freedom rights of the individual under our federal constitution."

"Professor Jervis," said student James Caldwell, "I can see why it had become impossible for you to continue working with Dean Hardbutt. It is clear to me that the Dean was not only against the homosexual because he did not want him to become a teacher, but because of political reasons. Your leaving, however, does create a problem for us, and, since such is the case, what do you recommend that we do?"

"Jim," responded Professor Jervis, "my leaving this University in no way places any one of you in jeopardy, although I will admit that it does create some problems. Someone will be taking my place here in a very short time, and, whoever it is, I am sure that he or she will be happy to continue to help you on your way to the doctorate. Of course, I would like to have continued working with all of you, and, had it not been for circumstances beyond my control, I would have continued my work here. If per chance any one or more of you would find it desirable to make the change with me, I would be most happy to have you come along."

With these remarks of Ron Jervis, the session ended. In the meantime, each of the students present came up to shake the professor's hand, and to wish him godspeed in his future position. If an outsider had been present, it would have been very clear that Dean Hardbutt had failed miserably in his attempt to downgrade the professor in the eyes of his students. It would have been evident to the observer that each one of these students had not only a lasting respect for their professor, but also for his outspoken integrity, and for his ability to establish a friendly and working relation with each one of them.

The extent to which Ron Jervis was being confronted by power groups in the academic world came out again in a controversy that arose between him and his publisher, over certain interpretations in his manuscript on the HISTORY OF EDUCATION IN THE AMERICAN CULTURE. As might be assumed, Ron Jervis, in one of the early chapters of his manuscript, had pointed out that, during the Colonial Period of American History, when the educational effort was controlled by Protestant groups, there was little freedom of mind among the people, only allegiance to a pattern of medieval dogma. Class consciousness, slavery, and indentured servitude were rampant in all of the colonies. To all of this, the Copy Editor took serious objection. Surely Ron Jervis was unfair to those church fathers such as Cotton Mather, Increase Mather, John Cotton, and Jonathon Edwards. When Ron pointed out to him that the well-known scholar V.L. Parrington, in his MAIN CURRENTS IN AMERICAN THOUGHT, had come to the same conclusions, his opposition to Ron's statements was dropped. On such matters as "The Role of Science in the American Culture," and "How the Political System Had Been Used to Betray the Cause of Freedom," no agreement was reached. The Copy Editor objected seriously to the idea that scientific knowledge had been used exclusively for profit, in total disregard for the general welfare of the people. So far as Ron Jervis was concerned, there was little relation between what the Revolutionary Fathers had visualized as the greatest contribution of scientific knowledge, and the way it had been used in the industrialization of the country during the nineteenth century. If there was a "Betrayal on Mount Parnassus" it was here. Free-enterprise capitalism, without an ethical and intellectual frame of reference, could only lead to more greed on the part of the wealthy and to more poverty among the poor of the world. This rape of science was the basis for the spread of Communism and the growing power of the U.S.S.R. To try to down the Communist movement by attacking it in a negative, militaristic way, by lies and the distortion of the facts, could only add to human misery for all of us. The only way to counteract this spread of Communist power was to demonstrate by deeds that the free democratic way of life was superior in terms of the GENERAL WELFARE. This we were not doing.

Nowhere in our cultural operations was our failure as a free society more manifest than in the way we conducted our political affairs. This Ron had spelled out in significant detail over the objections of the Copy Editor. It was clear to him that our political practices were fascistic, a bastardization of the ideas of the founders of the Nation. Again, instead of being operated on the basis of the common good, these operations were, almost without exception, anti-intellectual and power-motivated. Attack and tear down your opponent as if you were engaged in a boxing match with no holds barred. The way in which our politicians sought to gain the power of office was destructive for the Nation, and not an exercise of the principle of freedom. Since the public schools had been politically controlled throughout our entire history, it is not surprising that they have been marked by a high level of general incompetence.

The upshot for Ron Jervis was that, if he were going to get his book published, he had to compromise with the Copy Editor. The final result of his conclusion was that only a part of the manuscript was published, the part which dealt with the way in which the public schools were founded, their financing and their control. In so far as the contents of the book were concerned, Ron could say that in no way had he compromised his position. He would have preferred to have the book published in its original form, but that was not to be. There was no way in which he could dictate to his publisher what should be printed.

Before Ron Jervis could be accepted as a Graduate Professor in his new position, it was necessary that he appear before the Graduate Committee on Admissions to the Graduate Faculty. At the time of the meeting of the Committee, his record of teaching and research was reviewed with much care and with numerous questions. Professor W.O. Snyder of the English Department, who was later to become one of Ron's best friends, was the first to speak.

"Professor Jervis," said Professor Snyder, "let me first ask you a very personal question. Why, after more than fifteen years at your previous institution, did you choose to resign and accept a position here?"

"Professor Snyder," replied Ron Jervis, "this is not a difficult question for me to make a reply. The simple fact is that I found myself in such direct opposition to the policies of my Dean that I could no longer effectively work with him. Over a period of time, this situation led to much friction and a loss of personal respect. He is one of those trade-training Deans; whereas I, like many of my colleagues, thought that teachers being certified by our College should be qualified to serve as leaders of social thought in their respective communities. As you fellows know, the word TEACHER comes from the Latin word which means to lead. In my judgment, a mandate imposed on every state university professor and the public school teacher is that of operating in an ethical and intellectual frame of reference that would sustain and implement the education of free men and women in a free society."

"Professor Jervis," responded Dr. William Dean, Professor of Chemistry, "I find what you are saying of much interest, but I also find it difficult to believe that any teacher who operates in a community in the manner which you have prescribed could survive the term of her contract. A scientific mind is not what the majority of the people want or would tolerate. Also, it is my job to teach chemistry. That is what I was hired to do, and nothing else is expected of me. What happens to this country is not my responsibility. If a knowledge of the chemistry which I teach is used to kill my fellow man, that is not my baby. It is the philosopher's job to teach ethics, not mine."

"I have no quarrel with the idea of subject matter specialization, Professor Dean," said Professor Jervis, "but I do find serious objection to your idea of teaching your subject in a cultural vacuum, and that is what many of you in the College of Arts and Sciences are doing. I would call such teaching a betrayal of the faith of those who were responsible for the founding of the state university."

At this point, Professor Snyder re-entered the discussion. "Professor Jervis, your position on the role of the public school teacher reminds me of what William Shakespeare said when he wrote, 'There is a tide in the affairs of men which, taken at the flood, leads on to fortune. Omitted, all the voyage of their life is bound in shallows and miseries. On such a full sea are we now afloat; and we must take the current when it serves or lose our ventures.' "

"Yes, Professor Snyder," replied Ron Jervis. "No one has said it better than the great Bard. You will observe, Professor Dean, that when it comes to teaching, I am a generalist. The whole is always greater than the sum of its parts. In this case, the welfare of this Nation is tied up in the role which we assume as teachers. In the light of the reason why this state university and all the others were established, I see no way in which a public school teacher, or state university professor, can avoid his or her responsibility for promoting the education of free men and women."

"This last comment of Ron Jervis brought on a general discussion from all of those present. (There were seven of them.) The discussion was so heated that there was a tendency to forget the reason as to why they were there. Finally, Professor John Stuart, of the Psychology Department, turned the questioning back to the one that was being interviewed.

"Professor Jervis, I would judge from what you have been saying, that you are of the opinion that we do not, in truth, have a SCIENCE OF EDUCATION, only a Science of Methodology. Also, that such methodology is being used exclusively as a means of teaching this or that subject in total disregard as to how this subject will be used in the society that supports its teaching. Is that what you are saying?"

"Definitely so, Professor Stuart," replied Ron Jervis. "To have a SCIENCE OF EDUCATION there is need of an educational process in which the subject matter in question is directed toward an ethical commitment and an intellectual sense of responsibility. As we are now operating our public schools, we have no meaningful frame of reference, only an ethical and intellectual vacuum in which the free mind cannot possibly thrive."

"Gentlemen," said Professor Mangus of the Sociology Department, "I find myself in complete agreement with professor Jervis on the role of the teacher in a free society. He has put his finger on the basic reason as to why our schools are failing to meet the needs of our people. The leadership role and need for the teacher are irrefutable. So far as I am concerned, I am willing, without further discussion, to recommend Professor Jervis to a graduate professorship, with all the rights and privileges of such a position."

There was unanimous agreement on the motion of Professor Mangus. As the men departed for the evening, each shook the hand of Ron Jervis and complimented him on his performance. Each man expressed the hope that he would find his new professional life both challenging and satisfying. Professor Snyder was so taken with Ron's performance that he expressed the desire to get to know him better, and to meet with him again sometime in the near future. As for Ron Jervis, he was equally pleased with the outcome of his interview, and looked forward to many new challenges in the years ahead.

What kind of a state university was this institution to which Ron Jervis had now dedicated himself? In an operational sense, there was no fundamental difference between this institution and the one that he had just left. For Ron Jervis, however, the personal differences were very apparent. To begin with, there was a vast difference between the two institutions in terms of wealth and environment. Revenues from oil and gas made this state university one of the highest-endowed in the Nation. In contrast, the institution from which he had just departed had little or no endowment, making it heavily dependent on the state legislature for financial support. Also, Ron and his wife, Helen, now found themselves in a cosmopolitan community, literally a cultural oasis in a desert of cultural backwardness. This cultural change was pointed up in the fact that the community from which Ron had departed was known as Little Dixie because of the predominance of the traditional Southern influence. Again, in this new environment, there was little of the agricultural influence in the state university program, which was not the case in his former position.

As for the state legislature, the same kind of power role was being exercised as was true in all of the states, but here it was divided between the rural politicians and those coming from the growing urban centers. As a result of the expanding oil and gas business, the power of the petroleum corporations was becoming more evident in the acts passed by the state legislators. How this growing power was affecting the public schools system and the state university was the big question.

It was the discovery of oil and gas on the public lands that made it possible to provide a solid financial basis for the university plant, and for plant maintenance. Aside from the salaries paid to the faculty in the field of the Sciences, salaries in the other fields of knowledge were comparable to those paid in other state universities. The power exercised by the petroleum corporation lawyers was clearly demonstrated in the laws passed by the legislature relating to both the public schools and university.

It was not until Ron Jervis had become established as a resident in his new community that he came to realize how much technology had come to dominate every aspect of the everyday life of the people. The growing dominance of technology over the cultural life of the people correlated with the strong emphasis on methodology in the teacher education program, and with the emphasis on subject matter specialization. While the state university was being adequately supported on a comparative basis with other state universities, the same could not be said for the public schools.

The industrial development of the state had led to a high centralization of wealth in a few large urban communities. Since the idea of local support of public education still prevailed, and since most of the local school districts in the state were rural, equal education for all was no more than a myth. Also, since most of the people living in the southern part of the state were Mexican-American, there was an added language problem in their communities. Here, in these Mexican-American communities, there was little effort to enforce the compulsory state school attendance law, which accounted for the high degree of illiteracy found in these communities. Poverty was indeed a marked everyday characteristic of the life of these people. Is it any wonder that, in the light of the overall conditions in the rural communities, the state ranked third in technology in the Nation and fiftieth in cultural deprivation?

When Ron Jervis came to his new position he was well aware of the turmoil that had prevailed over a period of years in the administration of the university. This turmoil was a result of the differences in thinking between the Board and the Faculty. It had been, and was continuing to be, the opinion of the Board of Regents that the authority which had been granted to them by the state legislature and the governor was absolute, not only in matters of administration, but in determining what the faculty should teach and what books they could use. It should be recognized that this is a fascistic position and that such was the reason why the faculty opposed their position. On one occasion, of very recent date, the Board of Regents took the position that a Professor of History could not use John Dos Passos's book *History of the U.S.A.* in his classes as a reading requirement. When the President of the University refused to fire the professor, the Board proceeded to fire the President. Here we have a specific example of how the Boards of Regents in our state universities have violated, in thought and in practice, the basic principles on which the state university was founded.

The many examples of how the presidents of these state universities have assumed dictatorial authority over the faculty as well as the Board of Regents led to the professors organizing themselves into the American Association of University

Professors. It was the practice of this association to BLACKLIST any university that was proven to have violated the academic freedom or tenure of the professor. When Ron Jervis took up his new position, he was aware of the fact that his new institution had been so blacklisted. He had been informed by his friend Jack Knight, before leaving his former position, of the situation. At the same time, he had learned as to what kind of man his new college president was, and in particular as a university administrator. President Knight had expressed the opinion that his new President, although a "Cold Fish," was a man of strong character, and that this was the kind of man needed to protect the faculty from the tyranny of the Board. It was at his first meeting with President John Lothan that Ron Jervis raised the question concerning the blacklisting of the University.

"President Lothan," said Ron Jervis, "at the time I was considering the possibility of accepting a position at this University, President Jack Knight, who by the way sends you his greetings, and I discussed the fact that this University had been blacklisted by the American Association of University Professors. Since I am unfamiliar with the facts of the case, can you tell me how this came about?"

"Professor Jervis," replied President Lothan, "first, let me welcome you to our campus. Your former President, Jack Knight, recommends you most highly, and I want to assure you that our main purpose is to make this institution one of the outstanding state universities in the United States. Now, as to your question concerning the blacklisting of this University, I can give you the inside facts on the case, because I was involved in the controversy at the time that such action was taken. At the time the issue was raised, I was a Professor of Sociology and a representative of the Faculty. The Board of Regents had overridden the action of the President, and had fired a Professor of Economics because he had openly taken the side of a Labor Union involving one of the oil companies. I did not agree with the Board's action and I told them so. When the former President resigned because of the Board's action, and I was offered the position, I told the members of the Board that I would accept the offer provided that they would not interfere with my administrative policy. I am glad to say that thus far they have stuck to their word."

"It is good to hear you say that the Board has stuck by its agreement," said Professor Jervis, "for it creates havoc when the Board of Regents gets involved in the internal policies of the university. Also, the members of this faculty with whom I have talked are very happy to have a President who will stand up against the Board, for such Board action tends to belittle the university in the eyes of scholars throughout the world."

"Now let me ask you a question, Professor Jervis," said President Lothan. "Where do you stand on the issue of academic freedom and tenure?"

"President Lothan, I have no hesitancy in responding to your question," replied Professor Jervis. "It is my opinion that the state university is as much a child of the American Revolution as is the Declaration of Independence. As such, it has a clearcut obligation to contribute to the GENERAL WELFARE of this Nation. The concept of the general welfare is indelibly tied in with the idea of a free society. Since such is the case, academic freedom and tenure are vitally necessary if we are to have the kind of education necessary for the development of the Free Mind. The purpose of academic freedom and tenure was never to protect the vested interests of a professor. As is the case of all such policies, however, there are those who are ready to exploit the common good; but it is not the mark of intelligence to throw the baby out with the bath water."

"Professor Jervis," said President Lothan, "I have long defended the idea of academic freedom and tenure, but there are times when, as you expressed it, I am ready to throw the baby out with the bath water because of the arrogance of some self-willed professor. Also, it takes a lot of guts to stand up against a vested interest board member who wants some professor fired because he disagrees with him. For example, just now we are being confronted with the issue of who should be admitted to this University. We are being accused of discriminating against black students when the issue is not one of race but one of quality performance. I understand that you had some difficulty over the race issue at your previous institution. Tell me about it."

"President Lothan," replied Ron Jervis, "the issue which confronted me as a graduate professor involved the question of scholarly research and the responsibility which I had toward the graduate student who was doing his work under my supervision. Mr. Combs had included a chapter in his dissertation dealing with state school administrative officials and their educational policies. Although the chapter was thoroughly documented, I doubted that the new Dean of the College of Education and the Professor of Administration would approve of it because of the racial bias demonstrated by these state officials. Although I had told the student that he might be turned down by the committee, he insisted on retaining the material in his study, and I supported him in doing so. At the committee meeting, the two men in question did exactly what I had feared they would do. They turned Mr. Combs down, and told him that if he were to get his degree he would have to omit the material in question. At the time of the meeting, the student refused to omit the material, but three months later he acquiesced, and was approved for the doctorate. I can say that the data that were omitted from the dissertation were published in a national Negro magazine of some prominence."

"Professor Jervis," said President Lothan, "I think that you handled the situation most admirably. Now, on the question of admitting Negroes and Mexican-Americans into this university, the question is clearly a matter of standards. OF QUALITY PERFORMANCE. Because of the cultural and low level of performance of these minority individuals, very few ever graduate from high school, and , of those who do, many suffer from the same limitations. If this university is to maintain a quality performance, we cannot lower our standards below present admission requirements. As to discriminating against any racial group, that is just not so."

"President Lothan," replied Professor Jervis, "I too have been criticized because of my insistence on quality performance, especially by my former Dean. As you must know, many College of Education Professors are noted for handing out high grades to their students, even here in your institution. You will not find me guilty of such practices. This continuing warfare between the professor in the College of Arts and Sciences and the College of Education is clearcut evidence that we are not serving the general welfare of the Nation. If each one of these areas was thought of as a means and not as an end, we might be able to come to some common understanding."

"What common purpose do you have in mind, Professor Jervis?" asked President Lothan. "I am aware of the fact that although we speak of a liberal education there is no longer any such thing today."

"President Lothan," replied Ron Jervis, "I have particular reference to the purpose that was laid down by our Revolutionary Fathers in establishing the state university, that of providing leadership for the people in a free society. As I see it, such is not possible without the development of a free mind, and that we are not doing, either in terms of meaning or value."

"Professor Jervis,' said the President, "whether I agree with you or not as to why this university was established, I must agree with you on our present cultural condition. I would guess that this situation somewhat explains much of the conflict that exists in the thinking of the military and the civilian population. The military mind sacrifices freedom for the general welfare, whereas the civilian would sacrifice the general welfare for his FREEDOM."

"Your analysis of our cultural situation, President Lothan," replied Ron Jervis, "is very insightful. It is good to hear you speak from such a point of view. On the matter of the civilian being willing to sacrifice the general welfare for freedom, please note that our concept of freedom has been resolved into nothing more than the right to get rich. There is no doubt in my mind that our civilian population is suffering from a pattern of mind formation that comes out of early childhood. Parental conditioning that begins at this point is more attitudinally emotive than intellectual, and is based on belief rather than analysis. It is such people that exercise politcal power over the local school board. This kind of power over the teacher invariably is set against the development of a free mind and leads to regimented racial, political, religious and economic dogmatism. Note how this type of control shows up in the textbooks and library materials available for the classroom."

"Does this mean, Professor Jervis," asked President Lothan, "that you would give public school teachers the right to select the materials they use in their teaching? I know where you stand in so far as college professors are concerned."

"President Lothan," replied Ron Jervis, "it is my understanding that Thomas Jefferson held to the position that the state should defend the teacher in the exercise of his or her respnsibility, rather than define what that responsitiliby is. Our present pattern of operation is just the opposite of that proposed by Jefferson. We have turned out public schools into a form of political dogmatism. Under such conditions it is not possible to promote the kind of society visualized by our Revolutionary fathers. Yes, teachers, as agents of a free society, should not only have the responsibility of selecting their textbooks and other classroom materials but should have the freedom to examine any and all public issues. Our problem is not to deny the teacher his or her professional freedom, but to promote a quality of teacher education consistent with the development of a FREE MIND."

"Professor Jervis," said the President, "you seem to bring the issue down to the conviction that it is the state university which has failed us, and, in so far as teachers are concerned, it is the faculties of the College of Arts and Sciences and the College of Education that have been most directly involved."

"President Lothan, you have stated my position correctly. My position is that we are witnessing a betrayal of the faith and trust which those who founded this NATION placed on us," said Professor Jervis.

"Professor Jervis," said President Lothan, "I would like to continue this discussion for I find it most provocative, but I have an appointment coming up in five minutes. Let me once again welcome you to our campus. Be assured that I look forward at a later date to continuing our discussion on the role of the state university in a free society."

As Ron Jervis left the President's office, he felt much better about the man than he did when he entered. President Knight had told him that the man was "A Cold Fish" but he had not found him so after the ice was broken. What Ron did not know was that President Lothan had gotten the impression that he was a homosexual because he was wearing a pink shirt at the time of the interview. So far as Ron Jervis was concerned this personal impression of the President was not nearly so important to him as was the apparent evidence that the President was a man of character, the kind of man that would stand up against the personal intrusion of the Board of Regents in the administration of the internal affairs of the University.

Now that Ron Jervis had become acquainted with his new President, his next concern was his Dean. What kind of a man was he, both personally and professionally? It was this thought that ran through his mind as he sat in the Dean's office on the morning after his visit with the President. He had learned some things about his new Dean from Jack Knight, and from some of the members of his faculty. It might be expected that, from all of this background knowledge, he would have gotten some differences of opinion. Faculty members of the College of Arts and Sciences were generally negative about him, and for different reasons. In the first place, there was the generally negative attitude which such members display toward the faculty of the College of Education. In addition there was a negative attitude toward the Dean because of his desire to become President of the University. Finally, there was the known fact of his allegiance to a Presbyterian pattern of religious dogma. Most members of the College of Education faculty tended to go along with him because of his leadership ability. There had been a definite improvement in faculty salaries, as well as his securing federal aid for a number of research grants, especially in the field of Educational Psychology. As to his new Dean, there was no doubt in the mind of Ron Jervis that he was a considerable improvement over Dean Hardbutt. In this respect, Ron Jervis looked forward to years of solid professional service . As Ron reflected on these matters, the Dean's Secretary called out to him.

"Professor Jervis, you can go in now. The Dean is ready to receive you."

As Ron Jervis entered the inner office of Dean Lon Hazwell, the Dean rose from his chair and came forward with his hand out.

"Welcome to our campus, Professor Jervis," said Dean Hazwell. "It is good to have you with us, I am looking forward to what, I am sure, will be a significant contribution on your part to the program of our College."

"It is good to see you again, Dean Hazwell. I well remember the summer I spent on your campus as a visiting professor. Little did I realize at that time that I would become a member of your faculty. Let me thank you for providing the means to move my family. As I told you at the time, we just could not have made it had it not been for your generous help."

"Professor Jervis," replied the Dean, "I was glad to have the opportunity to provide the necessary cash so that you could move your furniture and household goods. We were fortunate in having sufficient private funds. I hope that you are well located, and that you are ready to begin work two weeks from now when we begin our registration."

"Yes, Dean Hazwell," replied Profesor Jervis. "We are located in a beautiful house in the northwest part of the City. Our furniture arrived two days ago, and we are settled down ready for the opening of the fall semester. While you are aware of the fact that I tried to help you find someone to fill Professor Basil's place (Basil had resigned during the summer months), I am most happy with your final choice."

"We did try to follow your suggestions," replied the Dean, "and intreviewed most of the men that you recommended, but not one of them was acceptable. Profesor Martinez was so bent on getting you here that nothing would satisfy him but have me call you, after you had turned us down. He was especially interested in you because you have a point of view that we are trying to promote in our teacher education program. As a result, you have been given the responsibility of organizing the undergraduate course which is required of all our students seeking the teacher certification degree. You will not find this an easy task because our students are more interested in what they call practical courses, those which help them in teaching their subject matter specialization. Very few of these students appreciate the need for a course that will help them grow in quality of mind, the foundation stone of any quality classroom teaching."

"Dean Hazwell," responded Professor Jervis, "You might be interested in hearing that this is where I found myself in disagreement with my former Dean. As he saw it, teacher education was nothing more than TRADE TRAINING, not an artistic and intellectual performance. Unless our state universities seek to provide that kind of education which contributes to the making of real leaders in all of our professions, we will not continue to survive as a free society. It seems to me that it is the absence of such a point of view in teacher education that is contributing to much of the conflict between the faculties of the College of Arts and Sciences and College Education. If we had a common purpose, such as that laid down by our Revolutionary Fathers, there would be little difficulty in resolving the differences between our two colleges."

"I agree with you, Professor Jervis," replied the Dean. "As you well know, those who are interested only in the advancement of knowledge are indifferent as to how this knowledge is used. This is especially true of those who teach in the field of the physical sciences."

"I have no quarrel, Dean," said Professor Jervis, "with the subject matter approach when it comes to the advancement of knowledge; but, when it comes to teaching, there is an imperative need for a concern as to how this knowledge is to be used. I think that this is true especially for the state university. It should be noted that this university was founded because of the need for leadership in this state. I know how close you have been associated with the Christian Orthodox Presbyterian tradition, whereas I am referred to by my friends as a John Dewey Pragmatist. I also know that on this matter of a free society we are in complete agreement."

"Very much so," said Dean Hazwell. "There is always the question as to how much can be accomplished in a given course. At least we can make a beginning and hope that the student will carry on from that point. It has been made evident to me that we have a need for teachers who have an awareness of the problem of quality teaching, especially when the GENERAL WELFARE of the country is involved. Also, by maintaining a quality standard, you will eliminate those who are unfit for the classroom. We need to eliminate the weak student who has been getting by because some professor is always handing out high grades. It will take a certain amount of guts to accomplish this purpose; but, from what I have heard about your teaching, you should be used to this kind of pressure."

"Dean Hazwell," said Ron Jervis, "I want to thank you for your consideration and interest in my future here on this campus. I note that I must move along now for a session with Professor Martinez. I am sure that we shall have other opportunities to discuss my work with you and other members of the faculty as the occasion arises."

Professor Martinez had found in Ron Jervis, during the summer that Ron had taught with him, a man to his own liking. His basic concern was not methodology or some specialized subject matter, but the general welfare of his people, the Mexican Americans. Martinez' genetic background was a mixture of Spanish blood with that of the Hopi Indian. He had grown up in the poverty of a mining village in the state of New Mexico, had worked his way through college, and had received his doctorate from one of the state universities in California. Since receiving his doctorate, he had made significant research contributions to his profession, in areas related to the poverty and educational conditions prevailing among his people. As a political activist, he had drawn the wrath of some members of the Board of Regents, as well as the university administration. While he was too politically powerful for them to fire him, they could and did keep him from getting any salary increases. Here was the same tactic that had been used on Ron Jervis by his previous Dean. When Ron entered the office of Professor Martinez that day, he was welcomed as a true friend and colleague. When he saw Ron walking toward him, he jumped from his chair and, with a big smile, was the first to speak.

"Well, Ron," said Professor Martinez, "when you were here two summers ago, you will recall that I spoke to you about joining us when and if the occasion arose. At that time, the door was closed and you spoke in a doubtful manner. Fortunately, for us, the chance arose for you to consider our offer, when Professor Basil resigned to go back to his native state to teach in an arts and sciences college. I did appreciate your sending me that long list of names, and we did check on most of them, but with little satisfaction. On the other hand, I was determined to get you back here if at all possible, and so I told Dean Hazwell. When you expressed doubt abut the possibility of your accepting our offer, I had the Dean call you. As for the rest of the deliberations, you know them only too well."

"Ricardo, you must know that, from the beginnings of our discussions," said Ron Jervis, "I had a number of reasons for desiring to join up with you; but I had to assure myself that both you and the Dean were fully satisfied with what I had to offer. I did have some personal problems, such as buying a new home and making sure that my wife and daughter were willing to make the move. Your Dean is a very persuasive individual, and when he offered to pay my moving expenses, the last barrier came down. I can assure you that I am most happy with my new position, and for many reasons. Things have settled down since my arrival, and I am ready to go to work.

Since you have already signed me up for certain courses, and have assured me that the necessary texts are here, it only remains for us to see how many students will register for my classes. I have discussed the matter of the required undergraduate course with the Dean, and am fully satisfied with what he had to say."

"Professor Jervis," said Professor Martinez, "have no worry about a sufficient number of students for your classes. We try to limit the number of students in a given class to thirty-five, but sometimes we have no alternative but to raise the limit to forty."

"That is no problem, Ricardo," said Ron Jervis, "since I have been teaching classes with up to a hundred or more students. The limit of forty students will be most welcome."

"On the graduate level," said Professor Martinez, "your classes will be much smaller, probably not more than twenty-five. We have a policy of requiring that all our Masters' Degree students take at least one course in the Philosophy of Education, and here you will be directly responsible for the course content. As of now, we have only two students taking the doctorate in your area, but I am hopeful, now that you are here, that there will be a significant increase in that number."

"Ricardo" said Ron Jervis, "it is good to have you express such confidence in my teaching, but what is your explanation for such a small number of graduate students taking their doctorate in our department?"

"Speaking quite frankly, Ron," said Ricardo, "we have not had anyone here in this Department who treated the field of Philosophy of Education as anything more than a watered-down Philosophy course. This kind of subject matter approach just does not appeal to those who are looking for the kind of cultural analysis which we consider of primary significance. Only by such an approach can we attract those in school administration and in historical research. The truth of the matter is that those who think of Philosophy of Education as a watered-down course in Philosophy should be teaching in the College of Arts and Sciences. One of these men, whom I admired very much, ruled this Department for a period of many years. He was a scholar in his own right, but was very dogmatic in his religious views. Compare this kind of mind with that of the graduate student to which I have just referred, and you can see why we have so few graduate students in this Department. Professor Basil was of the same mind, and Professor Buckley, whom we brought here only two years ago, is so ego-centered, and white-racist, that he drives students away from us. We would have many more Mexican-American students registering with us if they could only meet the standards set by the Graduate Record Examination. I know that you are critical of anyone who hands out so many high grades, but my reason for doing so is directly related to the language problem of my people. It would be better to deal with this problem at the elementary school level, but, as matters stand, I have no choice."

"I agree with you, Ricardo," replied Ron Jervis, "on the matter of dealing with the language problem at the elementary school level, but we get nowhere when we lower our standards at the graduate level of instruction. I am not sold on the use that we are making with the Graduate Record Examination, for it is being used to give preference to the Physical Sciences."

"You put your finger on much of the problem, Ron," said Ricardo. "Also, from time to time, I have protested to the State Educational Agency about the language problem, but I have never received a satisfactory response. The problem is definitely tied in with the poverty of my people and their working conditions. The state refuses to enforce the compulsory school law, and, to make matters worse, alien workers are allowed to come in and work at wages below the level required by law for our citizens. As a result, my people have a hard time finding work of any kind. Leadership is a fundamental need for the Mexican-American, and, in so far as it is humanly possible, I intend to help provide it."

"The need for providing a quality leadership for your people," said Ron Jervis, "is irrefutable. I can appreciate your deep concern on this matter. In principle, I agree with you wholeheartedly. If there is any difference between us it is that I think your approach should be universal and apply to all races. If we can get the kind of leadership that is necessary for a free society, the needs of your people would be realized. The lack of such leadership among the Anglos in this state is evident in the way you have been persecuted as an activist. This is demonstrated every day in the lack of quality school administrative leadership as well as that of quality teaching in the classroom. Now, not that I want to change the nature of this discussion but since I must be getting back to my place of residence, let me ask about your good wife, and how she is fairing during these hot summer months?"

"Very well indeed," said Ricardo, "but since you were here, she has undergone a thyroid operation because of cancerous growth. She is O.K. now, and fully recovered from the operation. They think that they got all of the cancer, and we are very optimistic about the future. How is that good wife of yours, and how is she taking this change of scenery?"

"Excellent indeed, Ricardo," replied Ron. "I would say that the truth is that she is the one who encouraged this move when she found out that you people were determnined to get me here. She was never happy with my former position, largely because they would not grant her a teaching position in the local community. The School Board and the Superintendent of Schools took the position that wives of the university professors would be seen as having an advantage over other applicants. It was all a matter of power politics, another example of why we are failing in our public schools efforts. She is convinced that she will have no difficulty in securing a position here."

"Again, Ron," said Professor Martinez, "we are most happy to have you with us, personally as well as professionally. Don't forget the Departmental meeting following registration. At that time we will discuss a number of problems which have arisen concerning the role of our Department in the College of Education."

That evening, as Ron and his wife relaxed in the family room of their new home, they went over the events of the day, and especially with reference to the promise of a good life in their new environment. They were well aware of how much they would miss their old friends and associates, but their new location held so much promise for the future that they could not help but feel that maybe, at last, they had found a place where they would be happier than they had been at any time in their last thirty years.

Economic insecurity had been a marked characteristic of most of Ron Jervis's life. As a fatherless boy, he had lived with his grandfather, on his mother's side, until he was thirteen. At that time it became necessary that he use all of his wits and energy to achieve the desired goals of his life. His mother had been responsible for much of his ambition, but not for his desire and sense of freedom. That had come from some internal creative desire, and from a determination not to believe anything that did not conform to his growing rational mind.

Ron's economic need, and his desire to further his education, made it necessary for him to work his way throgh the last three years of high school. This he did by serving as a waiter in a Greek Restaurant. From his earnings, he was able to build a small house on a piece of low-priced real estate. Thus, at the time of his high school graduation, he was able to sell his property at a good profit, and make his way, along with a scholarship, to his state university. Here, after three years of study and part-time work, he was able to graduate with a liberal arts degree, and enter upon a career of teaching and public school administration. It was in his third year at the University that Ron Jervis met the man that was to have a great influence upon his life, for, up to this time, he had never expressed any desire to go into the field of teaching.

Because of his poverty as a boy, Ron had learned much about the value of the free public school, that is, in terms of economics. Without these schools he could not possibly have finished high school, much less have gone to the state university. But he had found that public education, while free to him in the economic sense, was not free in the development of his mind. The quality of mind which Ron Jervis had sought was not found in his high school teachers. Most of them were old maids who were struggling for their economic existence. Two of Ron's teachers were men, however, one his high school principal and the other his teacher of American History. Each man was able to help him, not only in being able to work, and go to school at the same time, but to receive his scholarship to the state university.

It was in his sophomore year at the state university that he first came in contact with Francis Bacon's THE ADVANCEMENT OF LEARNING, a book which not only challenged him intellectually, but stimulated him to further intellectual pursuit. It was at this time that he began to grasp the full significance of the DECLARATION OF INDEPENDENCE and the BILL OF RIGHTS OF THE FEDERAL CONSTITUTION. From these great documents, it was made clear to Ron Jervis that *there could be no thing such as a free society without a free mind.* Also, that it was the obligation of the state university to provide the instruction and leadership if we were to develop a free minded society. If so, then why had there been a betrayal of those who were responsible for its founding, men such as Franklin and Jefferson? Although state universities had been established throughout the Nation, nowhere had they lived up to the mandate of their creators.

It was the insight that Ron Jervis had gained as to the origin of the state university, and the challenge which it presented, that continued to serve as a stimulant to him as he reminisced that evening in his home. His discussions with President Lothan, Dean Hazwell, and with Professor Martinez, had been most satisfying; but the experiences of the past fifteen years had made him equally aware of many of the problems which lay ahead of him. While there was no fear of economic insecurity in his mind, he knew that problems in the field of human relations would arise, problems between the administration and the faculty, between conflicting faculty interests, between faculty and students, and, yes, within his own family. It was on such a matter that Helen now spoke to her husband.

"Ron," said Helen, "during the time that you were at the University talking to your administrative officials, I had the opportunity to visit the City School Personnel Director, and talk to him about the possibility of a teaching position in the public schools this fall. As expected, he informed me that all positions had been filled, but, due to the fact that I had a certificate to teach science in the high school, I would be in great demand as a substitute teacher. Also, he was very optimistic about the possibility of my getting a full-time position next year, and especially so if I made good as a substitute."

"That is quite a contrast with the cold shoulder that you have been given all during these past many years," replied Ron. "I know how they used to excuse their attitude by saying that you were needed at home by our daughter, and how they feared that they would be accused of showing partiality to a professor's wife. When you consider the kind of salary that I was paid, they really put the squeeze on us. I now note that your dreams of returning to the classroom are going to be fulfilled. I hope that with this change there will be no great interference with our home life."

"To tell the truth, Ron," said Helen, "I am grateful for the fact that I will be doing only substitute teaching during my first year here, for it will give me adequate time to get used to the classroom again, and to put our home in order. Now that our daughter is in high school, there is not the slightest chance that I would want to spend all of my time at home. A woman of my education needs the intellectual stimulation that a teacher gets in the classroom. The fact that you like to cook, and always do as much in the kitchen as I do, provides for the kind of cooperation that is needed between husband and wife."

"Yes, Helen," said Ron. "You express my symptoms very well, but don't forget that what I know about cooking was learned during the three years that I spent as a boy, working in a Greek Restaurant. At that time, when I saw all of the other boys and girls running around, dating, and going to parties, I knew that I was being grossly discriminated against. Now, as I look back, I don't know, for it seems that by doing so, I was taught the value and satisfaction derived from creative labor. They surely wasted a hell of a lot of their time running around."

"All too true, Ron," said Helen. "But I have often wished that you would let up once and a while and take life easier. Tell me about your visit with President Lothan and with your Dean. How would you compare the latter with Dean Hardbutt?"

"As for President Lothan," said Ron, "I found him a much better man than I had expected. He was more pleasant and understanding than President Knight had thought. As for Dean Hazwell, he is much more considerate of my point view than Dean Hardbutt could ever be. However, we are miles apart when it comes to the matter of Christian dogma. Here he stands firm as a devout Presbyterian. We do agree on the idea that teachers should be able to provide quality leadership in their communities, and that they should operate from a meaning and value frame of reference consistent with the GENERAL WELFARE of a free Nation."

"And how did you find Professor Martinez?" asked Helen. "Is he as much of a political activist as he was when you were here two years ago?"

"Very much so, Helen," replied Ron. "You know, I like the guy better every time I see him. We had a long chat on his favorite subject, the plight of the Mexican American. He very much deplores the lack of a good public education program for his people, not only because of poor finance, but because of the language problem. Most of the public school teachers cannot speak Spanish, and find it difficult to communicate with these Mexican-American kids. He hopes to get his people fired up so that they will put more pressure on the State Legislature. But you know, Helen, it is not easy to get an impoverished mind changed into a free-thinking individual."

"Well, I must tell you, Professor Jervis," said Helen, "I have had enough of thinking and talking about teaching for one time. We still have a lot of work to do around here before we can say that things are in good order. So let us get to bed, and give our thanks to that great CREATIVE UNIVERSAL FORCE that brought us here."

As Ron and Helen walked toward their bedroom, they were buoyed up by the thought that there indeed must be some kind of creative force that had brought them here. No longer would they have to breathe and operate in the kind of oppressive environment in which they had lived for so many years.

Sleep did not come easy for Ron Jervis that night. The events of the day were such that he was unable to turn off his mind as if you were cutting off a water faucet. In spite of the assurance and support of his Dean and Martinez, he knew that the road ahead would not be strewn with roses. That did not bother him, however, for he was well aware of the challenge and the opportunity which his new position presented to him. Now that Helen would be teaching, his home situation would surely improve. He had no doubt as to his ability to build up the graduate program of his Department, this despite Buckley's failure to attract graduate students. It was the undergraduate course that concerned him most, for here he would come in contact with those who were to go out and become public school teachers.

Where were we headed with the public school program? How could the teacher be freed from the power politics which had curtailed the effectiveness of the public school for more than a century? How could we bring about greater financial support for the public school? The tendency of those of the middle class to place their children in private schools was a problem of major concern, especially now that forced busing of the students was destroying the neighborhood school. Yet he could not help but believe that, in the final analysis, it was the teacher in the classroom that determined the ultimate outcome of the public school program, and its role as a prime factor in promoting a society devoted to the cause of the OPEN MIND.

It was 2 a.m. before Ron Jervis finally drifted off into no-man's land and a deep slumber. He was awakened at the hour of 7 a.m. by Helen with a call to breakfast.

CHAPTER III

HIGHER EDUCATION IN A FREE SOCIETY

It did not take Ron Jervis very long to make an adjustment to his new environment. In a personal sense, it was, in many ways, a more satisfactory life than that which he had known in the past fifteen years. All fears of economic insecurity, which he had known for the greater part of his life, were now gone. Helen had become better adjusted in what she was doing, especialy in her part-time teaching in the local high schools. Now that he had his good friend Ricardo Martinez as a close associate, he no longer had to fight his professional battles singlehandedly, as had been the case in the past years of college teaching. While his new Dean was not all that he would have asked of an administrative superior, he was a considerable improvement over Dean Hardbutt. In a professional sense, he was not in conflict with his new Dean as to the role of Philosophy of Education in the teacher education program.

He knew that he was still in a decided minority on the "Role of Higher Education in a Free Society" with the various faculties of the state universities, but this did not minimize his determination to continue to devote his career to this issue.

On the issue of the "Role of Higher Education in a Free Society," Ron Jervis had found common cause with Frank Ruffner, to whom he continued to write. Now, in his new position, he had found a new friend in Professor W. O. Snyder of the English Department. Since his meeting with the Committee on Admissions to the Graduate Faculty, Professor Snyder had given him strong support on the responsibility of the Graduate Faculty to the GENERAL WELFARE OF THE NATION. The renewal of his association with Professor Snyder had come at the close of the first monthly meeting of the University Faculty.

"Professor Jervis," said Bill Snyder, "I have thought a great deal about our discussion at the time of our meeting with the Graduate Faculty Committee, and I am now fully convinced of the soundness of your position on the role of the state university. Your thinking, however, is so contrary to the thinking of your associates in the College of Education that I wonder how you ever came around to such a point of view?"

"It is a long story, Professor Snyder," replied Professor Jervis. "It goes back all the way to the time that I was an arts and sciences student. At that time, it was a Professor of English who encouraged me to read Sir Francis Bacon's THE ADVANCEMENT OF LEARNING, and I have never been the same since. I agree with the late Robert Hutchins that higher education should be defined and operated in terms of the search for IDEAS, the role of the intellect in the life of man. It was in my research on the 'Origins of the American State University' that I came to realize how much we had betrayed those who founded the institution. The central purpose of the university was to be the education of a free man for a free society."

"As you know, Professor Jervis," said Professor Snyder,

"that is the classical point of view, and that it is viewed by many of your associates as elitist and undemocratic."

"Very true, Professor Snyder," said Ron Jervis. "That is the tragedy of our present situation. If those who oppose that point of view had any knowledge of the history of higher education in Western culture, they would of necessity have come to realize that no society, democratic or otherwise, could long survive without a quality leadership that knew how to correlate the role of power with that of intellect and ethical responsibility."

"So it is your conviction, Professor Jervis," replied Professor Snyder, "that the condition in which we find ourselves is due, more than anything else, to the failure of the American State University to provide that quality of leadership which is fundamental to counteract the tyrannical power which runs like a thread throughout the history of the human race."

"Definitely so," replied Ron Jervis. "Power, naked brutal power, has come to dominate the life of our people, a trend which you can observe in almost every aspect of our culture. It shows up most tragically in our political life and in our capitalistic economy. In our political life, we are controlled by the idea of majority rule and, in our capitalistic economy, by the idea of getting rich in money. How could we ever have come to the conclusion that a majority vote which operates at the level of thirteen-year-olds was the essence of the democratic way of life? If we are to get intelligent citizenship responsibility, we must change the qualifications of those who teach in our state universities. As of now, there are no qualifications which are related to the science of teaching, only those of high scholarship in a subject matter field. There is everything right with the idea of high scholarship, but to limit the practice of teaching to this one attribute is to ignore the purpose for which the state university was founded. Subject matter specialization is fundamental for the advancement of knowledge, but the transmission of the known knowledge is equally fundamental to the growth of the human mind."

"So what you want, Ron," said Professor Snyder, "is a teacher education program for those who teach in our arts and sciences colleges. What surprises me is that you would advocate such a practice, what with the antagonism that is expressed toward the College of Education."

"Don't forget, Professor Snyder," replied Professor Jervis, "that I am as much a critic of the practices in our College of Education as is your College of Arts and Sciences Faculty, especially of those who are always handing out only A and B grades. What I am proposing is as much a need for the College of Education Faculty as it is for yours or any other division of the University. Actually, I would be tougher on the teacher education faculty than any other division of the University, since it is the members of this faculty that are responsible for certifying those who are going out to teach in our public schools."

"Professor Jervis," said Bill Snyder, "let us say that you are correct in your thinking about changing the qualifications of the university faculty. What I would like to know, however, is just what kind of subject matter content you would include in the program?"

"Well, to begin with," said Professor Jervis," I believe that it is imperative that we have a doctoral degree for university teaching. The Ph.D. degree is excellent for those who are going into research, but we need a degree that is comparable to that of the M.D. in medicine. We need a Certification and Review Board which has the responsibility to pass on, not only the qualifications of the teacher in subject matter, but upon the quality of mind of the candidate, especially his or her aspirations for a free society. Benjamin Franklin stated the case quite well when he outlined the requirements for membership in the Junto Club in 1727.

> " 'Do you sincerely declare that you love mankind of whatever creed or faith? Do you love truth for truth's sake, and will you endeavor to impartially seek and convey it to others to the best of your ability? Do you think any person should be harmed in his body or character for mere speculative opinion?'

"Much more was included in this pledge than I have presented here, but what has been stated will give you an insight into what I have in mind concerning the qualifications of the university professor. Actually this Junto Club, which later grew into the American Philosophical Association, could well serve with its pledge in the same way as the Hippocratic Oath has served the medical profession."

"Truthfully, Professor Jervis," said Bill Snyder, "I am beginning to see where your thinking would lead us. I find myself in general agreement with you, but what about the subject matter content of the teaching degree?"

"Bill," said Ron Jervis, "I would hold, as I think you would, that a liberal education is vital as a foundation stone for all public school and college teachers. What I am pointing to is not just the subject matter content, but to the meaning and value that goes with it — the quality of mind of the student who is to become a teacher in our public schools and in our state universities."

"Ron," said Bill Snyder, "can you give me a specific example of what yo have in mind?"

"Gladly, Bill," replied Ron Jervis. "One of the best examples that I can give you is to be found in connection with the use of the Christian BIBLE. You know, as well as I do, that there is no rational or scientific basis for teaching Jewish legendary history as the word of a divine God. The Christian BIBLE should be placed in the same category as the Islamic KORAN or the SAYINGS OF CONFUCIUS. These and other religious documents are as much man-made as the works of Shakespeare or the writings of Ralph Waldo Emerson. The Christian dogmatic mind has no more place in the public school than the dogmatic mind of the Communist or the Fascist. It is high time that we begin to think of freedom as a positive force, not as a cultural vacuum where dogmatic religions are freely taught in competition with each other."

"Ron," said Bill Snyder, "I note from the Wall Street Journal that the Editor has stated that the Ph.D. in History, Literature or the Classics had a negative return; whereas, the Ph.D. in Engineering or Computer Science was positively significant as an investment. Does this type of thinking represent what you have been saying about the limitations of the American mind?"

"Yes, Bill," said Ron Jervis. "You have put your finger on the issue, and without any reservations. We have historical proof that the study of literature is the most significant of all possible means for the development of the human mind. In this respect, it is most unfortunate that the Christian BIBLE was deified for, in doing so, there was a loss in the significance of the book as a contribution to the field of Human Relations. Those who are well informed know that the College of Liberal Arts pre-dates that of the Sciences by several centuries. No professor in a state university should be allowed to walk into the classroom without a thorough grounding in Classics, English, and American Literature."

"I can see, Ron Jervis," said Bill Snyder, "that you have given much thought to the role of higher education in the American culture. I note from my watch that the hour of six p.m. is approaching, and that my wife will be wondering just what has happened to her husband. I do want to continue our discussion at some future date, and especially with reference to the role of literature in the education of the state university professor. Since you hold a doctoral minor in the field of literature, you must have some interesting ideas about the significance of such a study."

"It has been good to renew our acquaintance, Bill," said Ron Jervis. "I would enjoy continuing the discussion when the time is convenient for you, and especially because there are so few of your associates that are interested as you are. I too must be getting along home. My wife will be wondering as to just what happened to me."

As the two men departed, Ron Jervis could not help but think that in Bill Snyder he had found a good friend and understanding associate. Ever since he entered college teaching, he had become increasingly aware of how little his fellow faculty associates concerned themselves with what was going on in the outside world, and especially the cultural trend of the times. By and large, they had wrapped themselves in a cocoon of subject matter. Only when the state legislators got involved in how many hours they should be in the classroom, or when their salaries were involved, did they seem to wake up to the realities of the everyday world. It was as if they lived in an academic world apart and aside from the market place. He would talk to his friend Martinez further about the matter in preparation for the departmental meeting that was to come up the following Friday afternoon. This would give him a couple of days to think about the action that needed to be taken. On Thursday of the next day, when Ron Jervis and Ricardo Martinez had a couple of free hours, Ron brought up the subject of a possible change in the title of the Department.

"Ricardo," said Ron Jervis, "knowing that your point of view on the role of our Department in the education of the public school teacher is much the same as mine, it seems to me that we should seek a change in the title of our Department. The title as it now stands is an academic subject matter title — History and Philosophy of Education — and in no way represents what we are trying to accomplish. The title does not point up the educational needs of the Mexican American or any other minority group. Stating our role in terms of subject matter makes it appear that we belong in the College of Arts and Sciences. I know that Professor Buckley does not agree with me, but I also know that he personally would prefer to teach in the arts and sciences college. If we are to make it clear that we are thinking in terms of our professional responsibilities, it would seem that the title of our Department should be changed to the Cultural Foundations of Education."

"Speaking to the point, Ron," said Ricardo, "it makes no difference to me that my work is not represented in the title of the Department, but I agree with you about the necessity to exemplify what we are doing. Such a change would reflect what our efforts are all about. At the meeting tomorrow I will back you up should you choose to make the recommendation on the change."

"Ricardo," said Ron, "I am sure that you are aware of the fact that Professor Buckley will oppose us in our efforts, but young McKinney will go along with us, since he has no firm convictions about the matter. We will find some opposition in the Administrative Council, but I believe that the Dean will go along with us, if for no other reason than he wants our support on two or three issues that are important to him. Now that we have covered what I wanted to talk to you about, I will move along and let you get to your morning mail."

As Ron Jervis departed from the office of his departmental chairman, he could not help but reflect on how much the conditions of his personal life had changed during the past few months. Yet, in spite of the improvement in his immediate environmental conditions, he was not laboring under any false illusion about the future. He was very much aware of the fact that his friend Martinez had paid a very dear price for his freedom, and for his efforts to improve the lot of his people. Also, Ron had become increasingly aware of the fact that the main financial support of the University was coming from those who were interested only in the develoment of the Physical Sciences. He knew that it was these same people that controlled the policies of the Board of Regents. Also, there were Professors, such as Buckley, who were interested only in their self advancement, and in kowtowing to the administration. As for the faculty of the College of Education, the great majority were little more than trade trainers, interested only in the methodology of teaching. Getting a change in the title of his Department would be a good first step in bringing about an improvement in the teacher education program. By having the support of his Chairman and that of young McKinney, he would have a majority vote of three to accomplish his purpose. As for the Administrative Council of the College, he would take care of that problem when the time came.

At the meeting of the Department, the issue over the change in the title of the Department developed as Ron had expected. It was Chairman Martinez who opened the meeting with several general comments concerning the status and present trends relating to departmental affairs.

"Gentlemen," said Chairman Martinez, "we have a number of important issues to come before us today so let us get on with our business immediately. The first of these matters has to do with the funds that are available for the year's operation. Among these funds are those that have to do with the hiring of one-half time student aid, and the half-time teaching assistants. This money is set aside to help the Professor do a more efficient job of teaching, as well as to provide financial assistance to our graduate students. Does any one of you have a question about the distribution of this money?"

"Professor Martinez," inquired Profesor Buckley, "am I correct in assuming that it will be possible to use my student aid share of the fund in hiring a student to do research work for me in the library?"

"Very much so," replied the Chairman. "There is no restriction on the nature of the use of these funds."

"Professor Martinez," asked Professor McKinney, "since I do not have any graduate students under my supervision, am I to assume that I will not have a teaching assistant?"

"Not at all, Professor McKinney," replied the Chairman. "The teaching assistant fund was set up to help every professor do a better job in his teaching, especially with the undergraduate students. Now let us turn to what is surely a controversial issue among us. Professor Jervis is advocating a change in the title of our Department and will speak to the issue."

"Professor Martinez," said Professor Jervis, "as you know from my discussions with you, I do not recommend a change in the title of our Department for trivial reasons. The issue which I raise is basic to the operation of every teacher education program in every state university in this Nation. As a Department in the College of Education, our function is not that of research in a subject matter field. Also, I am convinced that there has been far to much trade training in our schools and colleges of education. Our major purpose in our teacher education colleges is to provide the necessary leadership for our public schools, if we are to have a free society. If we are to have free men and women, then we must have teachers and school administrators who can assume the leadership role which is so necessary in our local communities. Subject matter areas such as THE HISTORY OF EDUCATION AND THE PHILOSOPHY OF EDUCATION are fundamental to this purpose in that they provide the necessary cultural content. The teaching of these subjects serves, however, only to the extent that they deal with the essence of our culture and throw light on the development of the human mind.

"It is well known that our public schools have failed us, in more than one hundred and fifty years, to provide the educasion necesesary for the development of the free mind. Much of this failure can be attributed to the fact that our state universities have not provided a quality of leadership for the public school teachers and administrators. It would be fair to say that, in this respect, our state universities have betrayed those who founded them. A change in the title of our Department would give due recognition to a long neglected significant educational need. By doing so, we can point to the fact that the overarching problem in our culture is directly related to the need for a free mind. Mr. Chairman, I therefore move that the title of our Department be changed to that of the CULTURAL FOUNDATIONS OF EDUCATION."

There was a second to Professor Jervis's motion by Professor Martinez, and, immediately following his seconding, Professor Buckley raised his hand to lead the opposition in the discussion.

"Professor Jervis," said Professor Buckley, "I find myself in total opposition to the change in the title of our Department. My first objection stems from the fact that this Department has a long and distinguished tradition, actually the oldest department in the entire College. With your motion, we would wipe out this glorious tradition and have to start over again. Also, we have no idea what the reaction of our colleagues will be. In such a change, I see a loss of respectability. Cultural Foundations of Education, what does that mean?"

"Professor Buckley," replied Professor Jervis, "I am sure that you are well-educated enough to know what is meant by the Cultural Foundations of Education. What I am primarily interested in, however, is giving some meaning and purpose to the courses which we teach beyond that of content. That meaning and unity of purpose can be found in the essence of our culture, where we came from, and where we want to go. Take, for example, the valuable work on the poverty and living conditions of the Mexican-American people, or, say, that larger field of Comparative Education in which you are primarily interested. Neither of these fields of need and interest are represented in the present title of this Department. I respect our departmental tradition, but even more that tradition of our Revolutionary Fathers where the guidelines of the educational needs of free men and women were laid down. As to our colleagues, we will be able to meet them on solid and well-justified grounds and, in doing so, ably defend ourselves."

"Professor Jervis," said Professor McKinney, "I had never thought of the role of our Department in the terms that you have so well expressed. I will frankly admit that I have been trained, and I hope educated to think in terms of subject matter specialization. But now I see how the leaders of the U.S.S.R. seek a sense of unity and purpose in their culture through the educational process, and thus the development of the Communist Mind. I can see that there is a real difference between what they are doing and what we are failing to do by not providing quality leadership for the public school teacher and administrator. But how do we do this without becoming involved in a process of blind indoctrination? I see a contradiction between theory and practice here."

"Dr. McKinney," said Professor Jervis, "you express yourself quite well. The fact is that we have had two thousand years of blind indoctrination in Christianity. Such is the major barrier to the development of the free mind in our Nation. We are not going to have a free mind if we continue to resort to the same kind of brainwashing as that perpretrated by the so-called Ministers of God. On the other hand, there is nothing of a positive sense of freedom to be found in the way in which these patterns of church dogma compete with each other. My point is that you don't get freedom or a free mind by giving the dogmatist, whether he or she be a religious, political, or economic slave, the freedom to express himself."

"Professor Jervis," said Professor McKinney, "if I understand you correctly you must think that you can get a free mind by suppressing the dogmatist."

"Professor McKinney," said Professor Jervis, "what is involved here is not the suppression of the dogmatist but the subtle suppression of the opportunity to promote the free mind in the education of our people. That suppression has found support in the vested interests of our religious, social, political, and economic endeavors. It has been especially true in the field of public education. Note how this has been done in the selection of the school textbooks and reading materials. Here the minds of the members of the local school boards completely dominate the minds of the teachers and the school administrators. When I read that there is no fundamental difference between what is taught in the public schools and what is taught in the church and private schools, I know that the public schools have failed us in not living up to their responsibility. I also know that this is largely due to the failure of the state universities to provide the kind of leadership that is necessary for the education of free men and women."

These last comments of Professor Jervis so incensed Professor Buckley that he could not refrain from responding in an emotional and illogical manner.

"Professor Jervis," said Professor Buckley, "I cannot sit here and be insulted by your accusations that I am a dogmatist. As an orthodox and loyal Christian, I believe in the principle of freedom just as much as you. My position is that the state university should, because of the right of freedom, stay out of all religious, political, social, and economic controversies and stick to the facts."

"Professor Buckley," replied Professor Jervis, "you have, by your remarks, given due testimony to what I have said. In short, you have doomed the state university to a mindless institution. Your knowledge of the History of American Education must tell you that the mere teaching of facts was not the reason for the establishment of the state university. Mr. Chairman, it is my judgment that there has been adequate discussion of the need for a change in the title of our Department, and that this discussion should be terminated. I so move at this time."

Dr. McKinney seconded Professor Jervis's motion, and, on a role call, the motion to approve the title of the Department was approved with one negative vote.

The agreement to change the title of the Department was very satisfying to Ron Jervis, even though it was a very small crack in the wall of the academic tradition. He was well aware of the fact that there had been a similar change in three other state universities. Surely, it was a change for the better. The next step in getting the change of title was the Administrative Council of the College of Education. First, he must discuss the matter with the Dean. With the support of his Dean, he was sure that he could overcome any opposition from the other members of the Council. That afternoon, at the end of the departmental meeting, Ron called the Dean's secretary and made an appointment to see the Dean on the following morning, at the hour of eleven.

When Ron Jervis walked into the Dean's office on the following morning, he found the Dean in an especially good humor.

"It is good to learn from your Chairman, Professor Jervis," said the Dean, "that you find your work here all that you had hoped that it would be. This pleases me very much, for there is nothing better for a college than to have its faculty in good spirits. Also, I am very gratified at receiving a letter from President Lothan expressing his pleasure on having received a good report on the growth of the College during the past year. You seem to have made a good impression on the President at the time of your interview, for he speaks in glowing terms of your manifest abilities. Now what can I do for you? My secretary tells me that you are here on an important matter."

"Yes, Dean Hazwell," replied Ron Jervis. "What I am asking of you is to me a very important matter, for it concerns the quality and significance of our teacher education program. At the last official meeting of the members of my Department, by vote of three to one, it was decided that the name of the Department be changed to THE CULTURAL FOUNDATIONS OF EDUCATION. This decision was made for the following reasons: 1. The present title of the Department in no way defines the content that is important to our responsibility in the teacher education program. 2. Subject matter listings in the title of the Department do not reflect the cultural need in teacher education. 3. There is a need in teacher education for an expression of the humanistic as well as the scientific part of the educational process. Now, without your support at the next meeting of the Administrative Council, I am sure that it will be impossible to get a majority vote for the change in the title of our Department. We believe that with your support we can not only get the approval of the Council, but the final approval of the change when the matter comes up before the University Council."

"Well, Professor Jervis," replied the Dean, "I will be pleased to give serious consideration to your proposal, but I would be interested in knowing just which member of your Department cast the negative vote and why."

"Yes, Dean," replied Ron Jervis. "It was Professor Buckley who, as you know, thinks in the narrow confines of subject matter specialization. Speaking quite frankly, Professor Buckley is of the opinion that the change will diminish his status as a Graduate Professor. As you must know, Professor Buckley thinks more in terms of a Professor in the College of Arts and Sciences than he does in the College of Education."

"Professor Jervis," said the Dean, "I think that your assessment of Professor Buckley is very much in order, but I must say that there are far too many members of our College who think the same way. Now, since I have another appointment coming up, I must close this discussion unless you have something else that needs to come up at this time."

"No, Dean Hazwell," replied Ron Jervis. "That is all that I had in mind at this time. I will be waiting anxiously for your decision on the matter."

"Yes, Professor Jervis," said the Dean. "I will let you or your Chairman know of my decision by tomorrow morning."

As Ron Jervis left the Dean's office he was convinced that he had made a good case for the change in the title of his Department, and he looked forward optimistically for the Dean's reply. When the reply came on the following morning, as the Dean had promised, it was positive. Now the stage was set for the meeting with the Council. Here an objection was raised by the Chairman of the Curriculum Department on the grounds that Ron was trying to monopolize the meaning and value concept of the teacher education program. The Dean, however, rejected this assumption on the grounds that the change in the title of the Department of the History and Philosophy of Education had nothing to do with the responsibilities of the other departments. It was at the meeting of the University Council that Ron ran into the most serious opposition. Fortunately for him, however, his friend Bill Snyder came to his rescue. The first faculty member of the University Council to express a negative attitude on the title change was Professor Steve Ryan of the Department of Philosophy.

"Professor Jervis," said Professor Ryan, "I have long questioned your College having a Department in the History and Philosophy of Education. Speaking quite frankly, Philosophy of Education should be taught in the Philosophy Department, and the History of Education in the History Department. If such is the case, then there is no place for your Department in either the College of Education or the College of Arts and Sciences. This would be true regardless of the fact that you seek to change the title of your Department."

"Professor Ryan," replied Professor Jervis, "as a college of arts and sciences graduate in an outstanding state university, I have no difficulty in understanding your point of view, but I must add that you are dead wrong in your assumption. As a member of the faculty of an undergraduate college of arts and sciences, your job is that of seeing to it that your students receive a liberal education. As to whether or not you are doing so, that has nothing to do with the issue under discussion. My job is to take liberally educated young men and women and see to it that they become effective public school teachers and administrators. Surely you are not supporting the idea that our College should be little more than a trade training school."

At this point Professor Bill Snyder came to the defense of the point of view being expressed by Professor Jervis. "Gentlemen," said Professor Snyder, "for years we have been complaining about the low level of the quality of the College of Education students. Now that Professor Jervis seeks to raise the quality of the performance of these students, I see every reason to support him in his efforts. I am very much interested in what he has to say about our efforts, for the College of Arts and Science is responsible for more than one hundred of the graduate hours of these College of Education students. I would be interested in what Professor Jervis has to say about the relation between the change being advocated in the title of his Department and our courses in the College of Arts and Sciences."

"Gentlemen," replied Professor Jervis, "I am most happy to reply to Professor Snyder's request. In doing so, I would like to point out that my thinking about the role of the state university is based upon many years of teaching and research in the field of higher education, at both the graduate and undergraduate levels of instruction. Let me say that the core of my remarks is directed at the state universities and not at the church and private schools and colleges. What disturbs me most is that we do not have, or give expression to, any central purpose in our efforts that would distinguish us from the church and private schools. Actually, our professors seem to be as indistinguishable as bricks when it comes to our practices. Our practices are in no sense consistent with the purpose for which the state university was established. What I note here is a similiarity between the difficulties experienced by our Revolutionary Fathers and what we have today. When the state university of North Carolina and the University of Virginia were founded, it was impossible to find professors who could or would assume responsibility for the education of those who were to assume political leadership in a free and democratic society. Note that the University of North Carolina was referred to at the time of its origin as THE RISING SUN OF SCIENCE. As to the University of Virginia, Jefferson writes about searching far and wide, even throughout Europe, for faculty for his institution, but with little success."

"Professor Jervis," said William Dean, a professor of Chemistry with whom Ron Jervis had become acquainted at the time of his interview by the Graduate Faculty Committee, "I would assume that in these respects you are referring to something quite different from specialized subject matter."

"Very much so, Professor Dean," replied Ron Jervis. "To understand what I am saying one needs both historical perspective and a knowledge of the history of higher education in the Western world. The importance of such was well illustrated in a lecture that I was privileged to hear some years back, a lecture titled 'Horizontal Thinking in a Vertical World.' The reason for the study of Latin and Greek in the Medieval University was not for subject matter specialization, but because these languages served as a means of bringing into reality the liberally educated man, Greek for its humanistic foundations, and Latin as the instrument of Christian theology. The origin of the practice of subject matter specialization is traceable to the German universities and the beginning of graduate instruction in this country."

"Professor Jervis," asked Professor Dean, "how can you imply that there is an anti-intellectual attitude pervading our culture when you know that we have made tremendous progress in the physical sciences during the past fifty years?"

"That is just my point, Professor Dean," replied Ron Jervis. "Our progress has been limited to the physical and the biological sciences, but when you come to the fields of religion and politics, the situation is very different. What is most frightening about our non-thinking is that, as a result of our cultural outlook, we are confronted with the threat of atomic war and the killing of millions of people."

"I get your point, Professor Jervis," said Professor Ryan, "but what can I as a university professor do to counteract this frightening trend toward the destruction of Western civilization?"

"Not much as an individual, Professor Ryan," replied Ron Jervis, "but, since the state university was created to provide leadership for the good life in a free society, we must question whether or not it has lived up to its responsibility. My belief is that it has not. In this respect there has been a BETRAYAL ON MOUNT PARNASSUS."

"That is a terrible indictment of the state university," said Professor Dean, "but, assuming that you are correct in your assumption, why has there been a failure on our part in providing the kind of leadership to which you refer?"

"Of course, Professor Dean," said Ron Jervis, "what I have said is a matter of judgment, but, in terms of historical perspective, I would say that my judgment has to do with my concept of the nature of man, and especially the way in which his mind is formed. One's concept of the nature of mind has everything to do with one's concept of how an individual learns. Prior to the publication of Charles Darwin's THE ORIGIN OF SPECIES, man's mind was thought to be that of the Neo-Platonic Christian. This concept historically was a source of major controversy between the Platonists and the Aristotelians. During the eighteenth century, as a result of the influence of Aristotle on the Medieval University, the Age of Reason became a reality with its concept of the rational man. Because of the influence of Jean-Jacques Rousseau on the concept of Democracy during the nineteenth century, however, there was a shift to the idea of man as an intuitive being, one that was both equal and good by his animal nature. It is this concept that has led to the anti-intellectual politics of power in our society, and to the false premise that majority rule defines tha nature of truth. As a result, we have no place for creative intelligence in our governmental operations. This is basically contrary to everything that Jefferson saw as fundamental to the role of power in our government. It was Jefferson's belief that there was an aristocracy of intelligence among men and that it was the intellectual and moral responsibility of the intelligent to provide the leadership necessary for a free society. It was this conviction that led Jefferson and other Revolutionary Fathers to support the founding of the state university."

"Today, we find our public schools committed to the Rousseau concept of the nature of man, the concept that has dominated our political life since the days of Andrew Jackson, especially the mind of the Democratic Party. On the other hand, it is the Jeffersonian concept of man as a rational animal that has dominated the thinking of our arts and sciences faculties. At the same time, there has been a substitution of the concept of subject matter specialization for the Jeffersonian concept of a LIBERAL EDUCATION. It is this substitution that has brought about the betrayal of the purpose for which the state university was founded. It is important to note that this allegiance to subject matter specialization was a result of the German influence on higher education in our country in the latter part of the nineteenth century. While extremely significant in the development of our graduate programs, this tendency has played havoc with our undergraduate concept of a liberal education. As of now, we think that an individual is liberally educated if he takes a number of courses in this or that subject matter area. Since there is no sense of unity or purpose in the number of courses taken, I must assume that the premise on which such a conglomeration of courses was taken is false. Investigations made to determine whether or not there has been a change in the thinking of the college students who have taken such a list of courses indicate no significant change in their thinking. So far as education for leadership in a free society is concerned, the end result has been a monumental fraud."

"Professor Jervis," said Professor Snyder, "I can see, as a Professor in the field of the Humanities, how we got sidetracked in the development of our graduate program. I admit that I have assumed in my teaching that if I just presented by lecture the subject matter in question, the rational student would do his or her thinking. What you are saying is that the student cannot think in a vacuum, and that there is a vacuum because there is no pattern of mind on which such thinking can be based."

"Professor Synder, that is exactly what I have been saying," replied Ron Jervis. "The eighteenth century assumption that man is a rational animal by his nature, that he or she is born with a mind or a pattern of thinking, is no longer supportable by virtue of the knowledge in the field of biology. As a result, what we are left with is that the mind is synonymous with brain, or is culturally acquired, and limited in its growth to time and place. If such is the case, then we are as mentally enslaved by Christian theology as is the Mohammedan by his Islamic faith. Jefferson understood the nature of this enslavement, but he was handicapped by the lack of scientific knowledge on the nature of man."

At this point Hugh Drummond, a Professor of Psychology, who had been sitting quietly on the other side of the conference table, spoke up with much feeling.

"Professor Jervis," said Professor Drummond, "I have listened very attentively to what you have said about the failure of the state university to provide the quality leadership necessary for a free society and, while I find myself in agreement with your idea concerning our mental enslavement by Christian theology, I see no justification for assuming that the human mind is anything more than the brain of man. I do believe that we face a grave crisis during the rest of this century because there has been a marriage of the filthy rich with the ultra-theological groups in our political life. This merger, if continued, will, in time, destroy our cherished freedom of thought and our national welfare. I know, as do most free thinkers, that the majority of our people have no penchant for truth, or for acting on long-term interests. Also, crimes, however hideous, have, at one time or another, been morally justified by evangelistic theologians. What we need to achieve your proposed leadership is to simply condition the brain to that end or purpose."

"Professor Drummond," replied Professor Jervis, "I am pleased to note that you agree with me on the matter of mental enslavement by our religious tradition, but I have extreme difficulty with your point of view when it comes to the issue of freedom. Your position, it seems to me, allows no place for creative thought, which is the essence of the free mind. I would also insist that we have a formation of mind as distinguished from the brain, but the formation of mind in your thinking is determined by those in the power role, a control from the top down rather than by the creative mind of the individual from the bottom up. This is my quarrel with the Marxist, as well as with the followers of Thorndike. Also, it is the same brainwashing method used by the Christians throughout the history of Western Civilization, Christian evangelists such as Billy Graham and Jerry Falwell. To adopt such a policy as yours in our state universities would not produce the mind of the creative scientist, but the scientific dogmatist, without any ethical commitment or feeling for ones fellow man. Such materialistic enslavement is far too prevalent in our culture today."

The two hours for which the meeting had been called had already passed when Professor Snyder, who was chairman of the Committee, brought the session to a close with the call for a vote on the issue of whether or not the title of the Department of the History and Philosophy of Education should be changed to the Cultural Foundations of Education. The results indicated four votes in favor of the change and one, that of Professor Ryan, against. Later, in discussing the reasons for Professor Ryan's negative vote, Professor Snyder had this to say to Ron.

"From what I know of the thinking of Professor Ryan," said Professor Snyder, "I would say that more than the specialization of subject matter was involved. Note that, in addition to his being an Hegelian in his thinking, he is a slave to the developing area of Linguistics. He has identified himself with that block of philosophers who think that they can find the answers to all matters philosophical in a science of language. As I see it, they are so hipped on the subject that they are prone to question anything that you or I might say or write. They have become, in a very literal sense, linguistic dogmatists. I am sure that it was your use of the word DOGMATISM that upset him. Underneath all of his dogmatism, however, is his belief that power defines the nature of truth, goodness and beauty. To me, this is the very essence of NAZISM, that which seeks to unify a people by creating an alleged external foe. Because of our lack of a sense of unity in our country, we are a dangerously fragmented society. By failing to provide a quality of leadership in our state universities we, as you say, are sacrificing our birthright for a mess of pottage."

"Bill Snyder," replied Ron Jervis, "I could not have said it better. You now see why I am so convinced that our salvation is to be found in whether or not we are capable of bringing into being a society of free men and women. There is no other institution in our culture today than the state university which is mandated to provide the leadership necessary to this constructive end."

Following these remarks, Ron Jervis bade his friend goodbye with an expression of appreciation for his help in getting the Committee to approve the change in the title of his Department. When Ron reached home that afternoon, he was greeted by a message from Helen. He was told that one of his female graduate students had called, and that he was to call her just as soon as possible. According to his wife, she seemed to be in a state of desperation. She said that her name was Bobbie Frank. Ron, having no idea of what the call was all about, dialed the given number and, after waiting a few seconds, had a response.

"Miss Frank," said Professor Jervis, "my wife tells me that you have been trying to get in touch with me. What can I do for you?"

"Professor Jervis," replied Bobbie Frank, "I am desperate and need to get in touch with you immediately. Can I come out this afternoon? I hope that you are not too busy to see me. It is very important."

"Miss Frank," replied Professor Jervis, "since you deem it so necessary to see me immediately, I could see you around eight p.m."

"Oh thank you, Professor Jervis," replied Miss Frank. "I will be out at the appointed time."

As Ron Jervis turned to his wife, he could not help but wonder why Bobbie Frank had called him in such a mood of desperation. When she did arrive, however, she was accompanied by Copeland Mason, a young married student who had followed Ron from his former institution. It was he who had advised Bobbie Frank to seek out Ron's advice because of the support he had received from him when he was in a similar situation. After admitting the two of them into the living room, Helen excused herself and left them in the care of her husband.

"Professor Jervis," said Bobbie Frank, "I would not have intruded on your free evening had it not been for the fact that I find myself in a desperate situation. I very much need the help of someone who would appreciate my position and give me some constructive advise. When I talked to Copeland about my condition, both he and his wife recommended that I see you immediately."

"Well Miss Frank," replied Professsor Jervis, "I do not know that I am the best possible help for you, but I do appreciate the confidence which Copeland and his wife have expressed in me. Now what can I do to help you?"

"Professor Jervis," said Miss Frank, "I hope that you won't be shocked when I tell you that I am pregnant. I am not a loose woman, and to tell you the truth, up to the time that I and my lover got involved, I had never made love with anyone. Having been raised in a very orthodox Lutheran home, I could not consider an abortion. Unfortunately, the man with whom I am involved is of Islamic faith. He says he loves me very much and wants to marry me, but I shudder at the thought of how my parents will react to my predicament, marriage or otherwise. Now that this is out of my system, what advice can you give me?"

"Miss Frank," replied Professor Jervis, "if I understand you correctly, there is no doubt in your mind, or that of your lover, that you really love each other, and that you do want to get married, except for the fears that you have expressed to me. Since he has asked you to marry him, and since you will not consider an abortion, you should go ahead and get married. If for no other reason, it will legitimize your child. After your marriage, if you find that it is impossible for you to live together, you should get a divorce. As to the objection of your parents, that is a secondary matter. You are adults and capable of making your own decisions."

"Professor Jervis," said Bobbie Frank, "by your straightforward and direct manner of speech, you have removed most of the cobwebs from my mind. I know that, in so far as the personal attitude of myself and my friend is concerned, we can get along well together, and that, as you say, is what counts. As to our parents, well, we will cross that bridge when we get there. I am sure that Mahmoud feels the same way as I do, although his parental relations are more closely tied than mine."

"Miss Frank," said Professor Jervis, "I hope that I am not intruding, but could the young man in question be Mahmoud Sadat? I happen to know, from what his adviser has told me, that he is a very fine young man as well as an excellent student. He is from Egypt, is he not?"

"Yes, Professor Jervis," replied Bobbie Frank, "and, from what he has told me, he is due to return home this coming June, after he has completed his doctorate. That is one aspect of my problem. Can I possibly live in a world of such rigid Islamic faith?"

"Miss Frank," said Profesor Jervis, "knowing you as I do, I know that you are not rigid in your Lutheran faith. As to whether or not you are able to live in the world of Islam it will depend to a large extent on the pressure which they place upon you. I would guess that this could arise when it comes to the question as to whether or not your child is to be brought up in their faith. If you are subjected to extreme pressure, there is always the possibility of your returning to the U.S.A. Your husband would then have to make the choice as to whether or not he will return with you."

"Professor Jervis," said Bobbie Frank, "you have made me supremely happy. Rest assured that I shall follow your advice, for it is constructively intuitive and rational. In the meantime, we will not forget you, and will write to you from time to time to let you know how we are getting along."

After Bobbie Frank and Copeland Mason had departed, Ron Jervis had much to say to his wife about the discussion with Bobbie Frank and his advice to her.

"Helen," said Ron Jervis, "I know that you are skeptical about my offering advice to a student on a matter that affects the entire future of two human beings, and that is what I have just done. Yet I would not have been true to my basic convictions about a teacher's responsibility if I had dodged the challenge which that young lady presented to me. The sad part about her situation is that here we have a microscopic example of a condition that deeply affects the peoples of the world. In this particular case, two aspects of the problem stand out: (1) the relation of the Christian world to the world of Islam, and (2) the relation of the Christian world to the world of Communism. Yes, it is true that we have provided a kind of freedom where both the Christian and those of other faiths can live together in peace, but it is an uneasy peace. The time will come, I fear, when one of these dogmatic groups will seek to dominate the thinking of all the others. Such a condition will surely lead to a state of brutal anarchy. It was such a situation that our Revolutionary Fathers sought to avoid by establishing the state university. It was their belief that our state universities would provide a quality leadership which, in time, would bring into being a people devoted to life in a free society, a people with minds free from the dogmas of the past. We are now confronted with the hydrogen bomb which, in due time, may lead to the killing of millions of people, and even the destruction of Western civilization."

"Ron," said Helen, "you must not continue to carry the burdens of man on your mind all of the time. If you continue to do so, as you are doing tonight, you will wind up a nervous wreck. Now go take a hot bath to relax yourself. It is past 12 p.m., and we both have an early morning class to teach."

When Ron Jervis arrived at his office the next morning, the first thing that he did was to call Bill Snyder, and seek an appointment with him. The idea that he had in mind was to continue the discussion on "The Role of the College of Arts and Sciences in the Education of Free Men." Bill acquiesced to his desire for a meeting, and suggested that they get together at the lunch hour in the dining hall of the Union Building. When they did meet, Ron began the discussion where they had left off at the meeting of the previous evening.

"Bill," said Ron, "you might be interested in learning that when I arrived at home yesterday, after your Committee meeting, I had a telephone call from a desperate young lady who is a graduate student of mine. To make a long story short, she, who is of devout Lutheran faith, had become pregnant to a young man who is of Islamic faith. The young man has asked her to marry him, but she, although expressing her love for him, is very reluctant to accept his proposal. It was this situation that caused her to seek my advice."

"But why should she seek you out?" asked Bill Snyder. "Why did she not go to the University Guidance Counselor?"

"Well," said Ron Jervis, "another graduate student, a young man whom I had helped on a previous occasion, had suggested that she do so. Yes, I advised her because her problem was of a cultural nature. My suggestion was that she should go ahead and marry the young man. Since I knew both of them quite well, I believe that they can cope with whatever problems arise between them. I might add that she left in a different state of mind from that in which I found here when she arrived."

"If I get your point, Ron Jervis," said Bill Snyder, "what you are saying is that we have a primary responsibility to our students. The subject matter which we teach is only a means to a purposeful end, not an end in itself."

"Exactly so, Bill," said Ron. "The human relations factor in teaching should always be primary. Isn't that why your area of subject mtter is classified as one of the humanities? If such is the case, then we are missing the boat in our state universities.

While we still retain the concept of a liberal education, and continue to think that the student is able to achieve such in four years of college life, nothing could be farther from the truth. All that the student is getting at the present time is a conglomerate of courses which adds up to nothing more than a statistic. The original idea of achieving a humanistic mind has disappeared in a mass of specialized subject matters."

"What you are saying, Ron, is all too true," said Bill Snyder. "But to what do you attribute this loss of a sense of unity and purpose in our state universities? Do you think that there is a relationship between this loss and our changing culture during the past century?"

"The answer to your question, Bill, is not a simple one," said Ron Jervis. "I do believe, however, that there is a relationship between this loss and the changing pattern of Western civilization during the past century. In the changing culture of the United States there are such factors as: (1) the negation of the concept of the free mind; (2) the negation of the role of reason in human affairs; (3) the dominance of the politics of power in the operation of our public schools; (4) the substitution of psychology over philosophy; (5) a rebirth of religious dogmatism as a power force in our culture; (6) the rise of corporate capitalism; (7) the influence of the German University on our graduate programs, especially that of subject matter specialization and research. On this latter point, and especially with reference to the idea of 'Freedom to Learn and to Teach,' we lost sight of the fact that, behind this idea in the German Universities, there was an acceptance of the power of DIVINE RULE as a frame of cultural reference. The German principle of freedom to learn and to teach, when brought over to the United States, had no unifying principle other than that of the physical sciences and a stripped down form of materialistic capitalism. As a result, subject matter specialization, rather than a liberal education, has become the end and purpose of the state university program. This vacuumatic freedom played into the hands of corporate capitalism, since it neutralized the study of the humanities. Since organized

Christianity and corporate capitalism had joined hands in a policy of you scratch my back and I will scratch yours, the end result has been a growing anti-intellectualism in our culture. If there is a unifying purpose in our culture today, it is that of becoming rich in material goods and powerful in political life. By so doing, it is believed that you can not only dominate the trends in our culture, but also those of the world."

"Professor Jervis," said Bill Snyder, "since I learned while studying a course in Physics that nature abhors a vacuum, what do you think will happen to us when we are confronted by an extremely stressful situation?"

"I think that you have a partial answer to your question, Bill," replied Ron Jervis, "in what happened in Germany after the First World War. The vacuum that was created during the period between 1917 and 1932 led to the rise of Hitlerian Nazism and the God State idea. I greatly fear that we are moving in a direction which is definitely anti-intellectual and nihilistic. There is a growing form of violence in our everyday life. Note how divided we were when the Japanese attacked Pearl Harbor, and how this attack unified us. When this divisional stress builds up, will we join in a Holy War against the U.S.S.R.? There is much evidence that such will be the case, and, if we do, it will be the end of Western civilization."

"Ron," said Bill Snyder, "I greatly fear that you are correct in your analysis of our present situation. I have noticed this rising tide of violence on a microscopic level in one of the young instructors in my Department. What caused this young man, who was thought by the other members of our staff to be an excellent teacher and scholar, to turn to such destructive, criminal violence is a deep mystery to me."

"Yes, Bill," said Ron Jervis, "I would like to hear what you have to say about the case. On the surface, it is difficult for me to understand why a young man with the reputation that he had in this community would turn to such brutal acts on another human being."

"Well, Ron," said Bill Snyder, "I had known Jim Thorpe, both as a brilliant graduate student and as a promising teacher in the field of the humanities. When it became known that two female students had disappeared, and that the last time one of them was seen was in the company of Thorpe, it was impossible for me to believe that he had anything to do with their disappearance. Also, when he volunteered to help in the search for the two students, I, and others in my department, discussed the possibility of something tragic having happened to them. Even after the passing of three weeks, when the decayed bodies of the two girls were found in a ditch north of this city, I could not believe that Jim had anything to do with their disappearance. It was not until he openly confessed his role in the death of the two students that I could believe that he had committed such a terrible crime as rape and murder. Here is the way he told of the incident in his written statement.

> " 'It was on a Sunday afternoon when the two girls had returned from home and sought me out for a visit in my apartment. I had been having a love affair with one of the girls, but the other girl was unknown to me. While visiting, the girl that was known to me decided that she would take a shower. That was after we had indulged in a number of martinis and were somewhat inebriated. When the girl whom I had not known before went into my bedroom to lay down, I stripped down for some love making with my girl in the shower. When she resisted my offer, on the grounds that her girl friend would not understand, I grabbed her by the throat and choked her to death in committing the rape. I then went into the bedroom, where the other girl was lying down, and raped her. In doing so, I choked her to death. I then hid the two bodies in my closet until after dark, at which time I carried them to my car, and later ditched them naked at the point where they were found.' "

"What a horrible story," said Ron Jervis. "If there was ever an example where an intellectual had failed humanity that was it, a microscopic example of where the state university, through one of its teachers, had betrayed those who had placed such great faith in its establishment. Surely there was something terribly wrong in the mental makeup of this young man. We have here a contradiction, not only of the role of the state university in a free society, but of the role of the intellectual in our Western culture."

"Ron," said Bill, "how far would you go back in our Western culture to trace the roots of our intellectual heritage?"

"In so far as the roots of the university are concerned," said Ron Jervis, "I would go back to the 12th century A.D. As to the roots of our intellectual and ethical heritage, I would go back to the ancient Greeks, to Socrates, Plato, Aristotle, Homer, Herodotus, Thucydides and Hippocrates. Also, there are the Jewish Prophets and the Roman scholars such as Cicero, Cato, Horace and Tacitus. It must be admitted, however, that it was the genius of Aristotle that provided the groundwork for the origin of the Medieval University. All during the period from the second century A.D. to the twelfth Century A.D., Neo-Platonism prevailed, a dogma rooted in the concept of the Man-God relationship and the idea of the Christ, as contrasted with the life of the man Jesus. With a rebirth of interest in the writings of Aristotle, and especially his logic, we have the origins of the University of Paris, the first of the Medieval Universities. In connection with the University of Paris, we have that beautiful and intriguing story of the lives of Peter Abelard and Heloise."

"Professor Jervis," said Bill Snyder, "I am amazed that a Professor in the College of Education would have the insight into our intellectual heritage that you have. I have some knowledge of the love life of Peter Abelard and Heloise, but not to the extent that you have. Tell me more."

"When I first heard of the romance of Peter Abelard and Heloise, I was an undergraduate student in the College of Arts and Sciences in one of our Eastern state universities. The professor in question was an able scholar, a dynamic and creative young man who showed tremendous admiration for the upstart Peter Abelard because he challenged a well-known scholar and teacher in the Cathedral School of Notre Dame, Paris, France. The controversy centered around the Doctrine of the Trinity, whether God the Father, God the Son, and the Holy Ghost were one or three. It was Abelard's position that the argument was foolish and inconsequential, for in true Aristotelian fashion, the issue was conceptual and rooted in the mind of man.

"The brilliance and arrogance of Peter Abelard was such that, in due time, when he became a teacher, he attracted students from all over Europe. As the jealousy of William of Champeau (the teacher whom Abelard had contradicted) mounted, Abelard was denounced as a heretic. This was largely because of the publication of his book SIC ET NON, which accused the Church of contradicting itself over a period of many years. If there was to be any valid church doctrine, it must be logically consistent.

"As if Abelard's heresy was not enough to convict him in the eyes of the Church Fathers, he was now to find himself in deep trouble because of his love affair with Heloise, a young music student in the Cathedral School of Notre Dame. When the love affair led to Heloise becoming pregnant, the wrath of the Gods came down upon his head. He tried to get Heloise to marry him, but she refused because it would destroy his chance to become a priest. In due time, the uncle of Heloise, an overseer of the Cathedral School, hired a number of assassins to waylay Abelard and castrate him. Following Abelard's castration, he was forced into retirement and went to live in an Abbey. Heloise, in return, retired into a convent where she became a nun. From their retirement, they wrote love letters to each other for a period of more than thirty years, or until Abelard's death. What they were not permitted to do in life, however, they were allowed to do in death. For centuries they have slept side by side in the Cemetery Pierre LeChaise which overlooks the city of Paris, France. This was the story my Professor presented in class, while I was still an undergraduate student. At the time, he suggested that, if I was ever in this international city, I should visit the tomb of these two lovers. That opportunity came when I was a special employee of the War Department, serving overseas in the ETO Theatre of Operations.

"Prior to the time that I had arrived in this historic city, I had fortified myself with the knowledge of how to get out to the Cemetery. After getting off at the entry gate and paying my entrance fee, I received a map showing the location of all the famous tombs. Here was the place where, throughout her entire history, many of the notables of France were buried."

"Ron Jervis," said Bill Snyder, "you amaze me. In addition to being an intellectual, I note that you are very much a romantic."

"Well, Bill," replied Ron Jervis, "there are some things that one can get romantic about, and the affair of Abelard and Heloise is one of those things. Since Alexander Pope and Jean-Jacques Rousseau responded in the same manner, I must not be in bad company. Now let me continue my story.

"It was drizzling rain as I walked toward the tomb of the buried lovers. The clouded atmosphere made it a perfect day to get the most out of my visit. Finally, I arrived at the tomb. Here Abelard and Heloise were laid out, side by side. Over the tomb there was a marble canopy, from which water was dripping out of the mouths of a number of medieval gargoyles. As I looked down on this picture of centuries past, wrought out in marble, my mind reflected on how well this tomb symbolized the combination of the intellectual life and the love of a woman."

"Ron," said Bill Snyder, "I note that you have not said anything about the role of language in the evolution of the human mind, because you have been thinking exclusively about the CULTURAL FOUNDATIONS OF EDUCATION. I know, however, that you are a strong supporter of the study of foreign languages as well as English."

"Very much so, Bill," said Ron Jervis. "I must tell you, however, that you have hit upon one of the week links in my educational background. I did study Latin and two years of French while in High School, as well as French, Spanish and German in College. That is one hundred percent better than most of our college graduates today. Also, I hold a minor in English and American Literature at both the under-graduate and graduate levels of instruction."

"To what do you attribute this lack of interest in the study of foreign languages in our high schools and colleges, Ron?" asked Bill Snyder.

"I think, Bill," replied Ron Jervis, "that the fact of our being thousands of miles away from the Continent of Europe has much to do with our attitude, not only in the study of foreign languages but also as to the cultures which they represent. While Jefferson and Franklin were internationally minded, such is not the case for most of our people. In this sense, we have another example of how the state universities have betrayed our Revolutionary Fathers. There is one interesting trend here, however, when it comes to a loss of present-day interest in the study of Latin."

"I would suppose," said Bill Snyder, "that what you have in mind has a relation to the tradition of the Christian Church, especially the Catholic Church and BIBLE study."

"Yes, Bill," replied Ron Jervis. "At the time of Peter Abelard, around the eleventh or twelfth century A.D., scholarship had deteriorated to such an extent over the Continent of Europe that there was massive ignorance even among the monks, priests, and rulers. With the discovery of Aristotle's writings came a rebirth of interest in the ancient Greek and Roman scholars. As a result, the limited efforts of the Cathedral Schools was expanded into the rise of the Medieval Universities and the study of law and medicine, as well as theology. This development called for the establishment of numerous Latin Grammar Schools to promote the study of the Latin language, a knowledge of which was necessary for entrance into the Universities. From the University of Paris came the University of Cambridge, England, and from Cambridge the establishment of Harvard University in 1636. In order to achieve the education of leaders for the spread of the Christian Protestant Faith, the establishment of Latin Grammar Schools was vitally necessary.

"At this point it is important to note the conception and the establishment of the state universities as an aspect of the American Revolution. The state universities were to do for the new state and national governments what the church colleges were doing for the Christian Churches. Proof of the fact that the state universities were established for this primary purpose is written into the records of the time. Latin and Greek were to be replaced by English and modern languages. The heart of the new curriculum was centered in the writings of John Locke, Adam Smith, Edmund Burke, and such French writers as Montesquieu, Voltaire, and Jean-Jacques Rousseau. Also much attention was paid to the work of the seventeenth and eighteenth century scientists."

"Ron," said Bill Snyder, "you have given me an excellent resume of the intellectual background of the Western world, as well as an insight into the thinking that was going on in the colonies during the eighteenth century. What you have demonstrated in a nut shell is the significance of a liberal education, and that the roots of such are in the humanities."

"There is no doubt in my mind," said Ron Jervis, "that such is the case. There is no substitute for a solid humanistic foundation for those who would serve as leaders in a free society. This should include all the major professions, especially those of teaching, law, medicine, business, government, the ministry, and yes, the military. It must be recognized that the significance of studying the humanities is not that of specialized subject matter, but that of developing a meaning and value frame of reference. The question that I would like to present to you, Bill, is to what extent are you and your fellow professors in the field of the Humanities seeking to promote a frame of reference consistent with the needs of a free society?"

"Ron," said Bill Snyder, "I will frankly admit that there is little in what we are doing today that even closely resembles what you have in mind. Even in our conference sessions, what we talk about has to do with such things as: How many hours of English should be included in the A.B. Degree, problems of attendance, what percentage of students in each class should be failed, what the content of a given course should be — and who should teach this or that course. I am positive that there is no unifying purpose in our teaching. A good example would be the way in which I teach a class in Shakespeare's *Macbeth*. First, I like to provide a solid background as to why and how the play was written; the genius and quality of the man; how the drama ranks along with the other plays of the author; a number of examples pointing up the genius of the writer; and finally, Shakespeare's grasp and knowledge of human nature. At no time do I try to tie the study of *Macbeth* in with an insight into the pattern of American life and culture. Also, I am sure that no other member of our faculty goes beyond what I have just said."

"Bill," replied Ron Jervis, "it is more than ironic to me that the Christian Church leadership, in so far as education is concerned, has no meaning and value frame of reference which can be identified with the education of leaders for a free society. Their educational program is still centered in the study of Latin and Greek, and with the BIBLE as the word of God. This pattern of study is the same as that found in the education of Christian Church leadership during the colonial period of the history of our country. I do not find anything during this period that is related in any way to the idea of a free mind, especially since the Christian teacher's role was that of parroting a pattern of dogma. Note how this is demonstrated every Sunday morning by the man in the pulpit who quotes from the BIBLE to support what he is saying. Such thinking, if you can call it such, is distinctly medieval, and in no way helps us to deal with our present-day cultural problems. It can be said that they have an otherworldly meaning and value frame of reference, which is more than you can say of many of our state university professors."

"Our main quarrel, Ron," replied Bill Snyder, "with your College of Education is the extent to which a narrow methodology or technology has taken over your teacher education program. This trend is a direct result of the elimination of philosophy as a teacher education requirement in the latter part of the nineteenth century. The truth of the matter is that you do not have a SCIENCE OF EDUCATION, only a science of methodology. I will admit that something of a similar nature is affecting teaching in our arts and science colleges for, more and more, a psychology of method is gaining prominence in our classrooms."

"I suppose, Bill," said Ron Jervis, "that you are referring to the way in which we are using objective tests in our teaching?"

"Yes, definitely so," replied Bill Snyder. "The kinds of tests that we are using tell us, in no uncertain terms, what we think is important. The controversy is one in which those who use objective tests extensively are willing to sacrifice the artistic humanistic approach in learning for a mechanical instrument."

"Bill," said Ron Jervis, "I am sure that you realize that I find myself on your side in this controversy. Objective tests, such as the true and false type, the multiple choice and word blank, especially when designed by an outsider, minimize the role of the teacher in the educational process. It definitely stifles the emphasis on learning as a creative process. The effect of such use has been deadly, and is showing up every day in our personal relations problems. Even more deadly is the effect of the use of objective tests on mind control. What we are getting from the use of these tests is little more than blind memorization of facts and mass conformity. I will admit that the number of students in our public schools and state universities is driving us in the direction of mechanized robots, but the end result will be a sacrificing of quality for quantity in our intellectual life. Is it any wonder that we are turning more and more to religious evangelism as an escape from a meaningless life?"

"Ron," said Bill Snyder, "what is needed is more emphasis on the quality of mind in our teachers as well as in our students. We come back to your conviction that those who teach in our public schools should be teacher-educated not just teacher-trained. Unless we seek to bring about a community of mind between those who teach in our colleges of arts and sciences and those who teach in our colleges of education, we are sure to end up as a militaristic, nihilistic Nazi Nation, one that is just as brutal and inhumane as was Germany during the era of Adolph Hitler.

"My goodness," said Bill Snyder, "I see that time has run out on me. Before we part, Ron Jarvis, I would like for you to agree to meet with the members of my Department some time in the near future for a continuation of the analysis of the problems we have been discussing."

"Gladly, Bill," replied Ron Jervis. "You set the time and I will be there. The role of the humanities in our culture is of such vast importance that all members of your Department should be vitally interested."

After the separation of Ron Jervis and his friend Bill Snyder, Ron headed toward his office. On the way he stopped over for a short visit with the Chairman of his Department. He found him there, as he had anticipated, but not in a very good mood.

"Ron," said Ricardo, "that goddamned Dean of ours is engaged in his dirty politics again, as you can see from this letter that I have just received from him. I am sure that you have a copy of it, for it is addressed to both of us. It would seem that he is interfering with something that is none of his damned business."

Ron was very much aware of the fact that no love was lost between his Chairman and the Dean, and that the conflict was a result of the way in which the university administration had penalized Ricardo for his political activities. He knew that Dean Hazwell had ambitions of becoming President of the University. This meant that he would do almost anything to counteract the conflict that existed between the faculty of the College of Education and the College of Arts and Sciences. The only way that Ron could be involved with Martinez was that letter which they had written in reply to a letter denigrating the faculty of the College of Education. Sure enough that was it, and what he now read was a stinker. It read as follows:

"Dear Professors Martinez and Jervis:
"It has come to my attention that you two

have written a letter which has been published in the student newspaper in response to a letter written by Professor Anderson of the Biology Department. It is true that Professor Anderson's letter was a scurrilous attack on the faculty of the College of Education, especially with reference to their competency. Such a letter, however, gives neither one of you the right to respond in like manner. What we need to do is to heal old wounds, not to create new ones. I trust that in the future both of you will act accordingly.

"Cordially yours,
Dean Hazwell"

"Well, Ron Jervis," asked Ricardo, "what do you think of this bastard telling us what we can not say or do? Who does he think he is anyway?"

"Ricardo," replied Ron Jervis, "in principle I think that you are dead right in what you say about the Dean's letter. Also, it is quite clear that Anderson is little more than a dogmatic subject-matter specialist who is terribly sensitive because of what his students have been saying about him. He definitely shows a sense of inferiority in his teaching, which indicates that he has no knowledge about teaching methods. Also, he is completely lacking in sensitivity to the feelings of his students. In a way, however, the Dean has a point. Why add fire to something that needs to be put out? I don't approve of the way in which the Dean has responded to our letter. He could have called us into his office and discussed the matter with us."

"Ron," said Ricardo, "I am aware of the fact that I am a hotheaded Mexican American, but surely I am partly justified in my response by the way my people have been treated throughout the past century. I do think that you have a point in what you say about not adding fuel to a fire that you want to put out, and I am willing to give what you say some consideration. I do wish, however, that some of these bastards would be more respectful in thinking of their colleagues. Too often, when a good professor is made into an administrator, he loses sight of his responsibility to his fellow associates."

"Yes," said Ron Jervis, "that is all too true, but to change the subject, I came by to tell you that I have just had a long talk with Bill Snyder about the role of the university in the education of free men and women; and that he is deeply aware of the need for more understanding between the Faculty of the College of Education and the Faculty of the College of Arts and Sciences. He is going to arrange for me to meet with his faculty in the near future to discuss the problem of our common role as members of a state university faculty. This I have agreed to do at his bid and call."

"Ron," said Martinez, "it is good to know that you and Bill Snyder have not only found common cause in your respective roles as members of this state university faculty, but that you are both willing to try to do something to improve the role of this university in the everyday life of our people. Bill Snyder is a good and able professor, both personally and professionally. There is no member of this faculty that is more respected than he."

As Ron Jervis left the office of his Chairman he was more determined than ever that he would seek support from his Dean, and the College of Education Faculty, in improving the quality of mind of those who went out to teach in the public schools. Equally, however, if not more, important was an improvement in the quality of the teaching that went on in the classrooms of the University. How could he possibly get university professors to see to it that they needed an ethical and intellectual frame of reference to give meaning and value to their teaching? This, he was sure, was the crucial issue facing the American State University in the twentieth century.

CHAPTER IV

THE RAPE OF SCIENCE AS A WAY OF LIFE

It was not long before Ron Jervis became convinced that the concept of a liberally educated man had given way to the idea that man was only a cog in a machine directed and controlled by mechanical law. This belief had been reinforced in his discussions with Bill Snyder and, in his growing realization, that the Classical Mind, the product of the Medieval University, had retreated from the reality of the modern world and lived only within the confines of the colleges and the universities. It was no wonder that the world of the academic man was a separate world from that of the man in the marketplace. Plato's retreat from the everyday world of reality had become a marked characteristic of those who were steeped in the humanities. They lived only in their books and in their tradition.

It was in such an academic world that the study of the

sciences had developed during the nineteenth century. Outside of the University, in the realm of the marketplace, the trend of the times was away from the dream of Jefferson's free society toward the rise of corporate power and the revival of Orthodox Religion. This change involved a basic anti- intellectualism toward the study of man in nature and a rebirth of the enslavement of the mind. This trend, when coupled with the rise of Jacksonian Democracy and the defeat of the Plantation South, provided evidence of the passing of THE AGE OF REASON toward the glorification of the mind of the common mind. The Rousseau concept of equality of identity had replaced the Jeffersonian concept of equality before the law. Within the universities, allegiance to the CLASSICAL MIND was giving way to the idea that the function of the state universities was to provide a training ground for those who served corporate industrialism. As a result, a study of the physical sciences began to replace the study of the humanities in terms of priority and value.

It was in his graduate research on the origins of the American State University that Ron Jervis became aware of the significance of the study of the physical sciences in the development of a free society. In the 1795 minutes of the first of the state universities, there was a reference to the fact that this institution was to be known as THE SUN OF SCIENCE, symbolizing the dawn of a new day in the life of the people of the new Nation. The study of physical science was viewed not so much as subject matter but as a means of developing a new type of mind. The role of the state university was to bring into being the new type of mind that was necessary for leadership in a free society. Without such leadership, the power of the people would not be directed by the ethical sense of responsibility or the intelligence necessary for the common good of all. It was with this thought in mind that Ron Jervis picked up the phone on the evening of January 10, 1958, and called William Dean. Fortuntely Professor Dean was at home and there was an immediate response to his call.

"Hello, this is Professor Dean, What can I do for you? Who is calling please?"

"Professor Dean," was the reply, "this is Ron Jervis, whom you will recall was interviewed by your Graduate committee on the matter of his admission to the Graduate Faculty. I am calling to see whether or not we could meet at lunch tomorrow in the University Dining Hall to continue our discussion of some of the issues raised at the time of the interview. I am particularly interested in discussing those having to do with the place of the physical sciences in our culture."

"Professor Jervis," replied Professor Dean, "it is good to hear from you. Since our meeting in the fall, I have thought about our discussion relating to the issue of the role of the physical sciences in our culture, and would be pleased to continue that discussion. I would be most happy to meet with you at lunch tomorrow in the University Dining Hall. Shall we say at about 12:30?"

"That time," said Ron Jervis, "is very satisfactory with me. It will be good to meet with you and renew our acquaintance."

When Ron Jervis turned to his wife, he commented on his good fortune in getting better acquainted with those faculty members who were teaching in the field of the physical sciences.

"You know, Helen," said Ron, "when you have something that is eating at your craw, it is better to get it out of your system than to let it lie there and rot. At the time of my first meeting with Professor Dean, I was impressed by his sincerity and the way in which he expressed himself. He is as critical of the church dogmatists as I am, but, in spite of this fact, we do have a fundamental difference on the role of the teacher in the public school, especially at the university level. I like the man very much, and believe that it is possible for us to establish an understanding relationship."

"Ron Jervis," said Helen, "you are a man with a mission and I love you for it, though there are times that I wish that you were a little more interested in your family life. For a man who came into the teaching profession by the back door, you amaze me. I agree with you, however, about the need for a more meaningful concern for the problems of this Nation and the role of the state university. I will be interested in how you come out in your meeting with Professor Dean."

When Ron arrived at the University Dining Hall on the following day, he found Professor Dean waiting for him in the lounge room. Since Ron remembered him from their previous meeting, it was not difficult to make an immediate identification. The two men shook hands and then proceeded toward the lunch counter. After selecting their food, they walked over to a table in the far east corner of the room where they could talk without much interference. During the intervening period, Ron observed that Professor Dean was much younger than he had thought at their previous meeting. Having obtained a full professorship at a youthful age, Dean obviously was a very bright young man. When they finished the eating of their lunch, Ron Jervis was the first to speak up.

"Professor Dean," said Professor Jervis, "I have a very good friend at the state university where I formerly served who is a Professor of Chemistry and now Dean of the Graduate School. His name is Henry Grant. I wonder if you know him."

"Very much so, Professor Jervis," said Professor Dean. "I know him personally and professionally. Over a period of several years we have been involved in a research project in the field of bio-chemistry. In the meantime, why don't we drop the formality of this relationship. I will call you Ron, and you can call me Bill. It is good to learn, Ron, that you and Henry Grant are such good friends. Any one who is a friend of Henry Grant is a friend of mine."

"All of this pleases me, Bill," said Ron, "for, to tell you the truth, it is easier to talk to a friend than it is to a stranger. Now, to get down to business, I would like to comment on the significance of this meeting. You will recall that at our previous meeting, I was concerned about the problem of the relationship of teaching in a state university to the purpose for which it was founded. You expressed certain opinions on this problem which I thought deserved further comment. That was my reason for calling you and asking for this meeting."

"One thing I would like to know, Ron," said Bill Dean. "How did you get involved in this subject of the role of the state university in our culture, and especially that of the sciences? Why are you so concerned about the sciences when you are in no way involved in teaching in this field?"

"Well to tell you the truth, Bill," replied Ron Jervis, "my interest in science goes back to my high school days. In so far as the role of the sciences in our culture is concerned, that began when I was doing research for the doctorate on higher education in a free society. It was our growing knowledge of the atom and the production of the hydrogen bomb that brought me face to face with my problem. Scientific knowledge, beginning with the seventeenth century, was first thought of as a means of bringing to an end the challenge of the Four Horsemen of the Apocalypse. Yet today it has become the instrument of death for the human race. WHY?"

"Ron Jervis," said Bill Dean, "many of the people who talk as you do are blaming the sciences for the predicament in which we now find ourselves. They quote from the *Bible*. 'He that eateth of the fruit of the tree of knowledge shall be damned.' You are not one of those people, are you?"

"Not at all, Bill," replied Ron. "On the contrary, what we need is more knowledge, not less. This is especially true for the field of the biological sciences. As you will know, development of the field of the physical sciences was retarded until they became a background for the Industrial Revolution. It was the development of the physical sciences that made it possible to provide vast quantities of food for the increasing world population, as well as better housing, transportation, and medical care. Along with such cultural improvements, however, came the modern weapons of war, and the means of waging modern warfare. What we have today is a hydrogen bomb in the hands of a primitive mind. The best statement that I have read on this is that which applies to Nazi Germany, SYNTHETIC BARBARISM."

"What you say, Ron, interests me very much," replied Bill Dean. "I cannot see that we can do very much about this synthetic barbarism. It seems to me that what you are talking about is nothing more than the nature of man."

"The nature of man in the realm of biology is one thing, Bill," said Ron, "but the nature of man in so far as the human mind is concerned is another. I am of the opinion that we can produce a new human mind, the kind of mind that we identify with scientific humanism. It was this kind of mind that Thomas Jefferson, Benjamin Franklin, and Thoman Paine believed could be brought into reality. Unfortunately, these men did not have a scientific basis for such an achievement; but, with the genius of Charles Darwin, there has come into being the possibility of the development of a new kind of mind, a truly human mind."

"Ron," said Bill Dean, "you underestimate the power of the Orthodox churches, and the hold which religion has over our people and much of the world. How do you expect a change with that kind of power against you?"

"Bill," replied Ron, "I am aware of the fact that the kind of mind with which we are dealing is the product of our religious tradition and the power of the churches. In the history of our culture, this church leadership has had little or no opposition that we need today; in fact, it is mandatory if the idea of a free mind is to become a reality. Note that the government of the U.S.S.R. provides a formidable opposition to the religious tradition, but it is an opposition which constitutes a DOGMA OF SCIENCE. What we need in our culture is the FREEDOM OF SCIENCE. Such a force of opposition to these religious dogmas would provide the needed competition in the field of human relations for a resolution of this problem. The men who founded this Nation, a nation 'conceived in liberty and dedicated to the proposition that all men are created free and equal,' believed that the state university was the logical institution for providing the necessary leadership for bringing into being the new mind. These state universities were to be responsible for the education of leadership in all of our fundamental professions save that of the Orthodox ministry. Instead of being Orthodox in their religious beliefs, this new type of leadership would be creatively and artistically religious, or, as Albert Einstein expressed it, have a 'feeling of oneness with the universe.' Such a pattern of meaning and value would, in due time, take the place of the present religious practice of worshiping a mystical God, with one of trying to understand the creative force in this universal world of reality. Love would take the place of fear in human relations, and social intelligence that of command obedience."

"Ron Jervis," said Bill Dean, "I am beginning to see that there is more of truth than fiction in what you are saying. For some time I have been aware of the need for greater perspective in our relation with planet earth. Our failure to develop world awareness, and a knowledge of the common background of all mankind, is surely the educational tragedy of our time. We need a sense of intellectual and cultural connectedness with the peoples of the world, for it is the lack of such connectedness that has led us to the brink of disaster. Where and how do we start toward this brave new world? I am not asking for a mass of data, but where and how to begin the endeavor?"

"Bill," said Ron, "we must turn to a naturalistic philosophy, one which seeks greater understanding of the relation between man and nature. In connection with this development of a naturalistic social philosophy, we need a selective teacher education program at the doctoral level for those who are to be qualified to teach in the state university."

"Ron," said Bill, "I want to throw in my two cents' worth about your teacher education program. If we do no better on the doctoral level than you people have done with the public school, then your dreams will be a complete failure as well as a waste of time and money."

"Bill," said Ron, "I find myself in complete agreement with you on the issue of my professional responsibility. At present, there is much of teacher training and very little of teacher education. As I have said many times to my colleagues in the College of Education, what is called a SCIENCE OF EDUCATION is nothing more than a scientific method of how to teach a given subject. Meaning and value in the cultural process are ignored by both professors and students. Psychology, which you choose to call a pseudo-science, dominates the entire process. It is a tragedy for our Nation that, in the latter part of the nineteenth century, philosophy was dropped as a requirement in the teacher education program. That is like throwing the baby out with the bath water. What was needed was a reconstruction of the philosophy requirement so that the scientific method could be used to attain the values and purposes of a free society. The kind of substitution that was made, however, when the great philosophical tradition was cast aside, was only a mechanistic frame of reference. All of this change brought about what I choose to call a BETRAYAL ON MOUNT PARNASSUS. You scientists, Bill, are just as guilty of failing to live up to our cultural needs as those of us in the schools and colleges of education."

"Ron," said Bill, "I do not see how you can arrive at such a distorted opinion about those of us who teach in the field of the physical sciences. I have consistently held to a high standard in regards to my grading of students. This is supported by the fact that upwards of 40 of my students fail the first time they take Chemistry I."

"Bill," said Ron, "speaking socially, we have to judge your teaching and that of others in your field by what happens to people who use this chemical knowledge. You told me on a previous occasion that what happens as a result of the use of the chemistry that you teach is no affair of yours. If the use of this chemistry is not your responsibility, then who is responsible? In a free society there is only one conclusion. Those who provide this chemical knowledge must be responsible for the results of its use. You and I are aware of the benefits which this knowledge has brought to mankind, benefits such as an increased food supply, protection against deadly diseases, improvement in housing and clothing, and better means of communication and transportation; but what of chemical warfare, of pollution of rivers and our water supply, and yes, even of the air we breathe? I am convinced that there are very few real scientists teaching in our high schools and colleges, only technicians. All of the true scientists that I know anything about, as a result of my knowledge of Intellectual History, had a deep insight in the meaning and value of what they were doing. Note how those of scientific mind have reacted to the discovery of the atom bomb."

"Ron Jervis," replied Bill Dean, "I can see the value of what you are saying about the need for teacher education at the state university level. It is evident to me from what you are saying that we have sacrificed the role of the teacher for the role of the research scholar. Speaking quite frankly, I see no reason why we should not have both the dispenser of knowledge as well as the creator of such. Both are equally important to a free society. For the teacher, there is the problem of human relations as well as the problem of knowing his subject. For the research scholar there is the challenge of the creative act and the advancement of knowledge. What is evident here is that eternal problem of the relation of the animate to the inanimate. Would you say that we who are teaching in the state universities are more responsible for the failure of our students than we realize?"

"I believe so, Bill," said Ron. "In recent invetigations concerning the attitudes and practices of college students there are some alarming facts. Uninspired teaching and poor academic advisement are a major factor in student failure. At least 35% or more of the freshmen who drop out at the end of their first year do so because of a loss of interest in their studies. A majority of the students at all levels of their undergraduate work say that they are bored with their life in the classroom. Overall, there is widespread cheating, ruthless grade competition, race conflict, cynicism, and a growing problem of crime against persons and property. From the report of these conditions, it can be concluded that there is an absence of committed teaching which, by the very nature of the case, points to the absence of challenge and the lack of a meaning and value frame of reference."

"Ron," said Bill, "you know as well as I do that there are certain pressures in the outside world, as well as inside the classroom, which tend to prove that no state university exists in a vacuum. These problems that you mention have a relation to what is going on in the outside world regardless of what I as a teacher try to do."

"That is true, Bill," said Ron Jervis. "It is a marked characteristic of those who refuse to take on the responsibility of leadership in our culture to pass the buck on to someone else. I would say, as the former President Truman once said, 'If you can't stand the heat, you should get out of the kitchen.' Teachers, by the nature of their position, must assume the responsibility of leadership. In the case of your field, Bill, I am sure that you know quite well how the role of science in our culture has been dictated by the role of the military and by corporate power."

"Yes, Ron," replied Bill Dean, "it so happens that I have been in a number of situations which show how these groups, and others, dictate the role of the science professor, especially in the physical sciences. This is done by money grants or by pressure on the university administration. Good Lord, Ron, look at the time. More than two hours have passed since we sat down at this table. I have a meeting coming up in less than fifteen minutes. We do need to continue this discussion for there is much ground that we have not covered. All of this has been very profitable to me, for I had never thought of my teaching in terms other than the transmitting of subject matter. I will be calling you sometime next week for a chance to continue our discussion. I hope that all of this finds you agreeable for another luncheon."

At this point the two men parted company, Bill going to his meeting and Ron Jervis to meet with a graduate student who was having difficulty getting along with one of his professors in the Philosophy Department. Over a period of years, Ron had become convinced that the role of the corporation in the American culture, while adding much to the supply of material goods, had, in a very large sense, contributed heavily to the RAPE OF SCIENCE as a way of life. This had been achieved by appealing to the emotions rather than the intellect, to material gain rather than mind growth, to individualistic greed rather than social need, to profit rather than human welfare. All of this, and more, was so much a marked characteristic of the cultural trend that those who had taken the lead in promoting this cultural abortion had been dubbed ROBBER BARONS. This was the subject that Ron Jervis wanted to take up that evening with his graduate students following his luncheon with Bill Dean.

Ron Jervis in his teaching, especially with his graduate students, had found it more challenging to discuss questions of a philosophical nature than to lecture from a text book, first because graduate students were a more mature and selective group, and second because they were more interested in the philosophical aspects of the educational process. As it turned out, the subject of this evening's discussion was to be one of the most heated of the entire semester. After the class had come to order, the first question that came up involved the place of the free enterprise system in the American culture.

"Professor Jervis," asked student Jim Rhodes, "since Adam Smith was a moral philosopher, how is it that the capitalistic system, as we know it, has been so closely identified with his name?"

"That is a very good question, Jim," replied Professor Jervis, "one that is worthy of much discussion. Would some one of you care to respond to Jim's question?"

Mary Ellis, an outstanding graduate student who had chosen Ron Jervis to serve as her graduate adviser, was the first to respond. "From what I have read, I get the impression that, since Adam Smith was a moral philosopher, he would have been very much opposed to many of the present practices in our economy. There is a significant difference between those who would use scientific knowledge only for material gain and those who think primarily in terms of human betterment."

"Miss Ellis," inquired student Henry Lodge, "don't you consider using this knowledge for the production of food a matter of human betterment?"

"Very much so," replied Miss Ellis, "but why would you destroy this food after it was produced, as was done during the period of the Great Depression of 1929 to 1940? Why? Because you could not sell it for profit at a time when millions of people the world over were existing only at the level of starvation?

I believe in the profit system as a means of production, but not as an end all of its own. Also, we must remember that man does not live by bread alone."

"There is a problem here which bothers me," said Henry Lodge, "a problem which Adam Smith saw very clearly, as did Jefferson and Franklin. The only source of progress or human betterment lies with the individual. The individual must have the freedom to create if he or she is to be productive, whether it be the freedom to build a bridge, to paint a picture, to write a book, or to grow corn. What would you say, Professor Jervis?"

"I agree, Henry," replied Professor Jervis. "It was this very lack of freedom that led Adam Smith to write his great book on THE WEALTH OF NATIONS which, interestingly enough, was published in 1776. Adam Smith was as much a revolutionist as was Jefferson or Thomas Paine. They belonged in the same philosophical company as did all of the eighteenth century creative minds. In this respect, we need to examine the cultural conditions prevailing in England and in the thirteen colonies at that time. In England, the great majority of the people lived in a medieval cultural pattern where there was little or no freedom, economic or political. It was for this reason that Adam Smith argued against the government passing laws affecting the economic condition of the country. When a law was passed, the benefits always fell into the hands of the landed aristocracy. What was the nature of the economy in the colonies? In addition to the slave economy of the southern colonies, indentured servitude prevailed in all of the colonies. There was the holdover, from medieval times, of the practice of primo-geniture and entail. The great majority of the people could neither read nor write, and only the property holders had a right to vote. By and large, the dogma of Protestantism reigned supreme. What appalls me is that, after more than a century and a half since the American Revolution, we remain totally ignorant of the cultural conditions that prevailed in the colonies, and their tyrannical implications. Since we continue to ignore the intellectual implications of our colonial heritage, and the significance of the American

Revolution, I have spoken of our present condition as a BETRAYAL ON MOUNT PARNASSUS."

"Professor Jervis," said Jimmy Ingle, "I would like to better comprehend what you have been saying. Are you implying that, having given every man and woman the right to vote, you do not think that Adam Smith would oppose the idea of government being used as an agency in correcting our economic injustices? Now, if that is the case, why is it that the laws that are being passed still favor the vested interests in our culture?"

"That is a good question, Mr. Ingle," replied Professor Jervis. "I wonder what the rest of you have to say in regards to Mr. Ingle's question."

"If I am correct about my knowledge of our history since the beginning of the nineteenth century," said Laura Procter, "I would say that there has been an educational failure at all levels of the public school system, and especially of the state university."

"Miss Procter," asked Professor Jervis, "why the distinction between the role of the public school and that of the state university? Do they not have the same basic obligation to the people?"

"Well," said Miss Procter, "if, as it has been pointed out by you and others in the field of public education, the state university was established primarily to provide the kind of leadership necessary for the development of a free society, then there has been a marked failure, at this level of the public school system, to provide qualified teachers for such service. Up to the present moment, I had little knowledge as to my primary responsibility in the classroom. There was little in my undergraduate training as a teacher that I would say was creatively intellectual. The content of the program was skill training, not creative thought. The major emphasis was conformity to the status quo, not leadership in free thinking. Because of such practices, the community mind in our culture has remained, and will continue to be, anti-intellectual. To speak of Christian Orthodoxy, I am of the opinion that not much has been changed since the American Revolution."

At this point, Henry Lodge came back into the discussion. "Your experience, Miss Procter, is much the same as mine. Our communities are dominated by the mind of the church people, especially in their influence on the local school boards. I believe that this is so because there is no competitive force which is able to offer more in our meaning and value relations than the traditional Christian leadership. Our public schools, administratively and in the classroom, are no different than the private and the church schools. The idea of a free scientific mind, as hoped for by the leaders of the American Revolution, has, at no time during our entire history, been a living reality."

"Is there any member of this class," asked Professor Jervis, "that would like to express an opposite point of view? If not, then let us move on to the issue which concerns the failure of the state university to provide the kind of teacher education program necessary for life in a free society. Why during the early part of the nineteenth century did these state universities fail to live up to their free scientific responsibilities?"

"Well, as an opener," responded Jim Rhodes, "I would say that as long as Christian medieval dogma prevailed, there was no possibility of our ever developing the free scientific society that we are thinking about. There is the fact that the physical sciences had come into full acceptance by the ruling majority of the people because they were a tool in the expanding Industrial Revolution. In a country like ours, which was vast and undeveloped during this period, economic expansion was far more important to our people than was the controversial issue of a free-thinking mind. The biggest drawback at this time was the plantation South, with its slave economy. With the liquidation of the plantation way of life, the corporation had a free hand to promote the dogma of a profit system."

"What you are suggesting, Jimmy," said Mr. Ingle, "is that the idea of free enterprise capitalism was taken out of the context of Adam Smith, with its ethical and intellectual sense of responsibility, and turned into a context of mechanical law of supply and demand. Such a change reduced the free enterprise system to nothing more than a means of exploiting the people and the natural resources of the Nation. From my study of the history of the United States, I have noted that all of the national resources were up for grabs to a few conniving individuals."

"That is my point exactly," said Jim Rhodes. "Please note that these conniving individuals achieved their desired end in many devious ways, for example: (1) by supporting Orthodox Christianity; (2) by buying off legislators and congressmen; (3) by controlling what is taught in the public schools; (4) by controlling the appointments to the U.S. Supreme Court; and (5) by having the corporation granted the same rights and privileges as a citizen. Toward the close of the nineteenth century one corporation head is credited with the statement 'We own this country, and by God we are going to keep it.' "

"Mr. Rhodes," said Professor Jervis, "I see that you know your American History very well. Can you tell me how the corporation got the power and rights of the citizen?"

"It is my understanding Professor Jervis," said Mr. Rhodes, "that this right came about in the way in which the Fourteenth Amendment to the U.S. Constitution was written. While the Amendment is said to have been written primarily for the Black Man, a clause was included in it which granted the same privilege to the corporation. With the growing wealth of the Nation, in the latter part of the nineteenth century, the corporation became a power in its own right, an economic government as powerful as the government of the United States. This power, for all intents and purposes, was absolute until Franklin D. Roosevelt became President. It was he who challenged this absolute power by extending the power of Big Labor. Since 1937 we have been confronted by a tug of war between the power of the corporation and the labor unions."

At this point the discussion had so upset student George Maxwell that he spoke up with great feeling. "You, all of you, are failing to take into consideration the good that has been done through the exploitation of the physical sciences. Without this exploitation how could we have conquered this country, built the railroads, produced all this food, developed our means of transportation and communication, invented the automobile and the airplane, and brought all the people of the world into closer contact with each other?"

"I will grant you, Mr. Maxwell," said student Ruth Young, "that much good has come about as a result of the exploitation of the physical sciences, but what about the price we are paying in terms of the value of human life? It seems to me that all of this industrial development was achieved without the ethical commitment that Adam Smith deemed necessary to the progress of the human race. Also, wasn't Thomas Jefferson convinced that a sense of responsibility to the GENERAL WELFARE was paramount if we were to have a free society? What we have now is not only the exploitation of our natural resources, but of our human resources as well. One of these corporation heads was quoted in my American History school text as saying that 'you could not run a coal mine without a machine gun.' When I look at what has been going on in our Nation since 1830, I see very little that points to a major concern for human beings. I see much that points to greed, scandal, corruption in high places, and indifference to human welfare."

"Professor Jervis," asked George Maxwell, "what is the origin of the ethical commitment to which you refer? Does it not come out of the Communistic philosophy of Karl Marx?"

"Not at all," replied Professor Jervis. "As I see it, the origin of the ethical premises of Adam Smith are traceable back to the thinking of the Jewish Prophets. You find the same pattern of thinking in the life of the Greek philosopher Socrates and in that of Jesus of Galilee. Also, as you must know, Karl Marx was a Jewish Rabbi."

"I agree with all that you have said, Professor Jervis," said Jimmy Ingle. "How does Jefferson's concept of the nature of man fit in with this ethical pattern of thinking? I would think that when he argues for an aristocracy of intelligence he could not be democratic."

"That depends entirely on what you think is democratic, Mr. Ingle," replied Professor Jervis. "If you think that all men and women are of equal intellectual ability then you are misinterpreting Jefferson. What he was defending was the idea of justice before the law. The ethical premise of the Fatherhood of God and the brotherhood of man are basic to his thinking. Jefferson definitely rejected the concept of Equality of Identity, a concept of the French Philosopher Jean-Jacques Rousseau. Placing ignorant and poorly educated men in the offices of government always resulted in tyranny, and in corrupt and ineffective government. I would say that Jefferson was democratic in his allegiance to the quality of individuality and opportunity. His thinking, in this respect, had its origin in the philosophy of John Locke, but his humanism can be traced back to the ancient Greek philosophers."

"If what you are saying is true, Professor Jervis," said Mary Ellis, "why do we allow just any citizen to run for public office, even at the highest level of government in our country? Would you not say that we have betrayed our Revolutionary fathers by doing so?"

"Yes, Mary," replied Professor Jervis. "We have betrayed them with our anti-intellectualism and with our Jacksonian sense of democracy. It was our religious ethic of equality in the sight of God that got us into this difficult political situation. By tying this belief to the thinking of Rousseau, the philosopher of the French Revolution of 1789, we came up with the idea of equality of identity in our political life, and with the concept of majority rule. We had no scientific basis for our thinking until Charles Darwin came forth with his concept of the nature of man. Since 1859, however, Orthodox Christians have been waging a holy war against the theory of evolution. It would be more accurate to say that they are against any scientific attempt to understand the origin of man."

"Professor Jervis," commented Laura Procter, "if I understand your thinking, what you are calling for is a shift from the subject matter classroom approach in teaching to a meaning and value frame of reference geared to the concept of scientific citizenship. This would involve the concept where man and the natural order of the universe are thought of as one and a part of each other, rather than the traditional belief that man and nature are two different things."

"Yes, Miss Proctor," replied Profesor Jervis. "That is precisely my thinking, and for a good reason. I am of the conviction that, if we continue on our present course, we will destroy our culture in a nuclear war."

"Professor Jervis," said Jim Rhodes, "tell us more of your thinking on this issue, and especially about some of the immediate educational implications of your thinking."

"Yes, Jim," replied Professor Jervis. "Let us look at the population issue which has come to involve, not only the matter of birth control, but that of abortion. One of our well-know professors in the field of genetics has been studying population growth during the past century. From his findings it is clear that if we do not take more direct action to control population growth, mankind will swamp the earth by the year 2000. If the nations of the world do not make a concerted effort to control world population, there is no way out but the killing of millions of people in a nuclear war. Also, mother nature is sure to take her revenge in starvation, hunger, and personal strife. Mexico is a good example of what I have in mind. Because the country can feed no more than 50 percent of her population, we are confronted with an increasing illegal alien problem. Our worldwide problem is unquestionably a result of the lack of quality leadership, an example of the failure of the state universities to live up to their obligation.

"The scientifically oriented citizen would not only be aware of the need for population control, he would understand the nature of the forces that constitute a road block to resolving the issue. The Christian dogmatists, and other dogmatic religions around the world, have opposed any form of birth control and abortion as a means of controlling population growth. Much of this dogma is tied in with the desire for cheap labor and the exploitation of the poor. Also, this is a marked characteristic of corporate business when it comes to the production and selling of goods in the Asiatic world."

"Professor Jervis," said George Maxwell, "I can see that we have never had the quality of mind which provides the needed insight into the nature of our cultural problems and their resolution. I recall how the history of our country points to this problem, the killing of the Indians, the importation of cheap labor, and the exploitation of those who worked in the mines and the factories. People continue to cry out for world peace, but, until we are able to bring into being the power of the scientifically social creative mind, we are sure to have more wars and more killing. Without such a mind, we will have to face hunger, and more hunger, conflict, and more conflict, crime, and more crime."

"Miss Young," asked Professor Jervis, "how do you view the population problem of growth in connection with the free enterprise system? Do you think the individual by his own effort can cope with the unemployment problem?"

"Well," said Miss Young, "it seems to me that we have gained some insight by noting the growing power of organized labor. With the coming of Big Labor we now have two competing giants, each fighting exclusively for its own interests. Free enterprise capitalism, where each individual's personal interests are paramount, has been supplanted by the power of organized labor, where the individual's interest in the organization is paramount. If the concept of the GENERAL WELFARE is to survive, then social planning becomes mandatory. Here, Jefferson's idea of the rule of creative intelligence and ethical responsibility is a social necessity, if anarchy, or its converse Nazism, is not to become a reality of our time."

"It seems to me, Miss Young," said George Maxwell, "all you are doing is imitating the Communists. How can the concept of freedom prevail if we are to have socialistic control?"

"I will admit, George," said Miss Young, "that there is some merit in the Communistic idea of a planned society, but this does not make me a Communist. The idea of form, of structure in relation to the world of matter, is as old as Aristotle. The Communist is unfortunate, however, in submitting to a dogma of science rather than operating from a theoretical scientific basis. Dogma always tends to destroy, to cramp individual initiative and creative thought. A dogma of science calls for a planned society, controlled from the top down by a few individuals. What I see, and deem necessary, is participatory planning, involving all of our citizens. Such participation should be directed, and creatively applied, by those representing the highest level of creative intelligence and ethical commitment. Science is not a dogma of analysis and reason, but a creative art form. As I see it, such scientific citizenship would be a force that operates on insight and intuition, as much as mechanical law and form. I would say that the U.S.S.R., with its dogma of science, is more in keeping with the needs of modern life than we are with our medieval dogma of religion and our laissez-faire individualism."

Just as Student Ruth Young ended her reply to George Maxwell, the bell rang; but, after the class was dismissed, several of the students gathered around Ron's desk to continue the discussion on the issue of a planning economy. It was Jim Rhodes who expressed genuine satisfaction on what Ruth Young had said, and proceeded to compliment her.

"Ruth," said Mr. Rhodes, "I think that you hit the nail on the head when you pointed out the real difference between an industrial democracy and a Communist state. Human growth is not something which is handed down from the top by a few individuals, but something which each individual achieves by creatively participating in a given situation. The failure of Christianity can be attributed to the fact that its dogma was such as to make it impossible for creative participation on the part of all. John Dewey pointed this out in his widely circulated book *Democracy and Education*. Here we come back to the thinking of Professor Jervis on the failure of the American State University."

"Thank you, Jim," said Professor Jervis. "Your class session this evening was one of the most satisfying I have experienced since I started teaching in this state university. If we could only get the majority of graduate students in our state universities to express themselves as your class has done this evening, we could bring about a revolution in thought in this Nation. Instead of talking about the RAPE OF SCIENCE, we could be talking about the SUN OF SCIENCE, and the coming light of a new day."

When Ron Jervis reached home that evening, he could not refrain from telling Helen about his discussion with Professor Dean, and of what went on in his graduate class. "You know, Helen," he said, "I am beginning to think that maybe I am making some headway with the faculty of this university and with the students. It is a long road, and the hour is late, but even a minor achievement has its merits."

"Don't you think, Ron," said Helen, "that you are becoming too involved in your crusade against organized Christianity and the corporation barons? One of these days the Old Guard will rise up against you, as they did against Peter Abelard. Even though we are the great exploiters of scientific knowledge, we continue to oppose the idea of science as a way of life."

"Very true, Helen," replied Ron. "It is increasingly apparent that the organized laborer is no more interested in the idea of scientific citizenship than the business mogul. Actually, since organized labor gained mass power, we have been confronted with two competing forces which seek control of our state and national governments for an expression of their special interests."

"Ron Jervis," said Helen, "are you not being a little hard on the labor organizations? I thought that you were a friend of the laboring man."

"I am Helen," said Ron, "but when the laborers adopt the same tactics as corporate business, and are concerned about nothing more than wages for themselves, they are no longer the defender of the poor and oppressed. They, like the corporation, have become a power-motivated mechanistic instrument without ethical commitment or intellectual responsibility."

"Ron, I wish you would cite me an example of the kind of organized labor practice that you are condemning. I am inclined to think that you are becoming a bit more capitalistic yourself," said Helen.

"Not at all, Helen," replied Ron. "What you have to take into consideration is whether or not the individual is ethically committed and intellectually responsible to the GENERAL WELFARE of this Nation. Speaking frankly, such commitment is no more evident in Big Labor today than it is in the Corporate Barons. A good example of what we are talking about can be found in the practice of commercialized athletics. Throughout the history of big league baseball, the players have operated in a pattern of slavery. Now that the players have organized, that pattern has changed. Baseball strikes, and the coming of the free agent, have given the players a balance of power which they are exercising to the tune of million-dollar salaries. It will not be long before single players will be demanding higher salaries than the market can stand. In this power struggle, neither the players nor the corporation give a damn about the welfare of the people."

"Well, Ron," said Helen, "now that you have made your point, I think that we should get to bed. The hour is getting late, and we must get up early because of the appointment that you have made with your Chairman. Also, I have some things to do before getting off to school."

"Yes," said Ron, "I am puzzled as to why he wants to see me at such an hour, possibly because he has no other free time during the day. My guess is that it has something to do with the Chairmanship of the Department. There is a rumor that he wants to step down, and, if so, he will want me to take over."

Ron Jervis was correct in his assumption that Ricardo wanted him to take over the Chairmanship of the Department, but he did get the surprise of his life in what Ricardo had to tell him about the reason why the change had to be made at once. After Ron had comfortably settled himself in a chair, Ricardo was the first to speak.

"Ron," said Ricardo, "I know that you are wondering why I wanted to see you so early this morning. I can assure you that I have good reasons for doing so. Let me get to the heart of the matter immediately. The Dean of the College is pressing me to resign from the Chairmanship of our Department as soon as I can get you to take over. You know how I feel about Buckley taking over the Chairmanship. He would destroy the very things that we have spent so much time in building up. Also, because of his subject matter convictions and his personality, he has been unable to attract graduate students for the doctorate. I am happy to say that the Dean agrees with me in every way. This being the case, and since it is necessary that I resign, the only one left who can take over the Chairmanship of our Department is yourself."

"Ricardo," replied Ron Jervis, "I am pleased to learn that you have so much confidence in me. You know that if it is necessary for me to take over the Chairmanship of our Department, I will be willing to do so. But why is it so necessary for you to resign at the present time? Why not wait until the beginning of the fall term?"

"Ron," said Ricardo, "unfortunately, that is not possible. Since much scandal about me will be in the morning paper, as well as in the next few days, I might as well tell you what this is all about. Miss Ida Hernandez, whom you know as a graduate student, has been a love companion of mind for some time. Of recent date she has become pregnant. As for my wife, ever since she had that thyroid operation, our relations have been going downhill, so much so that for some time she has refused to be my bed fellow. It was this refusal that drove me into Ida's arms. Talk about making love, what a difference between Ida and my wife. You remember the trip that we took to New Orleans several weeks back. You remember that I told you it had something to do with the publishing of my book. Well, as you must suspect, that was not my reason for going. The trip was made so that Ida and I could spend the weekend together. Celebrate, we really did, and with a bang, so much so that I am sure this is when Ida became pregnant. When my wife found out about our affair, through one of the university professor's wives, she took off for Santa Fe, New Mexico. I have been to see my priest about securing a divorce, but he has refused to give me any consideration. As a result, I have pulled out of the Catholic Church. Also, I have secured a lawyer who has seen to it that divorce proceedings are already in process. Speaking frankly, Ron Jervis, you have no idea how much stress I have been under during the past three weeks. For that reason, if for no other, I need to get out from under the responsibilities of the Chairmanship."

"Well Ricardo," said Ron, "since you feel so strong about the matter, let me talk to the Dean, and, if I find him agreeable, I will accept the offer. In the meantime, I am very sorry to hear about your wife, and, on the other hand, I wish you and Ida all the happiness in the world. I assume that you and Ida will be getting married as soon as your divorce has been granted."

"Yes, Ron," said Ricardo, "that is what we have been planning, but no date will be set until I have been granted my divorce. As you might well expect, it will be the beginning of a new life for me."

It was at this point that the discussion between the two men ended. The nature of the discussion was such that it led Ron Jervis to think about his past life. There were the ups and downs that had occurred between him and Helen, and the jealousies that had cropped up now and then. There was the time when Helen and her pipe organ instructor seemed to form a close attachment for each other. He well remembered when he exploded one night, when Helen refused to give him a reason for her being out so late. Thank God he had kept his emotions under control, for since that time he and Helen had found a good life together. He did recall the time when Helen had exploded at him, when she thought that he was having an affair with the graduate student that he had aided, because of the treatment she had received at the hands of the Dean of Women. It was not until that afternoon that Ron Jervis walked into the Dean's office to talk to him about becoming Chairman of his Department. Dean Hazwell was the first to speak.

"Professor Jervis," said the Dean, "as you must know, I have been in touch with Professor Martinez concerning the possibility of your taking the Chairmanship of your Department. May I say that I concur in the change most heartily, for I believe that you will make an excellent Chairman. I say this for several reasons: (1) It is impossible, under the circumstances, for Professor Martinez to continue; (2) while Professor Buckley has more tenure than you, and while he has asked me to consider his appointment, I do not believe that he would fill the position as satisfactorily as you; (3) I have complete faith in your ability to take over the leadership of this significant position, and to perform at a high quality level. I am glad to report to you that a number of the professors in this College, and in the College of Arts and Sciences, speak highly of your teaching and research. Now what do you say? Will you accept the offer of the Chairmanship?"

"Dean Hazwell," said Professor Jervis, "I am honored in that you have expressed such faith and confidence in me. The situation, being what it is, leaves me no choice but to accept your offer. It is my understanding that, with the acceptance of your offer, the change is to take place immediately, and that you will so notify the members of my Department and other administrative officials of the University."

"Yes, Professor Jervis," said the Dean. "Now, as your first act as Chairman of your Department, there is a very important meeting of the Administrative Council of the College which is to be held tomorrow morning at ten a.m., which I want you to attend. We will be discussing the relation of the mental health of the individual to the education process. As you know, Professor Ronald Reid of the Educational Psychology Department is Chairman of the Committee. Since he represents a point of view that is contrary to yours, the meeting should be very enlightening. We will be meeting in the Conference Room which is next to this office."

"Well, Dean," said Professor Jervis, "I can see that you know very well where I stand on the matter of mental health. You can count on my being present at your meeting."

At this point the conference with Dean Hazwell came to an end, and Ron, hoping to find Ricardo in his office, headed in that direction. While the hour was late for a professor to be around, Ron was fortunate in finding his friend still in the job. What he did not expect was to find Ida Hernandez present with him. As Ron entered Ricardo's office, Ida looked up and, with a friendly smile, spoke to him.

"Come in, Professor Jervis," said Ida. "My conference with

Ricardo is finished." Turning to her lover, she calmly remarked, "Then I will be seeing you tonight at the usual time and place. Don't forget for I will expect you to be on time." With these words she passed by Ron on her way out, but with a friendly wave of the hand as she departed.

For the next hour, Ron Jervis talked to Ricardo Martinez about his conference with Dean Hazwell. In addition to telling his friend that the Dean was pleased with his willingness to accept the Chairmanship of the Department, Ron talked of the coming mental health meeting of the following morning.

"Ricardo," said Professor Jervis, "I have some very strong opinions on the thinking of Professor Reid about the matter of mental health and wonder what your experience with him has been."

"Ron," said Professor Martinez, "he likes to think that he is very scientific in dealing with the issue but, the truth of the matter is, he is very individualistic. Without even knowing it, he is operating from either the Christian ritualistic premise of the soul, the so-called Democratic premise of Rousseau, or the atomistic biological premise of Thorndike."

"That seems to be the thinking of Dean Hazwell," replied Ron Jervis. "In this respect I intend to question Professor Reid about his position on the issue. Well, since you have an appointment with Ida coming up in the next hour or so, I will get myself out of your way and head for home. Helen will be wondering what is holding me up, and about my conduct, if I am not careful."

When Ron Jervis arrived home that evening, he had much to tell his wife about his appointment as Chairman of his Department, and especially about the affair between Ricardo and Ida Hernandez.

"You know, Helen," said Ron, "I had no idea that Ricardo was having an affair with Ida Hernandez. Also, the fact that he had kept a secret of the break between himself and his wife, and that Mrs. Martinez was no longer here. The fact that she was in Santa Fe, New Mexico came as a complete surprise to me. Ida Hernandez is a very attractive young lady. I had no idea that the old boy had it in him."

"That is the way you men are," replied Helen, "always on the lookout for some young piece of tail. So far as I am concerned, there is no difference between one woman's ass and another, but you men seem to always be on the lookout for a change."

"Now, Helen," said Ron, "are you not being a bit unfair? From what Ricardo tells me, the devil himself could not get along with that wife of his. As for myself, I am of the opinion that when you get the kind of split that you have between Ricardo and his wife, each must share a part of the responsibility. I doubt that Ricardo would have taken up with another woman had there not been a good reason. Since he is convinced that his wife is going to scandalize him, he has resigned from the Chairmanship of the Department, and I have been selected to fill his place."

"Ron Jervis," said Helen, "that is just great. It makes me very proud of you. Won't Professor Buckley be upset when he hears that you have been appointed over him? I know that he considers himself your senior on the job, and that he was very interested in becoming Chairman."

"Yes," said Ron, "he is very much of the opinion that he is superior to Ricardo and myself. He wanted the position, but more for the honor that it would bring to him personally than for the service he could render. Poor Buckley, I feel sorry for him. He has such an underlying sense of inferiority that he is always trying to cover up with a false sense of superiority. Now to change the subject, how was your day in school?"

"Very good, Ron," replied Helen, "except for one incident that will amuse you. I was showing a film to the class on Darwin's Theory of Evolution. When I asked for comments at the end of the film, one of the girls stood up and said, 'Mrs. Jervis, by showing this film you are contributing to the destruction of my religion. As I understand, no teacher has the right to interfere with a student's religion.'

" 'Well, Anne,' I replied, 'by not showing this film, I would destroy the freedom of the other members of this class. The truth of the matter is that no one should base his or her religious beliefs on ignorance.' "

"I think that you did a beautiful job the way you responded to the student," said Ron. "Here we have an example of what Andrew D. White in his HISTORY OF THE WARFARE BETWEEN SCIENCE AND THEOLOGY IN CHRISTENDOM, called THE GREAT DILEMMA OF OUR TIME. It was demonstrated in your class that the scientific citizen has not yet become a reality, and that the RAPE OF SCIENCE AS A WAY OF LIFE IS STILL WITH US."

"You know, Ron," said Helen, "there are times when I think that we are doing our daughter an injustice by not encouraging her to attend the church of her choice, but when I get the kind of reaction that I got today from that film, I am convinced that maybe she is not so bad off after all. We are not blinding her to the reality of our time, although she may suffer some loss in her social development. Many of the problems which we face today are not so simple as they seem. Of one thing I am sure, a good teacher should never assume the role of a dictator in her classroom. Now, having said my speech, I am going to hit the hay. I am very tired and feel like I am washed out."

With these comments Helen turned toward the bedroom, as Ron Jervis continued in his thoughtful mood while relaxing in his lounge chair. For one thing, he had a good idea of what the next day would bring forth, especially at the meeting on mental health. He knew exactly what he was going to say, for it was a subject to which he had given much thought. It would be a good session, for he expected to receive much support from Dean Hazwell. Soon he was on his way to the bedroom and a good might's sleep.

The Committee on Mental health and the Educational Process met at the hour ten as set by the Dean. After Professor Jervis had been introduced to the others as the New Chairman of the Department of the Cultural Foundations of Education, Professor Reid took over as the official Chairman of the Committee.

"Members of the Committee," said Professor Reid, "this meeting has been called to see whether or not we can, as the Advisory Committee to the Dean, come to a consensus as to what action should be taken on the matter of the mental health of teachers. Can we start with the premise that poor mental health is always an indication of an emotional disease, and should always be treated as an individual problem?"

"Professor Reid," replied Professor Jervis, "the point of view which you have taken is very controversial. I must say that for me your position is one which is far too prevalent among educational psychologists. I am of the opinion that your position is anything but scientific, in that you start from an atomistic point of view as to the nature of an individual. This individualistic approach is rooted in Orthodox Christianity, in the political philosophy of Jean-Jacques Rousseau, and in the theory of laissez-faire capitalistic individualism. It is in no sense an effort to understand the complex nature of the human mind."

"Professor Jervis," said Professor Reid, "you know as well as I do that there is no relation whatsoever between my position and that of Orthodox Christianity. I am a naturalist, first, last, and always. You cannot deny the fact, however, that the individual's problem is strictly that of a personal entity when you are talking about mental health."

"Very true, Professor Reid," replied Professor Jervis. "The point that I am making is whether or not the individual's problem is of an internalized nature or a result of some external social condition. I am ready to defend the position that there is a difference between the concept of science as method, and contrarily, that science is a process with a meaning and value frame of reference. What you are doing is trying to fit the individual into some rigid preconceived frame of reference. What you have is a refined technique which results in a slave-like submission to the status quo. Personally speaking, such an approach to the mental health problem is more like the RAPE OF SCIENCE AS A WAY OF LIFE, for it in no way provides for the growth of the scientific mind."

"Professor Jervis," said Professor Reid, "I get the impression that you are prejudiced to anything that smacks of a psychological approach to the problem of mental health. How do you reconcile your position with the fact that every college of education in this country is totally committed to my way of thinking on this issue?"

"Professor Reid," replied Professor Jervis, "if we are talking about a society in which the individual is to be regimented and made to fit into a groove, I would agree with you one hundred percent, but remember we are talking about a society of free men and women. If such is the case, as you say, we are betraying those who founded this Nation and were responsible for establishing the state university. There was full justification for eliminating the medievel philosophical approach in teacher education but, in doing so, we threw the baby out with the bath water. Instead of opposing the introduction of Educational Psychology as a scientific means in teacher education, I am very much a supporter of scientific methodology. But certainly not as a substitute for a philosophical meaning and value frame of reference. What I am supporting is the use of Educational Psychology in a teacher education program that seeks to make leaders of teachers for a free society. In such a program the students who graduate from this College would not only have a basic ethic, but would be intellectually responsible for initiating a program of public education that produced the scientific mind. Why have we not done so? I believe the answer to this question is bound up in the power of Christian Orthodoxy and Corporate Capitalism. What is missing in our teacher education program is a growth in the free mind of the teacher. We are not educating teachers, only training them to fit into some preconceived traditional pattern of conformity. Is it any wonder that we are the laughing stock of the professors of the College of Arts and Sciences?"

"Professor Jervis," commented Professor Lary Egan, Chairman of the Physical Education Department," "I have been of the opinion for some time that there was a need for more philosophical substance in our teacher education program. You have given us much to think about in connection with this need. I am sure that if we stop to think about the many problems that a teacher faces when she takes a position in a local community, we would realize that many of these problems are of a social nature. They cannot be solved by placing the blame on the teacher for every problem that comes up in the classroom. If a teacher is to operate effectively, she cannot do so by the singular process of emotional adjustment. At this point there is a definite need that the teacher have a meaning and value frame of reference from which to operate. The traditional Orthodox Medieval frame of reference, in which she or he has been brought up, has not met, and will never meet our present need. I believe that there is a need for this College to help every student develop the scientific creative social citizenship way of dealing with our community problems."

"You have expressed yourself quite well, Professor Egan," replied Professor Jervis. "I would be interested in hearing more of you express yourself on this issue, especially on the role of the College in the mental health of the teacher."

"Professor Jervis," commented Professor John French, Chairman of the Department of Curriculum and Instruction, "what I would like to see us do, in connection with the role of the College on the issue of mental health, is to have a series of weekly meetings where each one of us would assume responsibility for presenting a paper. I would recommend that Professor Jervis be the first to lead off, since it was he who opened up the issue. Mr. Chairman, I would like to put my thinking to a motion to see how this group responds."

The motion of Professor French was seconded by Professor Egan, and then carried with one dissenting vote, that of Professor Reid, who immediately called for an adjournment. From the action taken by the Committee, it was evident that there was general agreement with the position taken by Ron Jervis. To Ron, it was apparent that the members of the Committee were sensitive to the fact that learning to cope with the problems of the everyday world involved more than shrinking them to a size that would fit into the skull of the brain. Rather we should seek to intelligently change the world around us so as to make our lives more meaningful.

On Friday afternoon, after the members of his Department had been notified of Ron's appointment as Chairman, Ron called his first meeting. He wanted to make it clear that there was complete understanding between himself and Martinez. Also, he wanted to bring to each member of the Department the substance of the discussion at the Mental Health Meeting. After all were present, the first question came from Professor Buckley.

"Professor Jervis," said Professor Buckley, "since I am the senior member of this Department, other than Professor Martinez, I had the right to be appointed Chairman in his place. Don't you think that by usurping that right you have demonstrated a lack of professional courtesy?"

"Professor Buckley," replied Professor Jervis, "I can assure you that I had nothing to do with the Dean's decision. Actually, I much preferred to have Professor Martinez continue as head of our Department. Since that was not to be the case, the Dean called me into his office and presented me with an open challenge. I then and there accepted his offer. Now, Professor Buckley, let us get on with the purpose of this meeting.

"As you know, Dean Hazwell has a real interest in having every student who graduates from this College take a course in Educational Philosophy. That was the one thing that he stressed with me when I first came here. He was not sure as to the content of the course, but he was positive in the belief that the course should have a meaning and value frame of reference consistent with the fundamentals of a free society. I know that he is an Hegelian in his thinking, whereas I can be better identified with the thinking of William James and John Dewey. My point in all of these comments is that, regardless of your philosophical outlook, we in the American State University have an ethical and intellectual responsibility to the cause of the free and open mind. This places upon us the necessity of contributing our part to the education of the teacher so that she or he comes out of this College with a quality mind that is scientifically and socially creative."

"Professor Jervis," asked Professor McKinney, "you will recall that on a previous occasion I asked you about the problem of indoctrination. Surely you have not changed your mind on this issue and now seek to indoctrinate the student to your way of thinking?"

"Not at all," replied Professor Jervis. "No one in this Department is going to tell you how to teach or what you shall teach in your classroom. Since the responsibility for the course has been assigned to me, I must select the basic texts. I repeat, how you will teach the course and what the interpretations are to be are within your prerogative."

Since the course would be required of all students in the College, both Professors Buckley and McKinney would be teaching at least two sessions, along with the aid of a number of teaching assistants. This was sure to lead to a watering down in the quality of the product, but there was little that Ron Jervis could do about it. He knew that Professor Buckley would continue to go his own way and teach little more than fact; and that, while Professor McKinney would do his best to try to live up his responsibilities, he had a weak background in philosophical studies. At the close of the session, Ron made it clear that he would be meeting with the Chairmen of the other Departments for a period of several weeks on the thinking about the content of the course. The results of such thinking he would relate to each of them in due time.

It was toward the end of the acdemic year before Ron Jervis had another chance to talk to Bill Dean about how a number of corporations had violated their ethical responsibilities to the people for monetary gain. The opportunity to renew this discussion came when Professor Dean and his wife invited Ron and Helen over for a dinner and a get-acquainted evening. At the same time Helen was elated with the opportunity of visiting with Bill Dean's wife.

"Ron," said Helen, "I know that you have been looking forward for some time to continuing your discussion with Professor Dean. Little did I realize that when the opportunity came, I would become more involved with the university faculty women. What kind of an individual is this Mrs. Dean?"

"Frankly, Helen," replied her husband, "I do not know Professor Dean's wife any better than you. I do get the impression, from the grapevine, that she is a very pleasant lady and a free-thinking individual. I would surmise that you and she would get along beautifully."

When Ron and his wife arrived at the Dean household, it

was Dean's wife, Elizabeth, who met them at the door. Helen knew immediately, after being introduced, that she had found a new friend. During the period before dinner was served, all of the talk was of a gossipy nature relating to both friends and associates, the University administration, public school policy, and world affairs. It was not until after dinner, when the ladies had turned to cleaning up the dishes, that the men adjourned to Professor Dean's study. At this time, Ron turned to Bill Dean to continue the discussion on the corporate way of exploiting the interests of the people.

"You know, Ron," said Professor Dean, "I find myself in a very difficult situation. I know that you have much more to offer as a professor in this Institution than I do, and especially to the students that come under your influence. I know from the university records that your salary is only half that of mine and of the other professors in the field of the physical sciences. Why? Because one half of our salaries come from corporations that we personally serve. We are not here to teach students as much as we are here to do research in which these corporations have an expressed interest. You could say, because of this fact, that we have been bought at a price, and to a certain extent that is true. In a primary way, we are serving the corporations rather than the welfare of the people. If you think that what is good for the corporations is good for the Nation, you do not have a problem."

"That does not turn out to be true in a number of instances," said Ron. "You know, Bill, of cases where corporations have polluted the air and the land by surface coal mining, such pollution taking on the form of gases, bad odors, and dust storms. Our forest lands have been gutted of their timber, and made subject to flooding and soil waste. You must be aware of the fact that the world will face an ecological disaster of carbon dioxide that is being pumped into the atmosphere."

"Yes," said Bill Dean, "there is the possibility that in a period of not more than forty years the earth may get what is called the *Green House Effect*, a heating of the earth's atmosphere; and, with a melting of the polar caps, this will raise the level of the oceans. The end result, in such a development, would be an inundating of all the coastal cities of all the continents. Cutting and clearing the major forests of the world would be a major factor because trees remove carbon dioxide from the air."

"You know, Bill," said Ron, "it is unbelievable that we have learned so little from human history about how man has turned once great forest lands into desert areas. There is the biblical story of A LAND OF MILK AND HONEY that is today a barren wasteland. On the African Continent, at this very time, the same thing is going on among primitive tribes. With all of our technological knowledge, we fail to see what we are doing is the speeding up of the process of natural destruction. Why do we do it? The answer to this question is bound up in our gluttonous desire and in our ignorance of natural law. Our environmentalists tell us to take a harder look at what we are doing to mother earth. But the corporations reply that to clean the air and protect the land will drive them into bankruptcy. So the public, aided by the politicians, conforms to their wishes."

"You are quite right, Ron," said Professor Dean, "in your analysis of the way in which we have ignored the effects of the pollution of mother earth. What all of this demonstrates is that the human race does not see beyond the present moment. This same stupidity is exemplified in the way in which the heads of corporations have inflated their income far beyond any cultural need or justification. There is ample justification for the assumption that, in terms of the human good of a free society, the existence of a millionaire class in our society is an economic and cultural evil. Why should our corporate heads be allowed to pay themselves not only a salary in excess of that of the president of the United States, but, in addition, line up large pensions for retirement, receive bonus grants in profitable corporate years, be granted stock options at will, and, when retiring, be granted outlandish severance pay? It may be that such should be looked upon as acts of criminality rather than of justice. The tragedy of all this flaunting of wealth is that it has infected both the labor leaders and the politicians. It would appear that the end result is the abrogation of the GENERAL WELFARE."

"Bill," asked Ron, "what do you know about these charges

of lavish parties being thrown by the corporation heads at the expense of the public, at conventions, in the national and state capitols, and at super football and baseball games? If the charges are true, should not such activities be classified as gross corruption and manipulation of the power structure?"

"Ron," said Bill, "you would be amazed if you only knew just how much money is being spent by the corporations to control the votes of our state and national legislators and to sell a particular product. Bribery is the true interpretation of such acts, bribery in terms of money, liquor, a bed partner, or just anything that you might ask for such as air travel and ball games. Yet, since all of this expenditure can be deducted from the corporate income tax, the cost falls back on the public who pays the bill.

"One thing that you may not have noticed is how corporate industry has been able to control the voice of television by the kind of programs that are offered. What is most tragic about this activity is that the public is so ignorant of the nature of the operation as to think that they are getting something for nothing. The money that the corporations spend on televison programs is, once again, deducted from the corporate income tax. All of this would not be too bad if the programs were not so meaningless and exploitative, in other words cheap entertainment. Since the dominating purpose of television entertainment is to sell the product that is being advertised, there is the constant use of the young girl sex figure to hold the attention of the viewer. If there were ever such a thing as a BETRAYAL ON MOUNT PARNASSUS, this is it. Why can't our state universities turn out men and women who are intellectually and ethically so committed as to lead a crusade against these corrupt corporate practices?"

"One of the things that disturb me, Bill," said Ron Jervis, "is the seeming warfare between business and government. Do you think that there is a deliberate organized purpose on the part of the leaders in business to make sure that the people's representatives do not use the government for control over business affairs?"

"Yes, Ron, definitely so," said Bill. "I have attended any

number of these business affairs which were nothing more than propaganda sessions against government interference with business interests. The purpose of such meetings was to encourage our students to take a critical attitude toward government and organized labor."

"Bill," asked Ron, "what about the attempt of business to control the trustees of our state universities and the local school boards?"

"Ron," said Bill, "I do not know very much about the local school boards, but I do know something about the way in which business, and especially corporate business, attempts to influence the policies of the boards of trustees of our state universities. Take for example the state university with which we are identified. Every member of our board is in one way or another a corporate man. Rather than being CONCERNED ABOUT THE GENERAL WELFARE OF THIS NATION (we rank third among the states in technology and forty-nine in human welfare), these men are more concerned about corporate wealth, the profits of their corporations, and how much money they can gather for themselves. Their particular interests are in the realms of gas, oil, minerals and transportation. Here we have the reason why we have so many scholarships in the Physical Sciences. Also, adequate money is always available to bring to our campus any professor who is needed to promote their research interests."

"There is one aspect of this situation," said Ron Jervis, "that you have not said anything about which, in my judgment, is extremely important. That aspect, Bill, is the ability of these corporations to hire the best lawyers in the Nation to serve their purpose. I call your attention to the fact that there is a significant difference between the incomes of these corporate lawyers and those who are our next door neighbors. On the other hand, in so far as ethics and intellectual responsiblity are concerned, I see no difference between any of these lawyers. The motive of each is to win at any cost."

"Ron," said Bill Dean, "it would appear from what we have been saying that we are blaming the corporations for all of our failures. From my standpoint, that is not so. Actually, our entire culture pattern is much more complicated than we realize. Every thing that we do, whether for the GENERAL WELFARE or for profit, has to go back to the quality of the minds of our people. It was this realization on the part of Adam Smith, as a moral philosopher, that led him to the concept of a free-enterprise economy. What we have done to his free-enterprise idea is one of the great tragedies in the history of man. We have destroyed the original concept of economic freedom, based on an ethical committment to the welfare of man, and substituted the concept of monetary wealth and power, regardless of how we get them. Since this is the case, what do you think is the future of the free-enterprise system?"

"Bill," said Ron Jervis, "I would say that the future of the capitalistic system is not very bright. Capitalism, or the free-enterprise system as we now know it, will not survive this century. Strong anti-capitalistic sentiment is being expressed by our college students, and even by our economics professors. There is a growing labor monopoly across the country, as well as welfarism, inflation, and a growing crime wave in all of our large cities. If the great majority of the corporate heads would take the leadership in assuming direct responsibility for the GENERAL WELFARE, we would have more hope for the future.

"Looking abroad at the international picture, the world situation is no better than ours. Even though our sense of economic well-being continues to decline, I get the impression that nowhere in the outside world is there a better place in which to live than the U.S.A. Nowhere, around the world do I see any respect for international law and human decency. Violence and terrorism are increasingly rampant. Hunger stalks the land across the Continent of Africa. I must admit, however, that in our visit to the U.S.S.R., I was made aware of the fact that conditions in that Nation had improved considerably over what they were during the years of the Czars, both in literacy and in economic and social welfare. If mankind is to continue on the road of human progress, the world must have more creative minds directed toward a society of free men and women.

"What we need is more of the freedom of mind which brought forth the eighteenth century Age of Enlightenment. As we have moved away from (1) the era of slave labor, in which man struggled against the forces of nature to bring about (2) our age of technology and mechanical law, man has been reduced to a cog in a machine, an inaninate thing. If we are to have a new era, a truly humane civilization, dramatic changes of necessity must take place in our culture of violence. Benjamin Franklin expressed the human dilemma well when he said of the original Federal Constitution, "We have labored well, but what the future holds out for our people only time will tell.

"Ron," said Bill Dean, "in winding up our discussion for the evening, I would hope that, in some way or other, we could get most of our state university faculties to grasp the significance of their role in the culture of this Nation, and come to the realization that the subject matter which they teach pales into insignificance when lined up against their ethical and intellectual responsibilities. Quality of mind and an ethical sense of humanity are the fundamental ingredients of the future, not only of Western civilization, but of mankind in general."

"Well said, Bill," replied Ron Jervis. "Now that we are well past the hour of eleven, I must get hold of my wife and head for home, or you and your good wife will never have us over again."

As Ron Jervis and his wife headed home, each agreed that they had found two friends with whom they could converse in an open and understanding way. Ron could only wish that there were more minds of the quality of Bill Snyder and Bill Dean. Such a faculty would go a long way in living up to the dreams of those who founded the American State University, the bringing into being of a true scientific citizenship in the U.S.A. He knew that Jefferson's belief in the freedom of religion meant FREEDOM OF MIND, and that such lay at the heart of his philosophy.

CHAPTER V

THE POLITICS OF POWER IN A FREE SOCIETY

The politics of power runs like a threat throughout all of human life activities. Power in itself has never been a common good. Throughout the entire history of the human race, power has been used both for the common good and for the destruction of man. This has been true to such an extent that there is an old Chinese Proverb which holds that "power destroys, absolute power destroys absolutely." It is the politics of power with which we are concerned, power in the culture process. Power used negatively can be identified with either ignorance or a lack of ethical concern for the common good. The more Ron Jervis delved into the role of the state university, the more he became concerned about the role of power in the history of mankind. This was the subject of his discussion with his wife and daughter at the dinner table on the evening following his appointment as Chairman of the Department of Cultural Foundations of Education.

"You know, Helen," said Ron, "now that I have been appointed Chairman of my Department, I have become more conscious of the role of power than I had ever been during all these many years of teaching. There is one conclusion about this discussion that we have been having, and that conclusion is, power is organic in human life, and therefore in nature."

"Dad," said Betty Jane, "does the fact that power is organic in human life give you and Mom the right to exercise control over me?"

"Not necessarily, Betty Jane," replied her father, "but there are those, now and in the past, that have so believed and operated. The German Philosopher Hegel expressed it this way, 'Power defines the nature of truth, goodness, and beauty.' Note how this definition makes intellectual responsibility and ethical commitment secondary to the role of power. In terms of human history, there is much truth in what Hegel has said, for the great majority of mankind has always been subjected to the tyranny of the power role. What this means is that throughout human history, certain individuals have forced others to succumb to their will."

"Ron," said Helen, "how has this belief in the role of power been modified especially as it pertains to the rights of parents?"

"A very good question, Helen," replied Ron. "In my judgment the role of power has been modified as man became more civilized through the evolution of human thought. It is important to remember, however, that mentally speaking, the majority of the people of the world today still live in a primitive state. For example, those who have thought about the role of power continue to realize that power has been used both negatively and positively in human affairs. This is true whether or not we are talking about philosophy or science. It is possible to rationalize so as to justify the killing of a relative or a neighbor. Also, modern warfare has turned scientific knowledge into an instrument of death. The absence of power can be self-defeating, and even lead to the destruction of the self. In a very literal sense, when power fails, the lights go out. This is what happens when an individual dies."

"Then Dad," said Betty Jane, "what choice do we have as an alternate to the role of power?"

"Betty Jane," said her father, "since power is organic in the life of the human race, it should be used only with an intellectual sense of responsibility and with an ethical commitment to the common good. To so act calls for a high level of social intelligence, something which most of us do not possess. This conclusion tells us that we need more knowledge of the history of man if we are to acquire an understanding of the critical issues that create havoc in human relations."

"Then what you are saying, Dad," said Betty Jane, "is that you have the right to exercise power over me, but only to the extent that such use of power is directed by an ethical commitment to my welfare, and an intellectual responsibility for my growth and general development."

"You state the matter quite well, Betty Jane," replied her father. "It is because of the immature nature of the child that there is need for the family as a social institution."

"But, Ron," asked Helen, "where does the concept of ethical commitment and intellectual responsibility come into the picture?"

"That is where you find a major difference of opinion among those who have written and thought about the welfare of the human race. As I said before," replied Ron, "Hegel seems to be saying that goodness and intelligence are inherent in the role of power. Christians and other religious groups seem to be saying that they come from a divine source. I am of the opinion that they are products of the evolution of the human mind. For example, the power role seems to have had no contrary force until the birth of such religious thought as that of the SAYINGS OF CONFUCIUS, the RIG VEDA, and the OLD AND THE NEW TESTAMENTS. Historically speaking, orthodox religious groups have operated more on the basis of faith and the role of power than on social intelligence. Each religious group has assumed that it has a monopoly on God, and has been willing to use any necessary power to attain its ends."

At this point Helen spoke up. "I can see, Ron, from what you are saying why you are so critical of all orthodox religions. I can see that you recognize the significance of religion in the evolution of the human mind, but that you are convinced that such beliefs today are so tied up in the role of power that they lose contact with the needs of our day. You speak of this as a God complex which blinds the followers to what is true, scientifically speaking."

"Yes, Helen," replied Ron, "there is much emotional content in the dogmas of religion and little of social intelligence. Benjamin Franklin was so aware of this that he was forced to leave Massachusetts because of orthodox tyranny. Thomas Jefferson rewrote the NEW TESTAMENT, to bring it up to date, and Karl Marx saw religion as the opium of the people."

"I note that you use the words Social Intelligence, Ron," said Helen, "as one of the three components of a positive role in human relations. Do you make a distinction between intellectual activity and social intelligence?"

"Definitely so, Helen," said Ron. "Intellect can be applied to a method of action as well as to social relations. When so applied, it can be little more than word reasoning, the kind of thinking the scholastics did during the Middle Ages. The term intellect has been used to apply to the physical sciences and to the biological differences between individuals. So when talking about the use of intelligence in the social order, and to an ethical commitment to the common good, we are talking about the politics of power. I have specific reference here to the use of power as a means of deception. We speak of politicians as those who shed crocodile tears because they talk out of both sides of their mouths. Power politics is used in every aspect of human relations, and with negative effect, when there is an absence of ethical commitment and when the individual is interested only in personal aggrandisement".

"Ron," said Helen, "where does the role of law fit into this picture?"

"Helen," said Ron, "the problem of law and order is at the

very heart of the power role in that laws grant power to the legal authority that assumes power over man. Laws can be and are just or unjust in accordance with the meaning and value frame of reference on which they are supposed to be based. Their enforcement depends on the intelligence and commitment of those who exercise the power role. Former President Hoover stated the issue very well when he said, 'Ours is a government of laws and not of men.' There is a problem here, however, for if those who pass the laws do not have a sense of the GENERAL WELFARE in mind, and operate exclusively in the role of vested interests, then gross injustice is a result of the abuse of power in a free society. Every case involving a controversy between the citizen and his government that is appealed to the Supreme Court of the United States is rooted in the question of justice under the law."

"Ron Jervis," said Helen, "what disturbs me most, in the light of what you have said, is how we as teachers, who are supposed to be enlightened, are so abysmally ignorant of the fundamentals on which our well-being is determined."

"Dad," said Betty Jane, "to what extent have you found such practices in your university experience?"

"Unfortunately, Betty Jane," said her father, "there is more of the practice of the politics of power among the faculty, as well as the administration, than we like to admit. To be open-minded about it, the politics of power is found in all aspects of our culture where the relation of one human being to another is involved. As I have previously said, power is organic and is modified only as we exercise the role of intelligence in relation to our ethical comitment. From what I know about life in a state university, I would say that there is more ethical commitment and intellectual responsibility in a state university than you can find in any other area of government. You might be interested in knowing that I have arranged for a luncheon appointment tomorrow with Professor David Lucas of the Department of Political Sciences to get his thinking on the subject."

"Well, Dad," said Betty Jane, "all of this is too much for me, and now that I have finished eating, I will go to my room. I have much studying to do, as well as to call a girl friend to see what she is doing."

After Betty Jane had left the room, Helen picked up the discussion by inquiring as to what Ron knew about Professor Lucas. "I have heard you speak of Professor Lucas before, but what do you expect to get from him?"

"I do not know Professor Lucas very well," said Ron. "I do know students who speak very highly of him, especially the graduate students. He is a relatively young man who has risen very fast in his profession, and who is best known for his book on THE ROLE OF POWER IN WESTERN CULTURE. It is basically because of what he says in his analysis of the role of power that I have arranged to have this meeting with him. I am particularly interested in what he has to say about our relation to the U.S.S.R."

"It will be of real interest to me to learn about what he has to say about the Cold War," said Helen. "The involvement of the C.I.A. in this issue disturbs me very much. Now that I am going to find out more about this issue after you have had your meeting, I will get busy with my cleaning up of the dinner dishes. I have quite a bit of school work to catch up on before I can get to bed."

Before going to bed that evening Ron Jervis listened to a broadcasting of Mozart's *Don Giovanni*. He had developed a fondness for operas ever since he had listened to a performance of the Berlin Symphonic Orchestra in Berlin, Germany while he was serving in the E.T.O. in 1945-1946. The power of Mozart's dramatic feeling, as he expressed himself in this great opera, was the kind of religious sense that meant much to him, and which he needed from time to time as he sought for a sense of oneness with the universe. Life, as he saw it in its deepest sense, was a mystery and probably always would be. The best that one could do was to continue the struggle for that understanding and creative sensitivity which is so necessary for the progress of mankind. Now Ron looked forward to tomorrow for his meeting with Professor Lucas. He knew in his mind that it would be a meaningful one.

At the proper hour, on the following day, Ron Jervis walked into the parlor of the Student Union Building that adjoined the lunchroom and, while seeking out Professor Lucas, met up with his friend Bill Snyder.

"Hello, Bill," said Ron. "It has been some time since our last meeting. What is new in your world of activity?"

"Not much, Ron," replied Bill Snyder, "except that I find myself more and more critical of the way in which the Board of Regents is trying to dictate the kind of textbooks and reading material that we use in our classrooms. Just yesterday, at a meeting of Our Department, the Chairman informed us that serious objection was being raised by the Board about our use of Shakespeare's MERCHANT OF VENICE, on the grounds that it expressed a prejudice against the Jewish people. What is important to me is that such criticism indicates that there is a conflict between my conception of the role of a state university and that of the Board."

"That is the point that I have been making all along, Bill," sand Ron. "Since the members of the Board assume that all power rests in the Board, the members have the power to control what goes on in the classroom. Here we have both an anti-intellectual and an anti-ethical attitude. The politics of power being expressed by the Board is self-defeating, in that the function of the state university is to educate for a free society. Likewise, under such power of control, it is impossible for a professor to provide the quality of teaching demanded of him."

"I agree with what you say, Ron," replied Bill Snyder, "but what you have said implies that much more time needs to be devoted to the problem of communication, not only between the various departmental chairmen but between faculty representatives and members of the Board of Regents. Surely, the members of the Board must recognize that, on matters such as the use of texts in our courses, there can be no compromise on the principle of FREEDOM TO LEARN AND FREEDOM TO TEACH. Such is mandatory if we are to continue to live in the hope of attaining our goal of a free society."

At this point in the discussion, Professor Lucas walked into the room. Seeing Bill Snyder and Ron Jervis on the right side of the room, he walked over to introduce himself to Ron. After shaking hands with Ron, he turned to Bill Snyder with a pleasing comment.

"I see, Bill," said Professor Lucas, "that you and Professor Jervis are well acquainted with each other. Since such is the case, why don't you join us at lunch? I am sure that Professor Jervis will not object."

"Not at all," replied Ron Jervis. "In fact I am very hopeful that Bill will join us. He can contribute much to our discussion. What do you say, Bill?"

"I am more than pleased with your invitation," said Bill Snyder. "I have some idea that what you two fellows will be talking about has to do with the Politics of Power. Since David is a political scientist and has written on the subject, I welcome what he has to say, especially as to the relation of the power role to our political environment."

Following these words the three men walked into the lunch room, and after serving themselves cafeteria-style, found a table in a section of the room where they would not be bothered. It was not until they had finished their meal that Ron Jervis proceeded with an initiation of the discussion.

"Before we get into a discussion of the subject of Power Politics," said Ron, "I would like to hear from each of you as to when you think you became a free man mentally. Which one of you is to speak first."

"Speaking frankly, Ron Jervis," said Bill Snyder, "I think that you should initiate the discussion. You raised the issue. What do you say, David?"

"I agree, Bill," replied David Lucas. "I think that Ron should be the first to speak."

"I accept the challenge, fellows, so here goes," replied Ron Jervis. "When I was eleven years of age, I was baptized as a member of a Southern Baptist Church. That was my age of innocence. By the time I was thirteen years of age, I was in a state of rebellion. Why? Although I knew that age had something to do with it, there was more. I had seen my high school boy friend forced to leave school and go to work, to help take care of his younger brothers and sisters (there were seven of them) because of the death of his father. As for myself, I had been forced to go to work at the age of thirteen, if I were to continue my schooling. My job was in a Greek restaurant where, after school hours, I worked as a waiter from one o'clock in the afternoon until ten p.m. at night. The fact that I had to take care of my mother at such an early age, and work such abominable hours, in order to go to school added to my sense of rebellion. Thus, I became mad at the world for its being so unjust to my high school chum and myself. I, who had been an avid reader from the age of four, was more and more coming to the conclusion that what the preacher said about life made very little sense. His raving and railing about sin and God's love just didn't stand up. Also, what I had been told about every boy and girl having an equal chance in life was so much hogwash. The idea of every child having an equal opportunity to grow and prosper was not true. Therefore, during my last years in high school, I was inclined to become a revolutionist. It was this tendency that led me to idealize our Revolutionary Fathers, men such as Benjamin Franklin, Thomas Jefferson and Thomas Paine.

"What was it that made me become so negative toward the cultural pattern in which my life was unfolding, the pattern into which I was born, and in which I had grown up? I did not know it at the time, but it was what I now choose to call the POLITICS OF POWER, a power that I could not put my finger on, but it was there, and bigger than anything that I could comprehend. While I came to fear this power, and still do at times, I knew that I had to overcome its influence if I were to survive in this world. The big question was how. *I would submit my body, but not my mind to the status quo.* It was through the response of mind that I would overcome the forces that bore down upon me. It was thus that by gaining more insight into the world around me, and by learning to profit from every experience, that I was able to survive and to be where I am today."

"Can you give us some examples, Ron," said David Lucas, "that threatened your chance to grow up mentally and to become a free-thinking man?"

"Gladly, David," replied Ron Jervis. "That will be easy,

since most of such are related to my sense of economic insecurity. Since my rebellion was total, in terms of the principle of freedom of mind, I first sought freedom from the control of the Church. Through my study of the History of Western Culture, it became evident to me that what the preacher said was nothing more than legendary Jewish history. This, tied in with my study of biology, and especially with the life and work of Charles Darwin, brought about a change in my concept of the nature of man. Finally, it was a Professor of English who, during my junior year in college, put me in touch with Francis Bacon's NOVUM ORGANUM, a clear and convincing proof of the significance of the scientific method, not only in the physical sciences but likewise in the study of human relations.

"Even before entering the university as a freshman, I was confronted on two occasions with a threat to my being able to continue my high school education. First, the Superintendent of School attempted to interfere with my working and going to school at the same time. He did so by telling my high school principal that I could not do both, that I had to make a choice of one or the other. Fortunately, my high school principal, at the risk of his job, told the Superintendent that he should keep his hands off in running the high school, for that was his prerogative. This time the politics of power failed to dominate.

"The possibility of my continuing my high school studies was threatened even more by the possible loss of my job. This had come about as a result of the fact that the lovable Greek who had given me the job in the first place had sold a part of his ownership in the restaurant. The man who became his partner had a very dictatorial mind, a form of the politics of power at its best. To make a long story short, I knew that I could not continue working with him, but before quitting I found another job in a restaurant just two blocks from where I had been working."

"Ron," said Bill Snyder, "that is a fantastic story. I know that it must be true by the way you tell it. You must know, however, that there are very few young men in this university who, at your age, would have the guts to face up to the reality of life as you did. Frankly, I know that I would not have done so. My mental reconstruction did not come until I was a graduate student, and only as a result of the influence of a great and lovable man who was my adviser."

"The same holds true for me," said David Lucas, "but I still cannot put myself in the category of you fellows. Speaking quite frankly, I am a conservative when it comes to economic issues, a straight-laced free-enterprise man. I do have intellectual integrity and I look with utter contempt at those who choose to indulge in corrupt economic and political activities."

"Professor Lucas," replied Ron Jervis, "from what you have said, I would judge that you are a disciple of Adam Smith."

"Yes, Ron," said David Lucas, "and because of such I often find myself in conflict with the thinking of my associates. As you fellows well know, there has been a tendency for more than a century to define the role of the sciences in mechanistic and materialistic terms. This same tendency has been applied to the social studies such as economics, sociology, psychology, political science, medicine, and education. This tendency sets up a dualism between church dogma, which holds that man is a spiritual being, and the mechanist who sees man only as a cog in a machine. I reject this mechanistic concept of the nature of man, just as much as I reject the concept of the church dogmatists. It is my conviction that, to deal with the problem of man's relation to universal reality, we must operate on the assumption that there is a creative force in and through this universe of mechanical law."

"Your point of view, Professor Lucas," said Bill Snyder, "is well taken. It illustrates in a clear manner how we misuse and abuse the word ATHEISM. Do you not think that the most vicious use of the POLITICS OF POWER lies in the Holy War that we are engaged in with the Communist World, and especially with the Soviet Union?"

"There is no doubt in my mind," said Professor Jervis, "that such is the case. We have been engaged in this policy of containment of the U.S.S.R. ever since that Nation was established in 1917. Note how this policy has centered on the role of power. At no time has there been any discussion or analysis of the ethical and intellectual differences which divide the two nations. While there is much chatter about values, each Nation assumes a holy attitude toward the other. Bill, if you were speaking as a harsh critic, what weakness do you detect in the free-enterprise system?"

"I would say, Ron," replied Bill Snyder, "that while the Free-Enterprise Economy assumes that each individual has the same opportunity to be financially successful, it does not take into consideration the differences in wealth at the time of birth. We have no choice but to accept the natural genetic differences which exist at birth, both physically and intellectually. It is the differences in wealth at birth that are manmade and which contravene that which is natural."

"Can you be more specific, Bill," said Professor Lucas, "when you say that the free-enterprise system, as practiced, contravenes that which is natural and just?"

"Yes, David," replied Bill Snyder. "Research studies, without exception, establish the fact that unless a child has adequate food, shelter, and clothing, and a sense of love and security during the first six years of his or her life, he or she will not have the physical and mental growth to which every child is entitled."

"There is another weakness in the Free-Enterprise Economy," said Ron Jervis. "The weakness to which I refer is that those who support it confuse the concept of INDIVIDUALISM with that of INDIVIDUALITY. Since every individual grows up in a cultural environment, the laissez-faire individualistic concept contravenes that of natural law."

"If I did not know you two men," said David Lucas, "I would conclude that you were Communists. Can't you say something good about our free-enterprise economy, and our way of life? As you know, Adam Smith had much influence on the thinking that went into the making of the American Revolution."

"Yes, David," replied Ron Jervis, "from the standpoint of Adam Smith, there is much that is good in the theory of a free-enterprise economy. The very heart of human growth lies in the organic creative potential of the individual. Here Communist theory, with its mechanistic and materialistic concept of the nature of reality, is not only weak but dogmatic and unnatural. I commend the Communist for his grasp of the significance of social reality and his sense of the need of every child for adequate food, shelter, and clothing in the first six years of his or her life, but, in operating on a dogma of science, Communist thinking thwarts the creative thinking of the individual. It is because of such that politics of power dominate practices in the Soviet Union."

"David," said Bill Snyder, "where do you stand when it comes to comparing our political system with that of the U.S.S.R.? I have some reservations and firm convictions on this issue, and especially as it relates to our role as a state university."

"Professor Snyder," replied David Lucas, "I have thought long and hard about the way in which our political system operates. There is not much good that I say about the way in which we elect our representatives to public office. In my judgment, the whole operation is a colossal failure and can only do harm to the Nation. I speak as a political scientist who frankly admits that there is a significant gap between what I teach and what is practiced in public life."

At this point, Ron Jervis spoke up with much feeling. "Don't you see, David, that what you are saying points to a pattern of betrayal by those who are responsible for providing a quality education for leadership in the halls of our government? What we come down to in public life is nothing more than the POLITICS OF POWER, with no intellectual or ethical responsibility to the GENERAL WELFARE. What I would like to know is how could we have failed so miserably? I know from studies on the history of our Nation that men like Jefferson, Franklin and Paine committed themselves to a new way of life, but that they knew that this new way of life called for a new type of leadership in the affairs of government. To this end, they sought and promoted the establishment of the state university. Would you not say, David, that there has been a betrayal on the part of these who have assumed administrative responsibility for providing a quality leadership for our Nation?"

"What you are saying, Professor Jervis, rings true," replied Professor Lucas. "I had never thought of our problem in just that way. Like practically all state university professors, I have taught subject matter with the assumption that it would get across to the students for the common good. If not, then why was I teaching? I will admit that, unlike the profesesors in the University of Moscow, I teach my subject without a meaning and value frame of reference. This is what freedom to teach meant to me, not that to which the leaders of the American Revolution pledged their lives."

"Such being the case," said Bill Snyder, "what we have today is what we have been teaching, a virtual state of social anarchy. What we have been doing and saying comes down to a false concept of the DEMOCRATIC WAY OF LIFE, and of the FREE-ENTERPRISE ECONOMY. In the political sense, where in a specific way do you think that we have failed, Ron Jervis?"

"There is no simple answer to your question, Bill," said Ron. "There are some things which are clear to the researchers on this issue. It is very evident that there has been a failure of great magnitude in the field of education. Operating on the premise that democracy is defined by the will of the majority of the people, we have adopted an anti-intellectual and anti-ethical way of life. As a result, we have reduced our practice to the level of Hegel's concept of power, which in the final analysis is nothing more than NAZISM. Who should determine what is taught in the classroom, the parents or the professionally trained teachers? How much power should be invested in the local school board, the state legislature, in the Congress of the United States, in determining what the public school teacher should teach? Here the problem of vested interests stands out over and above the GENERAL WELFARE OF THE NATION. Because we place the public school teacher in the role of an animal trainer, it is not important that she be able to even define the word philosophy, much less operate in a meaning and value frame of reference."

"There is another problem that is related to this issue of defining the nature of the democratic process," said David Lucas, "and that is whether or not the profession of law has taken over the power that is vested in the people. Have the lawyers not defined power in such a way as to promote their particular interests? Since most of the men who took the lead in the American Revolution were lawyers, why has this power of the lawyer become a source of major concern?"

"The evidence seems to indicate," said Ron, "that lawyers of today no longer have the commitment, intellectually or ethically, to their country's welfare that was a marked characteristic of our forefathers. Our present-day lawyers are not as much interested in justice as they are in winning their cases. Thus, the power role becomes dominant ovr all their actions. Power and money go hand in hand, as each case begins and ends with the trial of the individual. Here, the end justifies the means, for there is no other purpose than that of victory over your adversary. Who is right and who is wrong? What is just and what is unjust? These matters are not important. What is impotant is that you win your case regardless of how you do it."

"It seems to me," said Bill Snyder, "that there is a relation between the lawyer who serves his client and the one who serves a vested interest when elected to public office. In each case there is the payoff, especially where corporate wealth and power are involved. Is it any wonder that so many people feel that voting is useless, that they no longer have any confidence in their elected representatives, and that there is so much corruption in high places of government? For the first time in our history a President of the United States would have been impeached had he not been pardoned by the man appointed to fill his place. When it comes to the matter of an innocent man, who has little or no wealth, being tried by a jury, what chance does he have when confronted by a ruthless prosecuting attorney?"

"I am aware of the corrupt political and social practices which are being brought to light involving the legal profession," said David Lucas, "having done much research in the area of legal practices in government. I do believe that we find ourselves in worse shape than you fellows have indicated. On the one hand, there are the outrageous practices of New York's high-price divorce lawyers, particularly those who engage in sex and scandal. Also, there are the corporate lawyers who engage in million-dollar law suits that wind up by destroying an honest business. Then there are the personal-injury lawyers who scandalize their profession by turning their client's injury into a deal involving hundreds of thousands of dollars. A good example of such would be those involving the medical profession. There are lawyers who make a living by suing other lawyers. Our situation is so bad that we have become an over-lawyered society, a society created by the legal profession."

"Under such conditions," said Bill Snyder, "how will we ever be able to free ourselves from this legal straitjacket?"

"Bill," said Ron Jervis, "before attempting to answer your question, there is one additional aspect of this condition that we need to consider that has to do with the educational process. Do we have the same conditions today as those which existed in the past, or, because of the POLITICS OF POWER, is our condition getting worse?"

"Ron," said Bill Snyder, "I can say to both you and David that the cultural condition of our times indicate a major trend toward the POLITICS OF POWER. This trend is indicated by our reliance upon military power in the field of international relations. During my lifetime we have fought two major world wars and two minor wars in Korea and Vietnam. For the first time in our history, we have moved toward Peace-Time Conscription. Our Revolutionary Fathers were opposed, and without reservation, to a reliance upon military power as a solution to our international problems. They, from their knowledge of history, saw how Roman civilization with all of its military might, failed to deal with its problems at home and thus drifted into economic and social chaos. Military power, by its very nature, represents an undulterated example of the politics of power, a total reliance on power by those occupying the seats of government. Note how this happened to modern Germany during the rule of Adolf Hitler. Up to the present we have been free from a total commitment to military power, but will such be true for the rest of this century? I cannot answer yes or no to this question, but I know that the trend of our times is toward the use of force in dealing with human relations. No one was more aware of this problem than was President Eisenhower when he warned us of the MILITARY-INDUSTRIAL COMPLEX. The power of this complex is growing in the Congress of the United States. Note how military officers are being placed in a special privileged luxury class, the same pattern as followed by traditional Western cultures such as Old Rome. Don't forget the power that we have given the C.I.A., a power contrary to those elements of a civilized society. There is no doubt that we are being placed in a mechanistic straitjacket from which there will be little possibility of a recovery."

"Ron," said David Lucas, "I assume that you agree with Bill on what he has just said about our increasing reliance on military power and the corrupting influence of the C.I.A. What I would like to know is, assuming that he is correct, whether or not there is something that we can do to correct this situation."

"The only way I can see, David, out of this legalistic and mechanistic straitjacket," said Ron, "is through a reform in our state university educational efforts. In the first place, this is necessary if we are to have a major change in the product of the public school. Also, this reform is necessary if we are to get an improvement in the quality of leadership in all of our professions, especially in law and in teaching."

"Yes, Ron," said Bill Snyder, "I agree with what you have just said to David about getting out of our mechanistic straitjacket. But where do we start?"

"I would start, Bill," replied Ron, "in the teaching of the Humanities. It is here that I would seek that sense of cultural unity and purpose which we have lost since the first World War. In so doing, I would hope that the professors in your area would think in terms of what a study of our great literary tradition can contribute to a sense of unity and purpose in a free society. In questioning my students at the senior level of instruction, I find an appalling ignorance of the ideas expressed by great Western thinkers such as Socrates, Plato, Aristotle, Herodotus, Saint Augustine, Cicero, Erasmus, Goethe, Voltaire, Francis Bacon, John Stuart Mill, Edmund Burke, Montesquieu, Samuel Johnson, Locke, Rousseau, Emerson, Walt Whitman, Dickens, Ruskin, Jonathan Edwards, and yes, even Franklin, Jefferson, and Paine. There was a time in our elementary schools, when students studied the McGuffey Readers and, while these individuals still extol the virtues of these readers, what is forgotten is that McGuffey was a moral philosopher with a cultural sense of the need for unity and purpose among our people. Today, we have shifted our emphasis to the significance of mechanical things, an interest more in mechanical things than in human values. In doing so, we openly attack our most outstanding educational philosopher, John Dewey. He is accused of advocating that a child be allowed to do his own thing, even at the expense of the common good, when in fact Dewey says, in his numerous publications, that the only kind of discipline which serves a free society is self-discipline, a quality in which we are greatly deficient."

"I would say," replied David Lucas, "that while we have done a good job of analyzing some of our basic ills, I am not as pessimistic as you fellows. Our democracy and our free-enterprise system will triumph over the Communist world, for we have the best way of life that man has ever devised. Before I leave, however, let me say that this discussion has been most enlightening, and I shall not soon forget it."

After David Lucas had departed, Ron Jervis and Bill Snyder had a brief discussion on what had just transpired. Of one thing they were sure. David Lucas was a man of high intellectual integrity. They could only wish that there were more university professors like him. Before parting they agreed that, at some time in near future, they would have another session with Professor Lucas, and that this time it would involve what each man had experienced within the university administration. At that time they would discuss the POLITICS OF POWER in a more personal manner.

Before calling the next meeting of the members of his

Department, Ron thought it necessary that he talk to Ricardo Martinez on some of the issues that were sure to come up. He thought he knew where Ricardo stood on most of them, but, in good Aristotelian manner, the power role should be exercised in terms of the art of compromise. He knew that, in view of the way in which Professor Buckley would respond, he needed the support of the former Chairman. To promote a sense of unity within the Department, he would have a social get-together. It was on this point that he addressed his friend Ricardo on the morning following his meeting with Bill Snyder and David Lucas. Meeting in Ricardo's office, Ron was the first to speak.

"Ricardo," said Ron, "now that I have taken over the responsibility of Chairman of our Department, I am going to need your help. There is no one else to whom I can turn if I am going to get the kind of support that I will need on some of the basic issues."

"Ron", said Ricardo, "you know that I am ready to back you at all times when I think you are right. Knowing me as you do, you know that I will oppose you when I think you are wrong."

"That is the reason why I am here, Ricardo," replied Ron Jervis. "It is fundamentally necessary that we work together if we are to achieve our goals. There are two things that I want to talk to you about. First, I want to call a meeting of the members of our Department this coming Friday afternoon; and second, I want a social get-together shortly thereafter to boost good will among us. On the matter of our departmental meeting, since Professor McKinney is going to take a leave of absence for the coming year, we will be needing a replacement. What do you propose?"

"Ron," said Ricardo, "I would suggest that we seek the help of some advanced graduate student, one who has completed all of his graduate work for the Ph.D. Degree except the writing of his dissertation. You, with your work in the National Philosophy of Education Society, must be acquainted with a number of professors who would have some available applicants. Why not write to them?"

"Very good, Ricardo," replied Ron, "I shall act on your suggestion. Now, on an issue of greater significance, it is my understanding that Professor Rigsby, a good friend of yours, is going to introduce a proposal at the next meeting of our departmental chairmen that the requirement for all graduate students in the College doctoral program to take a philosophy of education course be abolished. You will recall the difficulty we have had in getting Professor Buckley to go along with us in promoting a unified philosophy of education for our elementary education students. Now I expect him to go along with Rigsby in abolishing the Philosophy of Education requirement."

"You know, Ron," replied Ricardo, "I find it difficult to understand Buckley, always preaching national unity and waving the flag but never willing to cooperate with those of his Department on any policy matter. Actually, when it comes to a unified educational policy, he always undercuts both of us. As to my friend Rigsby, I am at a loss to understand his thinking, unless it is to get more students for himself."

"Well, Ricardo," said Ron, "it puzzles me, for I thought that he was the kind of professor, more than any other member in his Department, who would give us solid support. Yet I have noticed from time to time, at the faculty meetings, that he tends to express the narcissistic, individualistic cult of our times. How he can relate his thinking to the philosophy of John Dewey is beyond me. Rigsby should know that he is playing into the hands of those psychologists who play the POLITICS OF POWER."

"I agree with what you say about Rigsby's thinking," said Ricardo, "for it seems that everywhere I turn we are fighting a losing battle. Even if they do abolish the philosophy of education requirement, we will have students who want to take a course with us."

"That is probably true, Ricardo," said Ron, "but what is going to happen is that the educational psychology professors will load the doctoral programs of their students with so many educational psychology courses that little room will be left for anything else. There is one other matter which I should call to your attention. You are aware of the fact that the Dean has aspirations to become President of this University. What do you think?"

"Ron," replied Ricardo, "all this goes to prove what I have said many times about Dean Hazwell. He is power-drunk. That is why he has kept my salary down all of these years. He is afraid of my influence with the Mexican-Americans in this state. He thinks that my influence with them will interfere with his ambition to become President. You should know, Ron, that I checked on his background enough to know that he faked his doctoral dissertation. I know that he has been kind to you, and that he respects you, which is all to the good. That does not change things, however, in so far as I am concerned."

"Ricardo, you know," said Ron, "that I am opposed to what the Dean has done in keeping your salary down. Also, it is quite obvious that while he seems to give strong support to our Department, that support is more verbal than real. When the chips are down he allies himself with the power forces in this College. My prediction is that he will never make the Presidency of this University. He has too many enemies in the College of Arts and Sciences. He will be sidetracked into some job, such as a Vice-Presidency. This will be the end of it so far as I am concerned. As for myself, I propose to continue my efforts in the direction of making our Department a more dynamic instrument for the cause of public education."

Before moving on to his office, Ron spoke to Ricardo about the possibility of a departmental social get-together, to which Ricardo readily agreed. Also, Ron could not refrain from expressing the hope that his friend was enjoying life with his new girlfriend.

"Ron," said Ricardo, "you will never know what a relief it was to me to get rid of that wicked woman. She so dominated my life that I never had any peace of mind when I was at home. I now have my divorce, and Ida Hernandez and I will be married in a quiet wedding ceremony next Wednesday. Since your departmental social is not to take place until the following Friday, we will be greeting you as man and wife."

When the departmental meeting took place everything

turned out just as Ron had expected. Professor Buckley was so upset over Ron's being appointed Chairman that he could not resist commenting on the fact that he should have been chosen in Ron's place.

"Profesor Martinez," said Profesor Buckley, "will you explain to me why I, who have been a member of this Department two years longer than Professor Jervis, was not chosen Chairman?"

"Professor Buckley," replied Professor Martinez, "to be quite frank with you, Dean Hazwell was of the opinion that Professor Jervis would be the best man for the job, and I did not choose to disagree with him. If you wish to pursue the matter further, I would suggest that you take it up with the Dean."

"Professor Buckley," said Professor Jervis, "since I have no further comment to make on the issue of my appointment, let us proceed to the two matters which we need to consider. First, as you know, Professor McKinney will be on leave of absence during the coming year. We must find someone to fill his place. Professor Martinez, what do you have to suggest?"

"Professor Jervis," replied Profesor Martinez, "I would suggest that you contact some comparable state university departmental chairman and locate a graduate student who has completed all of his or her graduate work except for the dissertation."

"Gentlemen," said Profesor Jervis, "unless someone has a better idea than Profesor Martinez, we shall move ahead on the issue."

"I think that the idea of Professor Martinez is a good one," said Professor McKiney, "and I so move that we authorize the Chairman to proceed on the basis of the suggestion."

"I don't know that the suggestion is wise," commented Professor Buckley. "It will lower our standing with the other departments in the College. Why not let me see if I can get one of my professor friends to fill in for the year?"

"You forget, Professor Buckely," said Professor Jervis, "that the money available for the position is hardly enough to employ a man at the instructor level, much less that of a full professor."

"I second the motion of Professor McKinney," said Professor Martinez, "and move that the Chairman proceed as directed in securing a replacement for Professor McKinney for the coming year."

The motion carried with the usual one dissenting vote of Professor Buckley. The negative attitude being expressed by the Professor was even more apparent when the issue concerning the requirement on the Philosophy of Education course came up.

"Gentlemen," said Ron Jervis, "it has come to my attention that Professor John Rigsby of the Curriculum and Instruction Department is going to introduce, at the next meeting of the Chairmen of the College, a motion to the effect that all required courses be deleted from the Masters and Doctoral Programs in this College. This action I deplore for two reasons: (1) It will weaken our position in the graduate programs of the College, and (2) it will tend to weaken the sense of unity and purpose in our program for the public school teacher."

"Professor Jervis," said Professor Buckley, "I beg to disagree with you on both counts. If graduate students are free to take any course in our Department, they will take more courses not less. As to the matter of leadership, I cannot see that taking a course in the Philosophy of Education is any more important than a course in Statistics."

"Professor Buckley," replied Ron Jervis, "your position on the matter of course requirements in this Department amazes me, especially when you compare a Philosophy of Education requirement with Statistics. You, who preach so ardently for a liberal education, have committed yourself to a concept of education that is not only narcissistic but destructive of the common good. The greatest tragedy which our country is suffering from today is from an overdose of individualism. This narcissistic tendency carries with it no intellectual responsibility, and no ethical concern for the General Welfare."

Nothing more was said on the issue relating to the requirement of the Philosophy of Education course, and no action was taken because none was required. What had transpired at the meeting, however, indicated a source of future conflict within the Department, a source of vital concern both to the Department and to the College. That conflict, which was building up, came sooner than Ron Jervis had expected.

After contacting a number of professors in several leading state universities, Ron Jervis was able to secure the names of two young men who were interested in filling out for Dr. McKinney during the coming year. When these two young men were brought to the campus and interviewed, it was evident that neither was qualified to teach the courses assigned to Dr. McKinney. Because one of the applicants was a dark-skinned Hindu, Dr. Buckley held that he should be disqualified because he looked like a Negro. When it was finally determined between Ron and the Dean that neither of the young men should be offered the position, Professor Martinez exploded.

"Professor Jervis," Martinez said in a very angry voice, "I am amazed that you would bow to the pressure of Dean Hazwell and turn down the young Hindu because of the pressure of that bastard Buckley. Apparently you can't stand the heat of the kitchen either, as President Truman once said."

"Damn it, Ricardo," replied Ron, "there is not a word of truth in what you are saying. As a matter of fact, the Dean thought that it would be a good idea to employ the young man because he was dark, until I pointed out that he was not qualified to teach the courses required of him."

"I don't believe a damn word that you say," said Ricardo, as he exploded in an intense emotional state. "You have turned out to be nothing more than a corrupted hypocrite, just like the rest of you Anglo-Saxons. I never would have thought it of you."

Before Ron could reply, Ricardo walked out of the room. For two days he sulked in his office. Finally, late, on the evening of the second day, he called Ron at his home, and apologized for his temperamental Mexican conduct. He had found out for himself, from the young Hindu, that Ron Jervis had not capitulated to the Dean or to Professor Buckley.

Everything in the Department now settled down to a peaceful routine. Ron was able to get a young man, Dr. Karl

Johnson, who had been taking his doctorate with him at his former institution, but who had completed the degree after he had left. Since the young man was not satisfied at his job, he was happy to make the change. Fortunately for Dr. Johnson, Dr. McKinney, when his leave of absence was up, had taken another job and because of this Dr. Johnson was offered his position.

In the meantime, Dean Hazwell had been promoted to the position of Vice-Chancellor of the University, actually sidetracked as Ron had predicted. Who do you think was put in his place? A Professor of Psychology from the College of Arts and Sciences. Unfortunately for the College of Education, the new Dean knew little about the profession of teaching. All that he knew about the profession of teaching could be summed up as a narrow form of specialization in methodology. He had been selected by the President of the University so as to narrow and limit the role of the College of Education to certain testing procedures. At the first meeting of the Chairmen of the several departments of the College, the Dean, Dr. Jack Carson, spelled out his hope for establishing a better relation between the Faculty of the College of Education and that of the College of Arts and Sciences.

"Gentlemen," said the new Dean, "as you well know, I am no stranger to many of you. To those of you whom I do not know, I am sure that we will have no difficulty working together. I pledged myself, when I took this job, that I would do everything humanly possible, to not only make this a stronger College of Education, but to establish a sound and solid working relation with the Faculty of the College of Arts and Sciences. Ours is a task of discovering and providing the best possible methods of teaching the basic subject matters at all levels of the public school system and, yes, the college level as well. This shall be our primary task and purpose as a College of Education. In the meantime, I shall want to talk to each one of you to see how I can best serve you and your department."

Following these remarks, the Dean arranged for an appointment with each of the several Chairmen. Ron Jervis's appointment came on the second day after the meeting, and at the morning hour of 10 a.m. When Ron walked into the Dean's office, he was greeted with a friendly smile.

"Professor Jervis," said the Dean, "I have heard some fine things about you from a number of your colleagues and from members of the Arts and Sciences Faculty. Also, I look forward to a fine working relation with you and the other members of your Department. I have known your friend Dr. Martinez for a number of years, and I have a great respect for him becaue of what he has done for the Mexican Americans in this State. Now, tell me what you think are the real needs of this College and your Department. How can I be helpful?"

"Dean Carson," said Ron Jervis, "as you know we are a small department and, as a result, have very little power in this College. Thus, when there is a meeting of the Faculty of the College, we get little consideration because decisions are always made by a vote of the majority present rather than by the significance of the issue to us, or the worth of our Department in the College, In this respect, I cannot agree with you when you say that the primary function of the College is in the realm of methodology. There is an abundance of historical evidence that points to the need for teachers of high social intelligence and ethical commitment to the GENERAL WELFARE. The relation of the teacher to the life process, and to cultural reality in a free society, is paramount to any method of teaching a subject."

"I am not in disagreement with you, Professor Jervis," replied the Dean, "but what you are saying is the function of the College of Arts and Sciences, I would think that the teaching of the History of Education should be in the History Department and the Philosophy of Education in the Philosophy Department. Since we have separate departments, I propose to strengthen your Department by having some faculty members from the two departments of the College of Arts and Sciences added to yours. I will be recommending the same to the other departments in the College. This is what is being done in the Educational Psychology Department since I became your Dean. As of now, I have arranged for one of the members of the Philosophy Department to teach a section in the Elementary Philosophy of Education course."

"Dean Carson," said Professor Jervis, "are you sure that this is a wise thing to do? You are putting faculty members into our Department who have no responsibility for the future of the Department or for any of its members. Also, are you sure that a member of the Philosophy Department is competent to teach a section in elementary education?"

"Professor Jervis," replied the Dean, "I could not be positive about the success of this assignment, but we can find out by trying."

What Dean Carson had to say about having faculty members from the College of Arts and Sciences given membership in the Departments of the College of Education was a source of great concern to Ron Jervis. Giving a man voting power without any responsibility to the department in which he was teaching was self-destructive. He knew that the Dean meant well, but he knew that such a policy would give professor Buckley the chance to dominate the future policy of the Department. The Dean had promised to raise Ricardo's salary, and this was all to the good, but the idea of a professor in the Philosophy Department teaching a section in Elementary Education was indicative of how little he knew about the professional teacher. Well, it would only last for one semester, and that would be the end of it. So, upon leaving the Dean's office, Ron headed straight for Martinez to see what he would recommend as a course of action. Since he was in his office, and not too busy to see him, Ron sat down and proceeded directly to the issue.

"Ricardo," said Ron Jervis, "I have just returned from Dean Carson's office. I very much need to talk to you about the action that he plans to take in the College, for it will have a direct effect on the operation of our Department. I must tell you that I am very much concerned by what he has told me, especially on the matter of placing Arts and Sciences faculty members in our Department."

After Ron had explained to Ricardo the action which the Dean had planned in enlarging the faculty of the Cultural

Foundations of Education Department, Ricardo hit the ceiling.

"Damn it, Ron," said Ricardo. "What the bastard is doing is giving himself respectability in the College of Education Faculty. He knows little or nothing about professional education and is only a narrowly trained psychologist. Rather than giving our Department equal status with the other departments in the College, he proceeds to stack the cards against us. My guess is that he is acting under the direction of the President of the University, who is responsible for his being appointed Dean. In times past this president, who is a chemist, has made nasty remarks about this College and how he would reform it. He, like Dean Carson, is a very narrowly trained man."

"Ricardo," said Ron, "I know how to handle this problem as long as I am Chairman. I will not invite these new faculty members to any of our official meetings, I will be retiring from the Chairmanship after this year, however, and will not be able to control the situation at that time. That raises another issue. Our Dean has appointed Buckley to head the committee that is to look out for a new Chairman. You can be sure that, if Buckley has his way, he will be seeking a Chairman who follows his line of thinking."

"I have no doubt," said Ricardo, "that we are going to have to put up a hell of a fight if we are going to maintain any control over this Department and maintain our position in the College. While we are on this subject, what about the new man who is coming from the University of Karo. I found him well qualified, but I don't like his high-handed arrogance."

"I agree with you, Ricardo," said Ron, "but both Buckley and the Dean were impressed by his record. Also, his recommendations are all that we could ask from any candidate. As you know, before his final appointment, I wrote to the professors who had recommended him, and they assured me that he is very cooperative with faculty and students, that he has an excellent record, along with a liberal philosophy of education. Only the future will tell, and, if he turns out as we have feared, it will be tragic for all of us."

Unfortunately for Ricardo and Ron Jervis, the new man turned out just as they had feared. What made the situation worse was that the Dean, without the recommendation of the Chairman, gave the man an Associate Professorship. Associate Professor Potsby was not only arrogant, but active in manipulating his students against Ricardo and Ron. In short, he was power drunk. His game was that of the POLITICS OF POWER against those who were between him and the Dean. Because of such, he was not long in lining himself up with Professor Buckley.

Among the many things that Potsby did in violation of his ethical responsiblity toward his Department were (1) gossiping to his Colleagues in the other departments of the College about Ricardo's low academic standards; (2) restructuring his section of the elementary Philosophy of Education course into a methods course (this was done in order to play up to the Educational Psychology Department); (3) trying to run down his Chairman by saying that he did not have a major in Philosophy, although he did have a major in the Social Philosophy of Education as well as in Intellectual History; (4) belittling doctoral candidates on their oral examinations by asking them obscure and detailed factual questions which had little relevance to the quality of the student; (5) telling lies to the graduate students about the motives of the Chairman in the awarding of fellowships. After these practices had gone on for a period of time, Ron, at one of the departmental meetings, challenged Potsby on his conduct.

"Professore Potsby," said Ron, "it has come to my attention, now that you have been here for almost a year, that you have refused to cooperate with the policies of this Department. I would like to hear from you on what you have to say about your actions. To be specific, I note that you have refused to cooperate in the teaching of the elementary teacher education course in Philosophy."

"Professsor Jervis," replied Associate Professor Potsby, "I do not know what you are talking about. I have tried in every way possible to do an excellent job. Why don't you be more specific so that I can make an intelligent response?"

At this point Professor Martinez spoke up in a manner that expressed utter contempt for the Associate Professor. "Potsby," said Martinez, "there is no point in your trying to deny that you have deliberately and underhandedly tried to belittle me in the eyes of my associates. I do not have to make an apology to you, or to any one else, for the way I have worked for the betterment of the Mexican-American student. What you need to understand is that my people need leadership more than anything else, and that it is my intention to give it to them. My primary responsibility to this University is to help my people rise out of their poverty-stricken and illiterate condition. I understand that you have been very hard on our Lebanese graduate student, and have accused him of plagiarism before the University Conduct Committee. Is this because of your pro-Israeli dogmatism, or because of your dogmatic sense of superiority before a helpless student?"

"Professor Hernandez," replied Associate Professor Potsby, "I am very sorry that you think that I am prejudiced toward our Lebanese student. All that I have tried to do is to live up to my professional responsibilities, and to establish a high quality of scholarship, whether a student be Mexican-American or Lebanese."

"Well, Dr. Potsby," said Ron Jervis, "how do you answer the charge that you have lied to our graduate students about the Chairman's motives concerning the awarding of graduate fellowships?"

"I admit," said Potsby, "that I have talked to some of our students about the fellowship grants, but I did not accuse the Chairman of lying with respect to the way in which they were awarded. If a student told you that I had done so, he or she must have misunderstood what I said."

At this time the Chairman was convinced that it was useless to continue the discussion of the disloyalty of Dr. Potsby, so he turned to Professor Buckley to determine what action had been taken on the replacement of the Chairman of the Department.

"Professor Buckley," asked Ron, "please bring the other

members up to date on any action that has been taken by your committee."

"Professor Jervis," said Professor Buckley, "you will be glad to hear that we will have a man here for an interview on Monday of next week. His name is Steve Pooper, and he comes to us highly recommended by the Dean of his College. In the meantime, I will be letting you know the hour and the time of the interviews."

When Professor Pooper did arrive, it was evident that he was more of an academic philosopher than a philosopher of education, a rigid man in the most technical sense rather than a man of humanistic feeling. It was evident that he was lacking in a concern for leadership in the profession of teaching. Since his publication record was good, in addition to his experience in a state university, the Dean, along with Buckley and Potsby, was favorable to his appointment in spite of the objections of Martinez and Ron Jervis. He was recommended to the President of the University and employed.

After the opening of the fall semester, it was not long before conflict developed among the members of the Department over the admission of two faculty members of the College of Arts and Sciences into the Department. By admitting them to the regular meetings, and granting them the same rights and privileges, Pooper and Potsby had gained control over departmental policies. In doing so, they dropped Professor Buckley from their consideration, and turned to the outside for their power control. He was no longer needed to serve their purpose. The POLITICS OF POWER had gained the ascendancy. Was there not something that Ron Jervis and Ricardo Martinez could do about the situation? This is what they discussed after Ricardo entered Ron's office late on the afternoon following the day of the crucifixion.

"Ron," said Ricardo, "we are in one hell of a mess in this Department. I have been wondering what we could do to block the action that has been taken giving those bastards control over us. Althoug Pooper and Potsby have turned against Buckley, we can not count on him for any support."

"You are right, Ricardo," said Ron. "We cannot count on Buckley for any support, but there is something that we can do. We can call a boycott of their meetings. Since all of the graduate students are under our supervision, we can overnight kill any action on their part."

Before the next departmental meeting, Professors Martinez and Jervis had written their Chairman that they would boycott his meetings until there was a change in policy on the voting rights of the Arts and Sciences faculty members. Things dragged on for a number of weeks until Chairman Pooper went to the Dean to see if he would take action against Martinez and Jervis. Since the Dean was unwilling to take any action against them, he did suggest that a Committee of Three from outside the university be brought in to review the situation and arbitrate the dispute. At the same time, Dean Carson questioned Ron about the reasons for the unfortunate split in the faculty of the Department.

"Professor Jervis," said the Dean, "I regret that there has been a split among the members of your Department over the voting rights of the Arts and Sciences faculty members. Since both of the men are men of excellence and understanding in their role as professors, I wonder why you and Martinez are so opposed to them."

"Dean Carson," replied Ron Jervis, "we have nothing against the two professors. We are aware of the fact that each is a man of professional integrity and ability. Our position is a matter of principle. Since we are a small Department, giving outsiders power to vote means that they can override any action that we take on departmental policy. If we were a large department, like that of Educational Psychology, it would make little difference. In our Department, such a grant of power involves salary increases, promotions, course assignments, and recommendations for new faculty members."

"Now that I understand what this controversy is all about," said the Dean, "will you and Professor Martinez abide by the recommendations of the Committee of Three, especially since you participated in the selection of members."

"Definitely, Dean Carson," replied Professor Jervis. "We

are so sure that we are right that we have no doubt as to what the decision of the Committee will be."

After the Committee had made its investigation of the issues that led up to the boycott, it was three weeks before their report was in the hands of the Dean. As a result, the decision was a full justification of the position of Ron Jervis and Ricardo Martinez. The recommendation which followed held that the outside faculty be given voice but no vote. This action the Dean followed through on, and the matter was settled. No comment concerning the settlement came from Professor Pooper, Potsby, or Buckley.

It was not long after the settlement of the controversy over voting in the departmental affairs that Ron Jervis had a talk with his friend Bill Snyder about the difficulties that he had experienced while he was Chairman of his Department. The meeting took place in the usual Faculty Dining Hall.

"Bill," said Ron Jervis, "you must be aware of the fact that I, like you, am no longer Chairman of my Department. These past ten years, I am sorry to say, did not turn out as I had hoped. To a certain extent I find myself in the same position that William R. Davie, founder of the University of North Carolina, experienced when he searched for faculty to fill vacancies in the first of the state universities. Also, the history of the University of Virginia shows that Thomas Jefferson searched, both at home and abroad, for men who could fit into the purposes which he deemed necessary for the operation of his institution. In neither case could the needed professors be found. Truthfully, I find myself living in a kind of Platonic world, hoping for something that does not exist."

"Ron," said Bill Snyder, "the more I wrestled with my problem, and I must admit that I did a lot of wrestling, I was convinced that the hope for humanity rested in our ability to integrate the natural organic role of power with a quality of character and social intelligence that can come only from the culture process. To achieve that end, I, like our Revolutionary Fathers, am convinced that the state university offers the only hope for providing the leadership necessary for the GENERAL WELFARE OF THIS NATION. Why we have failed should be a problem of major concern to all of us, and especially to the faculty of this state university. That such is a factor of major concern is indicated by the extent to which we are living in a dream world, blind to the nature of the world around us. As for myself, I have no choice other than to continue the same course of action that I have been following during my professional career."

"Bill," said Ron, "I agree with you in every respect. I too find myself ready to go out and do battle with the forces of opposition. As for myself, the life that I have chosen to live is THE LIFE THAT IS GOOD TO LIVE."

When Ron Jervis arrived at home that night, Helen and his daughter Betty Jane commented on his cheerfulness and wondered just what had happened to him during the day. After relating his experience with Bill Snyder, Ron felt compelled to make these additional remarks.

"You know, Helen," said Ron, "if the people of this country could only learn to appreciate the power of the American Culture, we could develop from that knowledge the sense of unity and purpose which are necessary for the GENERAL WELFARE OF THIS NATION. We could bring our people to a realization that the accumulation of great wealth by inheritance has resulted in the creation of a power force that is destroying our sense of freedom and creative imagination. The right of inheritance of great wealth is a curse on our free-enterprise economy, in that it has always symbolized the POLITICS OF POWER. To be equal in the American Revolutionary sense, men and women must have an equal start in life, not having the cards stacked against them which is a result of the inheritance of wealth. One can rightfully conclude that it was the inheritance of great wealth that led to the destruction of the glory that was Greece and the grandeur that was Rome."

"Ron Jervis," said Helen, "are you saying that we need a more stringent inheritance law to achieve the purpose you have in mind?"

"Definitely so, Helen," replied Ron. "In the final analysis, it is the only way that we can ever begin to pay off our growing national debt, and, even more so, it is the only way in which our free-enterprise economy and our democratic culture can survive. Life is like having men and woman on a race track where, to be equal, each must start at the same given point. If such could be achieved, there is no telling what a future world of freedom and progress could be brought into being in our native land."

CHAPTER VI

LEADERSHIP IN THE CULTURE PROCESS

The more he taught, the more he read, and the more he researched, the more Ron Jervis became convinced that the survival and hope of a free society was dependent upon an improvement in the quality of leadership, especially at the high levels of government. On this matter he was to have numerous and continuing discussions with his friends Bill Snyder and David Lucas. But first, he had to clarify for himself as to what were the qualities of the leader in a free society.

As he studied the problem, he became increasingly aware of the fact that to be a leader in a free society was very much different from that of being a leader in a Communist or Nazi state. This produced the conclusion that there was no such thing as a leader in the universal sense. A leader serves in terms of the role he or she is to perform in a given culture. Since the state university had been engaged, for a period of more than a century, in the education of individuals for the various professions, Ron's first venture should be to contact some of these professionals and talk to them about their role in the American culture. It was on this conviction that Ron Jervis contacted his friend David Lucas. When he called him, David was just as anxious to continue the discussion as was Ron. It was thus at another luncheon hour that Ron Jervis and his friend found themselves together for a continuing analysis of their professional problems. Ron opened the discussion as he had done on the previous occasion.

"David," said Ron, "I know that you are just as much interested in the role of the state university in the education of leaders in our society as I am; but when you observe what is going on in our everyday life, you cannot help but wonder as to whether or not we are doing all that we should do in providing the quality type of leadership that is necessary for a free-thinking mind."

"Ron," said David Lucas, "I have given much thought as to why we have failed in our efforts to provide the kind of leadership that should be demanded of us. I think that we lost the battle during the first part of the nineteenth century because of the states rights conflict, and because it was impossible to find professors who were educated other than in the classical tradition."

"True enough," said Ron Jervis. "After the War Between the States, other than a few individuals like Eugene V. Debbs, there were few people who cared about the role of freedom in our culture. Don't forget that this was the period in which the Christian Church regained its power and, in doing so, waged an aggressive war against the State universities on the grounds that they were atheistic. It should be noted that the church leaders were aided by the growing power of the corporate industrialists who held that 'we own this country, and by God we are going to keep it.' "

"I would observe," said David Lucas, "that it was at this time when a new concept of the nature of the free-enterprise system was popularized, that of mechanical law. Gone was Adam Smith's intellectual and moral responsibility to the common good. According to the new Gospel, the free-enterprise economy was self corrective. Following this breakdown of the ethical frame in which the culture had been operating came a marked increase in political corruption, economic graft, and lawlessness. That the people of the states south of the Mason Dixie Line wallowed in their poverty and illiteracy was no concern of those who held the power strings in the Eastern states. It was good, as they saw it, that the people of the South pay for their sins, for they brought their destruction down upon themselves."

"The pervasive nature of the anti-intellectualism of the century was so marked," said Ron Jervis, "that it played into the hands of the supercilious bigotry of the conceited rich and well-born. The concept of freedom was stripped of all intellectual and ethical responsibility. By reducing the concept of DEMOCRACY to nothing more than majority will, it was easy for those who sat in the seats of power to control the minds of the people. This practice was so corruptive that it played into the hands of the ministers of God with their hell fire and brimstone tactics. Within the halls of the state universities, there was a retreat from cultural reality and the market place. In due time, the classical tradition was replaced by a glorification of technology and material progress. The concept of HUMANISM was swallowed up in the concept of the mechanized man. As corporate industrialism gained ascendancy in the American culture, the industrial laborer organized to combat the growing power of the industrial mogul. The call for economic justice and collective bargaining were more and more a part of the cultural climate."

"Ron," said David Lucas, "in the trend away from the agrarian economy of the nineteenth century, and the rise of an industrial urban society, where does leadershp fit into the picture?"

"David," said Ron, "there were a number of voices crying in the wilderness during the nineteenth century. After the death of Jefferson and Adams, I find no evidence of a power force that was concerned with the enhancement of the free, creative, scientific mind. There were such great humanistic minds as Emerson and Whitman, but the revolutionary thinking of a Thomas Paine was missing. The new type of mind was more inclined toward the interests of a special group, groups such as those of law, medicine, politics, engineering, teaching, the military, architecture, labor, and corporate industry. It is evident that the best minds had gone into those areas where the most money was to be found. As for the state university, faculty members had wiped their hands on what was going on in the outside world and confined themselves to their research interests. Thus, speaking generally, what we have is a concern for more and more about less and less.

"As to the first step to be taken, David, in determining why we have so few who are able to provide the quality of leadership necessary for a society of free men and women, what do you think of my interviewing several individuals who represent the interests of our several professions. What I would want to find out is how they would define the role of a leader in our culture. As a beginning, I would want to visit our University President to get a line on his thinking. What do you think?"

"Ron," replied David Lucas, "I think you have an excellent idea. After you have your interviews, let me know what you find out. Such interviews should give us further insight into the kind of thinking that is most prevalent today. Now that we have been at it for some two hours, I have just three minutes to make an appointment with my Dean."

Before seeking an appointment with President Forester, Ron thought that it would be a good idea to more clearly define for himself what qualities in an individual made for a good leader in a free society. This problem he would take up with his graduate students, as well as with Bill Snyder and Ricardo Martinez. In looking back over the years of his association with Martinez, he noted how well he reflected one quality which a leader in a free society must possess, that of dependent-independence. It was William Wordsworth, the English poet, who referred to these attributes when he wrote, "These two things, contradictory as they seem, go together, manly dependence and manly self-reliance." Martinez certainly possessed that quality of communication with others, with his feelings as well as with his mind; however, he suffered from a severe limitation, democratically speaking, a limitation rooted in the fact that his feelings were confined to the Mexican-American race. Instead of a universal concept of man, Martinez was limited to thinking only of the rights of his people, always blaming the WASPS (White Anglo-Saxon Protestants) for their plight. There was one other weakness in his make-up, a tendency to let his emotions dominate his intellect. This Ron had noticed in the way he reacted toward Dean Hazwell when he was Chairman of the Department. That night, after his meeting with David Lucas, Ron raised the question of democratic leadership with Helen.

"Helen," said Ron, as they sat in the living room after their evening meal, "I am planning to talk with President Forester (he had taken the place of President Lothan who was now retired) on the question of what makes a good leader in a free society; but, before doing so, I want to have an interview with several individuals in different professions. What do you think?"

"Ron," said Helen, "now that you have brought the matter up, I must admit that I have never given much thought to your question. I do know that, all during the years I was in high school and college, leadership was associated with power, especially that kind of power practiced by the military. I am sure that you must have had the same experience. Our history books have glorified and continue to glorify Ghenghis Khan, Alexander the Great, Julius Caesar, Napoleon, Robert E. Lee and Ike Eisenhower. Yes, we have extolled the virtues of Socrates, Plato, Aristotle, Jesus of Galilee, Shakespeare, John Locke, Thomas Jefferson, and Abraham Lincoln, but for true glorification leave it to the military. In our Nation, George Washington is glorified as the Father of his Country irrespective of his social, economic and political views. Along with Washington, the generals who have stood out in our Wars have wound up in the Presidency regardless of their qualifications. Ulyssess S. Grant for example. Making Eisenhower President of Columbia University was as much of a travesty as electing him President of the United States, for in no way was he qualified to serve in either position. Also, when our generals retire, more often than not they are made heads of our large corporations."

"Helen," said Ron, "don't you find that in most of the Latin American countries, and on the Continent of Africa, there is a belief that the military man is the one to bring unity to a country that finds itself in trouble?"

"Definitely so, Ron," said Helen. "The roots of the concept of the military man go all the way back into man's early history, probably because of the organic nature of the power role. This tendency is just as true in the Communist worlds of the U.S.S.R. and China. Only in the Anglo-Saxon world, and especially in the British Isles, has the military been placed in a limited glorified role. In our country, we have tended to follow the Prussian pattern of relating ourselves to the military mind. We have, in contrast to the English, set our generals up as untouchables, actually giving them special privileges like the monarchs of old. They live in a world of privilege, in contrast to the poor GI Joes. If there was ever an example of a privileged class, they are it. Here money is tied to that use of power which is so characteristic of our culture today."

"Would you say, Helen," asked Ron, "that this glorification of the military, even in our culture, tends to thwart the development of the concept of a leader in a free society? Where would you place the minister of God?"

"I see, Ron," said Helen, "that you are getting at the heart of my thinking. In some ways, there is a similarity between the status of a clergyman and the general. In both cases, we are mentally bound by the traditions in our culture. As you well know, I am not nearly as critical of the role of the priest in our culture as you are, though I will admit that I find your kind of thinking very similar to that of my father. What bothers me is that, with the waning influence of the Church, there has been a decaying of our ethical and intellectual responsibilities."

"Have you stopped to realize, Helen," replied Ron, "that the church people you are talking about may have contributed more than any other single group to the weakening of our intellectual and ethical responsibilities. This they have done by ranting and raving about the evils in our society without assuming any responsibility toward the solution of our common problems. These churchmen continue to preach a doctrine of conformity to God's will, which resolves itself into conformity to the status-quo. Devotion and worship to what is laid down in the primitive Jewish Culture BIBLE is contradictory to every thing that Jefferson and Thomas Paine held dear in our culture. As long as these ministers of God have a stranglehold over the minds of our people, we will continue to be victimized by the vested interests that are having such a negative influence in our society. You must know that it is these same clergymen who are at the root of the problem of dealing with the Soviet Union. In the final analysis, we must live with the people of the U.S.S.R., or die with them."

"I get your point, Ron," said Helen, "but you must admit that these people do much good for those in our culture who are poor and underprivileged, especially the children."

"I agree, Helen," said Ron, "but there is a price to be paid, and that price is mind control, the very opposite of the scientific approach to any problem. It is this scientific approach that has done so much in the eradication of starvation, as well as many terrible diseases. It is because of this scientific approach that we have our advanced birth control measures, these measures which are vitally necessary to control the advancing world population. Without such control, we are headed toward the destruction of our Western civilization, if not of mankind. But let us turn to another area of the human struggle where we are directly involved, that of school administration. What do you think of our school administrators as leaders in our free society?"

"While my experience in this respect is very limited," said Helen, "I must admit that I do not have a very high opinion of the school administrators I have known. In general, they have been very well educated but they act more like servants than like free men, seeing their role as one of conformity to the will of the school board. They tyrannize over the teachers under their supervision rather than communicating with them as equals. Actually, they are more interested in their athletes than they are in quality scholarship. While my experience is very limited, I have never known a school administrator who stood out as a leader in the community."

"How can you say such a thing, Helen?" asked Ron. "Have you forgotten that I was once your school administrator?"

"No, I have not forgotten, Ron Jervis," replied Helen. "How could I, when I taught under your supervision for two years. You must admit that you were not the typical school administrator, for, even before we were married, my mother, more than I, recognized your qualities. She once said to me, just a few months before she died, 'That boy has real character, not that I want you to marry anyone just now, but that young man is going places.' Your research and your teaching in four state universities is clear proof that her faith in you was not misplaced."

"Yes, Helen," said Ron. "Your mother was a very perceptive woman. But to get back to the social intelligence of school administrators, I must agree with you on your assessment of their lack of the qualities of leadership. I do not know of a single school administrator who could be said to stand out as a leader in public affairs. This being the case, what can we say about the quality of the public schools for which they are responsible? Not very much, if your concept of quality has any relation to required teacher qualifications and the attention being paid to those teachers who have potentiality as leaders in a free society, to high intellectual ability, and to a genuine concern for the GENERAL WELFARE."

"What you are saying, Ron," said Helen, 'is a far cry from the present operations. It may well be that teachers are adequately paid, though I doubt it, for what is expected of them. The contrast, however, between what a classroom teacher is paid and that of the school administrator is a mockery of the concept of justice. Such salary differences are obviously due to the POLITICS OF POWER, a situation similar to that of the manager in a factory and the worker. Unfortunately, the concept of trade training dominates our teacher certification, not teacher creativity and a high order of social intelligence. The entire history of the public school movement in the United States shows that our public schools have never been financed at a quality level of instruction or of administrative leadership. It is clear, upon an analysis of their operation, that the role of the administrator is to keep teachers in line with school board policy and with the pattern of conformity set by those who control the politics of power. Freedom and creativity have never been a marked characteristic of our public schools. Throughout their entire history, women have played the underdog role, often required to sign a contract that made them promise not to become pregnant during the school year. It is well known that they were brought into the classroom because they were more submissive to the dominance of the male administrator and because they would work for a lower salary. On the other hand, Ron, what would you say about the role of the administrator in our state universities?"

"Well, Helen," replied Ron, "the pattern is not the same, but the results are not different. The state university is not educating for leadership if we are talking about the GENERAL WELFARE. For such a failure our people are paying a very dear price. When dealing with the various professions, our state universities have done a satisfactory job if you are thinking in terms of the mechanics of the operation. This is especially true of the military, medicine, law, and engineering. If you are talking in terms of justice, the legal profession has been a miserable failure. All of this would indicate that the state universities have lost sight of the purpose for which they were created, of their ethical commitment and intellectual responsibility to promote quality leadership in all areas of human endeavor. What has been done is a substitution of the quality of means for the purpose for which the state universities were established. Note how the law of the land has been corrupted to the point of throwing out all pretense of justice for money and victory over your opponent. In teaching, a watered-down dose of child welfare has been substituted for the welfare of all. Why? Because of our ignorance as to the nature of the child and as to how the human mind is created and operates."

"Ron," said Helen, "I can see that your respect for the public school teacher is not very high, but I understand why. In general, I agree with you; but let me turn to a problem of more immediate interest, that of the well-being of our daughter. I have noticed that she is coming in after 12 o'clock. If I say anything to her about it, she flies into a rage, saying that I do not trust her and that she is old enough to make her own decisions. I wish you would speak to her. It may be that she will listen to you."

"I will be glad to speak to her when the occasion arises," said Ron, "but right now, I need to do some reading in preparation for my tomorrow's graduate class. What I want to find out is how our graduate students see the role of the teacher in the public school and in the university. Such a session will be of great help to me when I get around to talking to President Forester."

After these remarks, Ron Jervis retired to his study where he read until after midnight. It was one in the morning when his daughter tried slipping into the house so as not to awaken her parents, only to be confronted by her father as she walked into the kitchen to grab a bite from the refrigerator.

"Why, Dad," said Betty Jane, "I am surprised to see you up so late. You are not spying on me are you?"

"Now, Betty," said her father, "you know better than that, but your mother is very much concerned about your coming in after midnight. She worries about your health and about your school work, and so do I. We have been proud of you up until now, as a sweet and beautiful girl, and we don't want all of that achievement lost by thoughtlessness."

"Dad," said Betty Jane, "I know that I have upset Mom by coming in so late, but she should trust me. All of my girl friends are doing the same thing."

"I know," responded her father. "But do you always have to conform to the will of the crowd? At somewhere along the line you must wake up to the reality of the need for leadership in our society, and you are just the kind of person to do it."

"You know, Dad," replied Betty Jane, "I never realized until now what you and Mom were trying to tell me. I now know that what you are saying is not just a matter of trusting me, but of my realizing that I should have an obligation and purpose in life far above the will of the crowd. I promise you that things will be different from now on, and, since it is getting very late, we both need to get some sleep. Goodnight, Dad."

"Goodnight night, Betty Jane," responded her father. "You are a daughter of which any father should be proud."

The next day, when Ron Jervis met with his graduate class, he was fully prepared to stimulate his students, and so opened up the session with a shocking statement.

"It has been said that we are a people with little or no respect for our Declaration of Independence or the First Amendment to the Federal Constitution. Now, how or why should such a statement be made? Are we not constantly proclaiming our freedom to the Communist world, and, every Fourth of July, celebrating the birth of our Nation with songs and jubilation?"

"The question you raise, Professor Jervis," said Jan Procter, a major in Social Studies, "would seem to have some relation to the investigation carried out by a newspaper reporter in the state of Wisconsin on how many people knew what the Declaration was all about. When the responses were tabulated, the great majority of those who responded said that the Declaration was a Communist document. Also, when the First Amendment to the Federal Constitution was presented to one of our college freshmen classes, the majority of those present said that it was too radical. It would appear that the mass mind of our country has not as yet caught up with the mind of Jefferson."

"What you have here," said Ralph Jones, a student majoring in English, "is a clearcut example of failure on the part of the public schools and the state universities to promote an understanding of our cultural heritage, and especially the basic concepts on which this Nation was founded. It would appear that the predominant concept of Democracy today is that of DOING YOUR OWN THING."

At this point Professor Jervis raised the question as to what Jefferson had in mind when, in 1820, he said, "I tremble for my country when I think that God is just, and that his justice will not sleep forever."

"Professor Jervis," said Sara Engle, "I get the impression that what you are implying is that we are grossly deficient in creative mentality, which, it seems to me, is what justice is all about. I am of the opinion that we are deficient in our thinking today, just as the people were in 1820, on the nature of Freedom."

"Yes, Sara," replied Professor Jervis. "That is precisely what I am saying. The question which comes to my mind is, why have we had such a poverty of leadership in our country, especially since 1830, and why do we continue to default on our commitment to a Nation of Free Men and Women? The truth of the matter is that the great majority of our people have never had the quality of mind necessary to promote an ongoing free society. Since this is the problem facing us, we must conclude that the state universities have failed to provide the necessary education for such a quality mind, neither during the formative period of our country nor at the present. What we have is an intellectual vacuum in which the traditional forces of Orthodoxy and class privilege have gained ascendancy."

"Professor Jervis," asked Susan Gregory, an elementary education major, "are you saying that, with the passing of our Revolutionary Fathers, there was no one to take their place?"

"That is precisely the point," replied Professor Jervis. "Other than Abraham Lincoln, there is not a single President during the remainder of the 19th century who stands out with a quality creative mind."

"What about Andrew Jackson?" asked Sara Engle. "Was he not the founder of the Democratic Party?"

"Sara," replied Professor Jervis, "I was hoping that one of you would ask that question. Yes, members of the Democratic Party trace their origin to Andrew Jackson. It is important to remember that Andrew Jackson got his reputation as a military leader, for his attacks on the banks, and for his dispute with John Marshall. In no sense did he possess the quality mind of a Thomas Jefferson. I find him totally lacking in that intellectual and ethical sense which is necessary for a creative mind."

"Professor Jervis, now that you have disposed of the Democratic Party," said Sam Postum, a major in the Physical Sciences, "how about Abraham Lincoln and the Republican Party?"

"Sam," said Professor Jervis, "Abraham Lincoln came close to representing what Thomas Jefferson sought as a leader in a free society, in spirit if not in mind. But the Republican Party since the death of Lincoln has been dominated by corporate capitalists. The Republican Party, although claiming Lincoln as its founder, has rejected everything that he sought to achieve. We need to take note of the fact that the planter aristocrat of Virginia, which Jefferson, Madison, Monroe, and Washington represented, gave way to a commercial-oriented planter class after 1830. Since the American State University was born in the Southern states, it was this property-minded slave class that controlled the state university operations in their formative period. It was the determined policy of this class to see to it that no quality mind such as that sought by Jefferson ever came out of these universities. Increasingly on the defensive, this slave-oriented society finally saw its demise in the War Between the States. With the death of the Old South went the passing of the culture which best symbolized the life of Old Europe. What was left was an uneducated poverty-stricken mass of humanity which increasingly found itself confronted with an ever-growing group of greedy corporate industrial barons."

"Professor Jervis," asked Jan Procter, "in respect to what happened in our culture during the past century, where would you place Woodrow Wilson? Also, what about Franklin D. Roosevelt?"

"Jan," replied Professor Jervis, "Woodrow Wilson and Franklin D. Roosevelt were entirely different in the way in which they used the power of the Presidency. The main difference between them was that Woodrow Wilson thought in narrow religious and academic terms, whereas Franklin D. Roosevelt thought in pragmatic social terms. Actually,

Franklin D. Roosevelt was the first of our Presidents who creatively faced the problems confronting our Nation. As a devout Presbyterian, Woodrow Wilson was limited in his concept of a free society, which is to say that he believed in freedom so long as it was in the framework of Christianity. The idea of a person being a Communist was rank heresy to him. You must know that the U.S.S.R. was not recognized as a nation until Franklin D. Roosevelt was President. My judgment is that he is the only President during this century who stands out as a leader of a free society. He possessed the cultural, ethical, and intellectual qualities, as well as the sense of power necessary for the office of President."

"Professor Jervis," replied Jan Procter, "why do you think that we have failed to produce the quality of mind necessary for our present-day political leaders, minds such as that of President Roosevelt?"

"A full and adequate response to your question Jan is not easy," said Professor Jervis. "There are some things, however, that can be said in connection with your question. History tells us that man, in a genetic sense, has the creative ability to cope with his problems, this depending upon the quality of leadership. In the Western world, down to the seventeenth century, the concept of mind was limited to that of an Orthodox Christian, a mythological belief of a non-physical or spiritual nature. I must add, however, that this belief did provide for the need for ethical commitment and an intellectual sense of responsibility to the welfare of man. This need was evident in the power exercised by the Catholic Church, and in the rise of enlightened despotism in the governments of Europe. What was missing was the concept of a natural creative evolutionary process."

"Professor Jervis," responded Robert Miller, "if I understand you correrctly, what you seem to be saying is that, while we think our political system is serving the people, it is really serving the party members."

"Precisely so, Robert," said Professor Jervis. "What we have in our Nation is two self-serving political parties, not distinctly different parties which are constantly exploiting the people rather than serving or leading them. In the truest sense, they repressent the special interests of those able to exercise power in their communities. Play up the idea that taxes are evil; that we as a people represent all that is good in the world; shed crocodile tears over the miseries of the poor; and brow beat your opponent, if you expect to win. Seldom, if ever, do our politicians exemplify that quality of mind necessary to cope with the needs of a creatively free society. There is a need for our becoming conscious of the potentialities of the human race. By doing so we can develop the institutions that will enable us to deal creatively with our industrial, urban, and international problems."

The two-hour session with Ron Jervis's students had come to an end. As the students, fifteen in number, filed out of the classroom, each commented to Professor Jervis on the significance of this particular session. One student, Jan Procter, had this to say about the class, "Dr. Jervis, I have spent fifteen years of my life going to public school and to this University, but you are the first Professor that has opened my eyes as to what a free society is all about and the role of leadership in bringing into being a society of free men and women. Thank you for your honesty, for your intelligence, and for your contribution to the GENERAL WELFARE of our country." The response of his students, after that two-hour session, helped Ron Jervis to feel more secure about what he would say to his President, the meeting with whom was to take place on the coming Wednesday morning, in his office at 10 a.m.

Before meeting with President Forester, Ron had done some checking up on the man so as to know how to approach him on the matter of leadership. All of those to whom he had talked, and especially his Dean, commented on President Forester's genial nature, his desire to become better acquainted with his faculty, and his broad cultural background. As a Professor of the French Language, he had taught for a number of years in a sister state university before getting into the field of university administration. When Ron Jervis entered his office that morning, he was greeted in a friendly manner.

"Professor Jervis," said President Forester, "I am glad to have you drop by for a discussion on university administration. Too often, I find that members of our faculty think that the administration is on one side of the fence and they are on the other. University administration should be thought of in terms of a unified approach to our problems rather than as a divided responsibility. Along with my vital and continuing interest in administrative relations, I am always glad to get better acquainted with the faculty, men such as yourself who I understand is greatly respected by your Dean and fellow colleagues."

"President Forester," replied Professor Jervis, "it is good for me to have this opportunity to get to know you. I too have heard a number of nice things about you, both personally and professionally, so much so that I feel that you have a real interest in the problem that I wanted to discuss with you, namely, the role of the administrator in the state university."

"Professor Jervis," replied President Forester, "that is a subject I have thought long and hard about, especially after becoming President of this University. During this time, I have found that many of my colleagues know very little about the history of the state university, why it was founded, and what its role should be in our urbanized, mechanized culture. They come to this position with little more than a knowledge of their subject matter specialization. You know as well as I do that few of our state university presidents have any preparation as a leader in the intellectual community, much less that of knowing how to relate the various subject matters into a common purpose for our national well-being."

"I take it for granted, President Forester," said Ron Jervis, "that you make a distinction between managing the affairs of an institution and the need for providing leadership to the students, faculty, and citizens of this state."

"Very much so," said President Forester. "*Management* I think of as a science of getting things done through people; whereas *Leadership* is the art of getting people to do the things that should be done. The appointment of a man or woman to this position does not necessarily carry with it the ability to either manage or lead. In my judgment, however, the greatest weakness in the administration of our state universities today lies in the area of leadership. That is the number one problem in our higher institutions of learning today."

"President Forester," said Professor Jervis, "could you give me an example of what you have in mind on the role of leadership in our society, and what you have learned from your years of being a university administrator?"

"Yes, Professor Jervis," replied the President, "one of the most difficult problems that I have faced as President of this university is that of delegating authority to my subordinates. It makes no difference how bright a mind you have, if you cannot delegate authority intelligently you will come out a poor administrator. Also, a subordinate should be willing to accept challenges which are over his head, and even make mistakes, but he will not do so unless he or she receives encouragement from his or her administrative superior. The real test of a leader comes about in planning for the future, for unless the administrator has creative imagination, backed by a knowledge and understanding of where he or she is going, he or she fails, whether the failure is realized or not. This is the real challenge in our Nation today, if we are to gain the necessary power and sense of purpose in dealing with the nations of the world. Professor Snyder tells me that he had discussed this problem with you in some detail."

"Yes, President Forester," replied Professor Jervis. "I find Professor Snyder a very insightful man when it comes to the role of the state university in a free society. He, as you know, is very much concerned about the need for reviving the revolutionary spirit which gave birth to our country. He is disturbed by the prevailing idea that there is a poverty of leadership in our Nation, that leadership implies followership, which sets up a class structure that calls for thinking from the top down."

"Unfortunately," said President Forester, "that is one of the prevailing dogmas in our present-day culture, and especially when applied to our political structure. Actually, our concept of democracy has been so watered down that we are led to believe that anyone, by virtue of birth and citizenship, is qualified to be a governor of any one of our states, or even a president of the United States. Nothing could be farther from the truth. The effect of such thinking has been devastating, in that it has produced massive incompetence in our political life since the days of Andrew Jackson. How can you make any sense out of the fact that we require some intellectual qualifications for a science teacher in our public schools and none for public office?"

"President Forester," said Professor Jervis, "I could not agree with you more, especially when such practices involve the state university. The men who were responsible for the founding of the state university knew that it would be impossible to offset the mind control of the Christian Church leadership if provision was not made for the education of a new kind of leadership. As for myself, I would say that end result has been a BETRAYAL ON MOUNT PARNASSUS."

"Professor Jervis," said President Forester, "ever since taking the office as president of this University, I have realized that there is a gap between our present-day political practices and our cultural heritage of freedom. Actually, we train for monetary success in all of our professions except the professions of teaching and the clergy. As for teachers, we expect them to sacrifice themselves and their economic well-being for the general welfare. Knowing and believing that it is extremely difficult to change the course of a nation or a university, I do appreciate your efforts and those of Professor Snyder, but I am not optimistic about the future. What disturbs me most is that we have entered a new era in our relation to the several countries all over the world, especially the Soviet Union. We need to recognize that we are grossly lacking in that quality of leadership so necessary for our present-day world problems. As things now stand, we are in danger of destroying ourselves, both within and outside our national boundaries, by engaging in an atomic war. The leadership of the Soviet Union can be faulted on many counts, but as long as we follow a policy of containment of the U.S.S.R., there is not going to be any resolution of the growing world conflict."

"President Forester," replied Ron Jervis, "I see that my time for this interview has come to an end, and, knowing that you are a very busy man, I should be getting out of your office. I do appreciate your good will and your constructive efforts to provide a quality leadership for this University. If I can be of any help to you personally, or professionally, all you need to do is to give me a ring. Good day, and thank you so much for taking your time with me."

As Ron Jervis left the office of his President, he could not help but wonder how a man of his qualities had been able to survive the power struggle which goes on every time a university presidency is to be filled. Surely Bill Snyder must have had some influence in bringing his election about. He would talk to Bill about this very thing at his meeting with him on the next day, as well as about some other matters concerning the role of a state university in a free society. What would happen to President Forester if he did take the bull by the horns and sought to force a change for what he believed to be the common good of this Nation? On the following day, when Ron Jervis sat down at lunch with Bill Snyder, his first remarks were directed toward his meeting with President Forester.

"Bill," said Ron, "I had a very interesting and profitable meeting with President Forester yesterday, and found him to be a very enlightened and responsible man. It is most unfortunate that we do not have more Presidents like him in all of our state universities. He spoke very highly of you, Bill, especially with reference to your stand on the role of a state university in a free society."

"You know, Ron," said Bill, "I had not said anything about the President to you because I wanted you to find out for yourself just what kind of man he was. I am glad to hear you confirm my conviction about him. Why is it that we do not have more men of his type at the head of our state universities? What a difference such men would make, not only in the operation of the universities, but in the meaning and value of culture in the life of our people."

"That is very true, Bill," replied Ron Jervis, "but when I look at the way in which our country evolved, and the way in which religious dogma prevailed in the minds of our people at the time of the Revolution, I can understand why the dogmatic mind has continued to prevail over the insights and hopes of our Revolutionary Fathers."

"You seem to be talking in riddles, Ron Jervis," said Bill Snyder. "I think it will be possible to understand you better if you will be more specific."

"Yes, Bill," replied Ron, 'I will be glad to get down to brass tacks. You are aware of the fact that we were told while we were growing up that our fore-fathers came to this country for religious freedom; whereas they came across to promote their particular brand of religious dogma. I am convinced that they had no idea of what religious freedom was all about; and, if they did, wanted none of it. The weight of the historical evidence establishes the fact that on the whole these early immigrants came over here for land and economic well-being. Land was that which would bring wealth and social status. Please note that at the time of the American Revolution this dream had not changed, nor has it changed to this very day. As a matter of fact this dream of wealth and power has dominated the entire history of our Nation, and is possibly greater today than at any time in our history. It was the desire for wealth and power that led our people to run roughshod over the rights of the native Indians and the Mexican Government. Herein lie the tragedies of the War Between the States — a war over the freedom of the Black man, it is said, although property rights and power were at the heart of the conflict. Violence has been a marked characteristic of our entire cultural heritage. Note how crime has been on the increase ever since World War I. This trend in our culture has only given the Ministers of God a chance to grow fat and powerful on the body politic of the people. Note how they continue to rave and rant about our sins, just as they did during the Colonial Period of our history, but what have they ever contributed to an improvement of our record of violence?"

"You make yourself quite clear, Ron," said Bill Snyder. "I must agree with you that with all of our education and wealth, I see no improvement in the quality of the mind of our people. As for myself, I think that things will continue to get worse until a basic change of some kind or other is forced upon us. That is the problem that exists in Poland. With the anarchy which is sure to come, there will follow a military dictatorship."

"What you are saying, Bill," said Ron Jervis, "is that our failure to develop a constructive change in our meaning and value frame of reference, and in our culture, has brought about a serious breakdown in our allegiance to law and order. The fact that there is no creative recognizable leadership to bring about a basic change in our culture has resulted in a major crisis for our time, a time when world leadership is of such paramount need, if we are to have a semblance of peace in the world. While I do not know very much about the limitations of the church and private colleges, I do know that, by the very nature of their commitment, they contribute little to the progress of the human mind. In this respect, Bill, you must know more about these colleges than I do."

"Ron Jervis," said Bill Snyder, "from your knowledge of the history of this country, you must be aware of the fact that these colleges were not designed to serve the purpose of the free mind. Church colleges have a unifying purpose, and have had ever since Harvard was established in 1636. The power of these colleges, however, is in the hands of a Board of Control which sees to it that the dogma which led to their establishment is fully adherred to in the classroom. This predetermined dogma has a pattern of meaning and value, regardless of whether or not we are talking about Protestants, Catholics or Jews. In such colleges, it is necessary that the President succeed in getting adequate funds for the financing of his institution, as well as conformity to the institutional dogma by the faculty. A good example of such would be Baylor University in Waco, Texas. In recent times, there has been a tendency for faculty and students to revolt against such a pattern of control, but the power of tradition still reigns supreme. Do not forget that it was because of such church power over the minds of the people that the state university was conceived and established."

"What about the so-called private colleges and universities?" asked Ron. "They come under a different pattern of control, don't they?"

"Yes indeed," replied Bill Snyder. "In a sense they may be said to cover the waterfront, from those which grant a large amount of freedom to both students and faculty to those which are controlled by a pattern of dogma, whether left or right. Most of these institutions appeal to those of wealth and social prestige. I well recall the blackballing of the University of Pittsburgh, by the American Association of University Professors, for the firing of two of its liberal professors. One well-known artist, at the time this happened, referred to the administrative policy of this institution as A POET BUILDS A CATHEDRAL OF LEARNING."

"What you have just said, Bill," replied Ron Jervis, "explains why there has been a betrayal of the hopes which Thomas Jefferson and William R. Davie had for the future of this nation. With a President such as Dr. Forester, we have a golden opportunity to bring about a major change in the educational program of this institution. I would suggest that, in this respect, we begin with the education of the faculty."

"Ron," said Bill Snyder, "it may sound strange to you, but if the change which we seek is to ever take place the requirements for becoming a member of this faculty must be changed. There is a move in this direction, by having every faculty member become more competent in the teaching of his particular subject. While I am in favor of such a change, methodology will in no way solve the problem of quality teaching, for such is due to the lack of a meaning and value frame of reference. The significance of such is pointed up in the fact that when the American state university was established there was a recognized need for a major change in the curriculum of the institution, a change in substance as well as in method. Ron Jervis, you have done more research in this area than I. What have you to say about this need for a change in faculty requirements?"

"Bill," said Ron Jervis, "I know as a matter of historical fact that Benjamin Franklin, in his academy, and William R. Davie, as well as Thomas Jefferson, not only had a desire to change the subject matter content in the new institutions, but likewise sought to do away with the dogma of Medieval Christianity. It is clear that they sought to replace that dogma with a scientific and socially oriented frame of reference. The curriculum of the colonial colleges was limited to Latin and Greek, and sometimes Hebrew, along with a detailed study of the HOLY BIBLE. Every college established during the colonian Period of our history, 1607-1776, was a church college. There was, of course, Benjamin Franklin's Academy. In short, those who sought the establishment of the State university looked forward with the hope of bringing into being the FREE HUMAN MIND. To do so, a new curriculum was in order — the modern languages including English and French; mathematics and the sciences; elocution and the modern philosophers, especially John Locke, Adam Smith, Sir Isaac Newton, and Montesquieu. In order to bring this new mind into being, it was necessary to separate the church from the state. Thus a change in the power role of the church was to be brought about. The significance and need for such a change is pointed up in the First Amendment to the Federal Constitution."

"Ron," said Bill Snyder, "do you think that the Revolutionary Fathers underestimated the power and influence of the church leadership? It would appear that they erred in assuming that once knowledge was freed from censorship, the power of the church over the human mind would gradually disappear."

"I would doubt that, Bill," replied Ron Jervis, "but I do know that their concept of the nature of man was faulty. The fact that they assumed that man was a rational animal has something to do with their failure to bring about a change in the beliefs of the people."

"How so, Ron?" said Bill Snyder. "I do not see the connection here."

"The intellectuals of the eighteenth century, both in Europe and in the colonies," said Ron, "believed that human beings were different from the rest of the animal kingdom by virtue of an inborn rationality. At that time there was no evidence to support the evolutionary hypothesis concerning human nature. The argument centered on whether man was born in sin, as the Orthodox Christian believed, born good as Jean-Jacques Rousseau assumed, or born rational as was held by the philosophers of the Enlightenment. As rational animals, when given the facts, men would arrive at the truth. These beliefs and assumptions were abrogated by the publication of Charles Darwin's THE ORIGIN OF SPECIES. Is it any wonder that the Christians have continued to wage a holy war against Darwin and his disciples? During all of the nineteenth century leaders of the Christian churches led a verbal attack on the state universities, holding that they were atheistic godless institutions. Also, to this very day, they continue their efforts to make this a Christian nation by amending the Federal Constitution. All of which brings us around to the need to change the requirements for membership in our faculty."

"If we take a lesson from the efforts of our forefathers," said Bill Snyder, "we should have the state call for a certification of those who assume positions on our university faculties. A three year certification program beyond the four years undergraduate degree should be a minimum requirement. The contents of this degree would be similar to the present Ph.D. degree, but would necessarily include studies in the History of Higher Education, Cultural Foundations of Education, Origins and Purposes in the Establishment of the State Universities, and the Psychology of Teaching. Also, what is very much needed are studies in the Role of Leadership in a Free Society."

"Bill," said Ron Jervis, "I can anticipate much opposition to your proposed program of requirements for teaching in the state universities; but I believe that, once the significance of the proposed changes is realized, our faculty would back you up. I know that President Forester would welcome such a proposal. So far as those who are now on the faculty are concerned, no effort should be made to provide for such a requirement, but we should have campus lectures along the same line for all of our faculty."

Following the meeting with Bill Snyder, Ron Jervis devoted

much time during the month to interviewing a number of individuals who stood out in their communities as potential leaders in their professions. Those individuals included: the Chairman of the Board of an electronics corporation, a Brigadier General at a U.S. Airforce Base, the head of the State Medical Association, the President of the State Bar Association, a United States Senator, the Manager of one of the National Football League teams, the President of a large labor union, and the Superintendent of a large city school system. While all of these individuals were well educated in the academic sense (three of them had a doctoral degree), not one of them had a concept of leadership outside of his professional obligations.

Although it would take an inordinate amount of time to detail the conversations that took place on each of these occasions, it is necessary to elaborate on some of the essentials which indicate the limitations of our present national and world outlook. As to the Chairman of the electronics corporation, Ron Jervis found him to be an affable gentleman, as well as one who was able and well informed in the operations of his corporation. When Ron asked him as to how he would distinguish between management and leadership, he did not hesitate to reply that management was a process of getting things done through people, whereas leadership was the subtle art of getting people to do things. He did recognize that appointing an individual to manage a corporation did not necessarily carry with it the responsibilities of a leader. To offset the differences in these two concepts, Ron learned that a number of corporations had dual operations, A PRESIDENT and a CHAIRMAN.

The head of the State Bar Association expressed the opinion that there were two types of executives, the judge and the director. The judge-type of executive always appointed deputies of high quality and then let them run the business. The director-type had a tendency to make all of the important decisions, leaving little for the deputies to do except to obey orders. The idea of leadership being something other than management was not in his thinking.

The Brigadier General thought only in terms of leadership, but leadership to him was dictatorial and autocratic. To the General, as he expressed himself, there was no place for free thinking in the military order of things, only command and obey.

Interesting enough, it was the labor union leader that expressed the most interest in the men for whom he was responsible. He expressed the opinion a number of times that a leader must be sensitive to the needs and wishes of his fellow workers. A leader, he said, must have determination, be able to stand on his own feet, stand up to management in the interests of the laborers, and not be overweening in his ambition. A labor leader, he argued, should seek to persuade, but not push, for there is a limit to driving any one. An expert on his job, thought Ron, but, as to leadership in terms of the GENERAL WELFARE, that was a nebulous thing to him.

Of all those to whom Ron Jervis talked, only the head of the State Medical Association placed emphasis on ETHICAL responsibilities. This was a tradition in the field of medicine that dated back all the way to Hypocrates. There were, as he said, doctors who did not live up to their professional responsibilities, but that was not a professional matter. When he was asked about excessive medical fees, he agreed that they were high, but not so when compared with the money paid to actors and athletes. The United States Senator turned out to be the most evasive and sweet-talking of the lot. While the senator talked a great deal about serving his public, it was clearly evident that he was more interested in remaining in office than in facing up to the quality issue of leadership. Much of his thinking, since he had the background of a lawyer, was similar to that of the head of the State Bar Association. What bothered Ron Jervis about his responses was the lack of an ethical commitment to the people, and his being more interested in winning votes than in being a leader in a free society.

As in the case of the head of the electronics corporation, Ron found the Superintendent of the city schools an affable and cooperative individual. He did demonstrate, in his comments about the school administrator, a genuine interest in the welfare of the school child. Yet his concept of leadership fell far short of any thing that could be classified as something more than management. There was little in the man that could be identified as creatively artistic. He knew little of the history of the public school, or of the purposes for which it was founded. His role as a school administrator was to have a well-oiled machine, in the day-to-day school operations — teachers who could maintain discipline in the classroom and who conformed to the ideas of the administrative superior. What was most disturbing to Ron was the way in which he capitulated to the will of the School Board, especially with reference to teacher salaries, classroom load, school supplies, and football boys.

Following the completion of his last interview, Ron Jervis determined that he should have another talk with his friend Ricardo Martinez. After that he would confer with his Dean, as a final gesture toward formulating his thinking on the SIGNIFICANCE OF LEADERSHIP IN A FREE SOCIETY. Also, he wanted to hear from his Dean on the importance of the state university for such leadership education and training. There was no longer any doubt in his mind, if there ever had been, that those who had been handed university leadership responsibilities had betrayed the founders of the institution. Not one single person that he interviewed saw his role as a leader outside of his chosen profession. In plain English, what we had was nothing more than a mulligan stew. Expressed in different terms, we can say that we had all the parts of a car, but no car. Well, he would see how Ricardo reacted to his thinking. It was this idea that he had in mind as he walked into the office of his friend.

"Ricardo," said Ron Jervis, "you might be surprised to learn that I spent much of yesterday afternoon in talking to our city school superintendent. What do you know about him as a leader in the field of public education?"

"You damn well know, Ron," replied Ricardo, "what I think about our dear school superintendent. You know that he has no intestinal fortitude. If he did he would let that WASP

School Board of his know what he thinks about the discrimination that goes on in the schools of this community. When I last talked to him he was very outspoken about the discrimination against the Mexican-American children; but when he talks to the School Board, he says something quite different. He may well be good at management in school affairs, but as a leader he is a flop. To me a leader would see the classroom teacher as an individual, as a whole person, and not just a hired hand. Also, he seeks to follow mechanized standards in all of his operations, whether he is talking to the School Board, parents, teachers, or students. To have effective leadership, we must have understanding, execution, and follow-through, none of which he has."

"Well, Ricardo," replied Ron Jervis, "I do think that you are a bit hard on him due to the fact that our public schools nationwide are politically power-centered. The school administrator, whatever his qualities, is at the mercy of the public school board. As things now stand, leadership in our culture is thought of in terms of emotional responses, whereas management is identified with professional competence. Our people select those who serve them in government on the basis of charismatic appeal. Where the individual, like F.D. Roosevelt, has the ethical qualities and a high order of social intelligence, you come out with a great leader; but where these qualities are lacking, you wind up with an Adolph Hitler or a Richard Nixon."

"Ron," said Ricardo, "while I understand you quite well on the matter of leadership, I note that you put much emphasis on the concept of leadership with the reference to a free society. Just how do you make a distinction of this nature? Isn't a leader a leader whether or not we are talking about a free society or a totalitarian one?"

"Well, Ricardo," replied Ron Jervis, "I have noted over some period of time, and especially since the interviews, that we seem to be more concerned with the means than with the ends when we are talking about leadership. This is illustrated by the way in which Joe McCarthy attracted public attention, and the way in which McCarthyism gripped the Nation. Politicians know that people vote more on the basis of the dramatic than on the basis of logic, or intellectual responsibility. The mass mind moves in the direction of the individual who plays on the emotions, rather than toward the individual who seeks solutions to complex social problems. This complicates the role of the individual who seeks to be a leader in our society. Because of the prevailing conditions in our political arena, the real leader must combine the role of art and feeling with intellectual responsibility and ethical commitment to a free society. Since communication is always bound up in the feeling relations of people, it is not enough that the leader be ethically committed to the human cause, or that he be of high social intellectual responsibility. Here is the reason why so many university professors fail in the classroom, and why we need a three year doctoral teacher education program, and a degree to parallel the present Ph.D. Of recent years we have come to realize that emotional maturity is as fundamental in human progress as is the role of intellect."

"Ron," commented Ricardo, "while I agree with you in all respects about the role of leadership in our society, you must be aware of how difficult it will be to bring about the changes which you deem necessary for the common good. Another aspect of leadership in our society involves an identification of the crucial issues which are fundamental to our ethical commitment and intellectual responsibility. How would you identify them?"

"The question that you have raised, Ricardo," said Ron, "is of greatest importance, especially in dealing with role of the state university. In some respects we have a common sense knowledge of what they are, but we do have a compelling need for the knowledge of the research scholar and the scientific mind. As of now, from what I have learned in my research, and from my teaching, I would list the following issues. In doing so, I recognize that the underlying priority is what individuals seek to know in order that they may believe, in contrast with the orthodox dogma of belief before knowing. In dealing with these issues, how can one doubt the need for the quality leadership necessary for a society of free men and women? 1. Population control. 2. Energy Resources Development. 3. Reordering of Our Economy. 4. Reordering of Our Political System. 5. University Teacher Education Proram. 6. One World Community. 7. Protection of Our Environmental Resources.

"While each of these issues is interconnected with all the others, each is fundamental to the GENERAL WELFARE. While each issue involves a long-time adventure, it is fundamental to the common good of all mankind. Since some of these issues have been discussed in our previous sessions, they do not need further discussion. Comments are needed on some of the others. First, let us look at the issue of Population Control. Here we have a need that grows increasingly critical with every passing year.

"At one time in the history of the race of man, growth in population was necessary for the survival of the tribe. Tribal wars, starvation and disease were an everyday threat to human survival. Within each tribe, there was one or more individuals who provided the leadership necessary for continued tribal existence. This leadership was provided by the warrior, the medicine man, the wise old patriarch, or the scribe. As these patterns of leadership were developed, they became a vital part of tribal existence. So much so that today they have a value that is detrimental to human welfare, largely because of their power role. What is now needed is creative leadership, the mind that made it possible to increase the food supply of the tribe when Mother Nature no longer could do it alone. Knowledge of how to plant seeds, how to fertilize the soil, and how to cure the surplus food for future use came in due time, as well as how to control the deadly diseases which destroyed the physical body. Unfortunately, along with the advancement of knowledge that was used for constructive ends, there was the knowledge that was used in the art of war. Since man, over the many centuries of time, had been conditioned to the killing of his fellow man, this new knowledge was used, not only for the killing of animals for food and tribal protection, but for human sacrifice. Christian nations of the Western world, during the past two thousand years, have demonstrated how easy it is to justify mass killing in the name of human brotherhood, justice, and mercy.

"It is during the past three hundred years, however, that the new knowledge has made possible such an enormous growth in population, a growth that threatens the very existence of man, both socially and biologically. If population control does not become a common practice in all the countries of the world, massive starvation and atomic warfare are inevitable. Much of such starvation is with us on the continents of Asia and Africa and Latin America, but what we have today is only a sample of what lies ahead if man does not make a revolutinary change in population growth. In this respect a new type of religious leadership is in order around the world. Dogmatic authoritarian religions must give way to an ethically committed scientific social attitude, which today can come only from the Western world."

"Ron," said Ricardo, "I can see why you are so committed to the belief that the state university which, in its origin had a commitment to mankind, has failed to live up to its responsibility."

"Ricardo," said Ron Jervis, "I have one more interview in this connection, and that is a visit to our Dean tomorrow morning. It is my sincere hope that he will, in some way or other, try to bring about a major change in our teacher education program. In doing so, it will be necessary for him to work with President Forester to bring about a university teacher education program for all university professors."

"Ron," replied Ricardo, "in these respects I wish you well. Now that we have a new Dean, it may well be that you will get a positive reception."

That evening, before retiring, Ron Jervis talked enthusiastically with his wife on what he expected to say to Dean Carlyle about the reordering of the teacher education requirements and including in such a change requirements for a program of training for all university professors. Now, he was more aware than he had been at his last interview of our creative potential to meet the growing world challenge. We had the technology and the resources to bring about a major revolution in the reordering of the pattern of our national life, toward the well-being of all mankind. If we could only get enough creative minds in the university faculty, the hope for a new world order could become reality. Just think, it could begin on our campus!

The new Dean of the College of Education was a long-time friend of Ron Jervis and very sympathetic to the role of the Cultural Foundations of Education in the teacher certification program. He was not a brilliant man, in respect to his creative intellectual potential, but he knew how to delegate authority and to communicate with his faculty. As Ron walked into his office that morning, he was greeted with a smile and a handshake, which was the Dean's way of expressing his friendship to the members of his faculty.

"Ron," said the Dean, "it is good to have you drop by for a visit, and especially so since I have for sometime wanted to congratulate you on your success with your graduate program. As I understand from our telephone conversation, you wanted to discuss with me an issue related to our teacher certification program. I am sure that you know that our teacher certification program is tied to certain specific state regulations, though we do have control over the requirements for the degree Bachelor of Education."

"Yes, Dean," replied Ron Jervis, "I am aware of the differences between the state certification program, and the Bachelor of Education Degree. My major interest, however, is not only in what goes into the education of the teacher for public school service but in the development of a doctoral teacher education degree for our university faculty. I have discussed these matters with President Forester and find him very sympathetic with my thinking. I am very pro-research in respect to the university's role in society, but you know as well as I do that being a good research scholar does not necessarily make for a good teacher. There is a significant difference between teaching what is known and trying to discover the unknown. Teaching involves a quality of communication between two or more individuals, whereas research is a matter of creative individual endeavor. Subject matter specialization is vitally important to the research scholar, but the role of teaching should be centered on the growth of the mind of the free citizen. Here the leadership role of the professor becomes paramount."

Professor Jervis," said Dean Carlyle, "President Forester has spoken to me about your interview with him and, in doing so, expressed the hope that you would discuss the matter with me. It is good that you should bring the matter up at this time, and especially so while my visit with the President is fresh on my mind."

For over a period of two hours, Ron Jervis and Dean Carlyle discussed the problem of the role of the teacher in a free society, and especially the significance of leadership in the teacher education program, not only at the public school level, but especially for the university professor who operates in the classroom.

"As you are aware of the fact, Dean Carlyle," posed Professor Jervis, "teacher education throughout our Nation has been adversely criticized for being little more than trade training. The enrollment records of the university tend to support this criticism, in that the poorest students, academically speaking, enroll in the Colleges of Education. This, can in part be attributed to the low salaries of teachers in our public schools, but also because we seem to be more concerned with numbers than with quality performance. Personally speaking, I think that we should forget about numbers and concern ourselves with quality teaching, but the state legislatures won't let us. This confronts us with a major dilemma. We cannot expect the support of the Faculty of the Arts and Sciences Colleges in the development of a doctoral program in teaching unless we raise our standards in the Colleges of Education."

"Professor Jervis," replied Dean Carlyle, "what you are saying is all too true and, although there are political reasons which tend to interfere with our overall responsibility to the GENERAL WELFARE, I think that we must take the bull by the horns and move ahead as our minds dictate. As a doctoral major in the field of Public School Adminstration, I know how serious these limitations are when it comes to the education of public school adminstrators. It is in many ways our fault that our public school adminstrators care more about management than about leadership in a free society. We have let power politics dictate our educational practices. It is time that we take the lead in determining the future course of public education in this country."

"Ron," continued the Dean, "by definition, higher education should deal with ideas and the significance of ideas for the future of mankind. Here is where we have betrayed the founders of this Nation. Today, our national crisis has become so demanding that we can no longer shirk our professional responsibility. To achieve the necessary result, which is to provide able free-minded teachers and school administrators for our public schools, we must organize for power. I for one, along with your help, will seek to bring about a major reform in the requirements for teaching in our public schools and in our state universities. At the same time, I will seek to bring about a selective admissions policy in the College so that only those who show high promise as community leaders will be allowed to continue toward graduation. No longer will we pass the buck to others, or labor in the illusion that it is democratic for students to determine the content of our courses. Get out of our rut we will; and, in doing so, let us welcome wholeheartedly the turmoil that we are bound to create. If a new age is upon us, let it be the age of free men and women in a free society."

When Ron Jervis arrived home that afternoon he was feeling like a born-again professor. A new world seemed to be opening up for him, one in which he would find a place for his creative mind and for his surplus energy. He reflected back on the years he had spent, first as a boy working in a Greek restaurant in order to be able to go to high school, and then as a public school administrator and teacher, trying to get himself established as a leader in the public school program. His years as a college teacher had not been easy ones, for these were the years of the Great Depression. He vividly remembered the time when he drove over the mountains of

Pennsylvania, in ice, snow, and fog, from one community to another, trying to help upgrade the quality of teaching in the public schools. Then there came the opportunity for a university professorship on a state university campus in the Midwestern part of the Nation. At first, the job was challenging and personally satisfying; but then old Hardbutt had become Dean of the College, and a new struggle had set in for him. Had it not been for a number of his friends, the struggle would have been self-defeating. In the long run it was his graduate students who had provided him with the genuine satisfaction which comes to every progressive-minded teacher, and the feeling had continued into his present position.

At this point Ron Jervis, in his most creative and intuitive sense, expressed his allegiance to that creative universal force that had so markedly been a part of his entire conscious life, that force which had made it possible for him, both in body and in mind, to be a free man; and, as he believed, a leader in the field of human progress. What was ahead for him he could only hope, but he did know, from his past experience, that he would give every situation the best that he had, and that is all that could be asked of anyone. As far as he could tell, from personal experience and from his knowledge of the evolution of the mind of man, only a small percentage of individuals were born to lead, to move out in front of the masses of mankind, to be creative in the areas of life, areas of music, painting, exploration, and especially in the realm of social thought. If such is not so, why in looking over the vast thousand years of man's history had there been only the few such as Socrates, Confucius, Lao-tse, Jeremiah, Plato, Einstein, Aristotle, Leonardo da Vinci, Shakespeare, Benjamin Franklin, Ralph Waldo Emerson, Walt Whitman, John Dewey, Voltaire, Homer, Tacitus, Tachowski, Sibelius, Goethe and a host of others? Why in his own family had not one of his grandfather's or grandmother's children or their children, other than himself, sought the light of a new day in human development and in human thought? The key to all this human endeavor was the OPEN MIND.

CHAPTER VII

COMMERCIALIZED ATHLETICS: A CANCER IN THE BODY POLITIC OF THE UNIVERSITY

Over a period of years, actually since his first year of teaching, Ron Jervis had been concerned about the relation between the physical well-being of the individual and that of the GENERAL WELFARE of the Nation. More and more, he had come to the conclusion that the massive trend of the people away from the farm to urban centers of living had created a major problem of personal adjustment. There was, in addition to the mental aspects of the problem, the matter of health and physical well-being. How should the public school deal with this increasingly troublesome condition?

On the university level, Ron Jervis had become convinced that the problem was essentially one of leadership; whereas, on the public school level, the problem centered on the need for a sound body and a sound mind. It was the failure of the state university to provide quality leadership for the public schools that had contributed to the failure of public education as an instrument for the GENERAL WELFARE. It was on this point that Ron Jervis had a meeting with his friend Lynn Edwards, a Professor in the field of Physical Education, on an afternoon following a heated discussion at the faculty meeting on whether or not prospective teachers should be required to take at least two courses in physical education for certification.

"You know, Ron," said Professor Edwards, "I think that our colleagues in the Curriculum Department are concerned with nothing more than the methodology of how to teach a given subject. The end result, however, is that they don't give a damn about how the kid functions in the community, or about the GENERAL WELFARE OF THIS NATION. Under such conditions, the future does not look bright for any of us. As for myself, there is no alternative to having a sound mind in a sound body if we as a nation are to survive."

"Lynn," said Ron Jervis, "I appreciate the interest that you have shown in the work of the Cultural Foundations Department, and I am sure that you are aware of the fact that I make a clearcut distinction between the work of your Department and the binge our state universities are on when it comes to commercialized athletics. I would say that the efforts of your Department have great educational significance, but, as to the role of our athletic teams, I put them in the category of commercialized entertainment. Unfortunately, such commercialized entertainment has led the public to forget the true function of the university and to become so emotionally involved that academic excellence is no longer important in the rating of an institution. Personally, I see a direct relation between the weakening of the quality of public education and the growth of commercialized athletics. Our situation has become so critical that I would say that our athletic programs have become a CANCER IN THE BODY POLITIC OF THE UNIVERSITY."

"That is rather strong language, Ron," replied Lynn Edwards. "You are sure to get a great deal of backfire from the public if your thinking on the issue becomes well known. Such thinking will be especially counteracted by a howl from both students and alumni. I gather from what you have just said that you think these programs are tending, not only to undermine the overall purpose of this University, but to having a very deleterious effect on the public high school."

"Exactly so, Lynn," replied Ron Jervis. "There is a deep-rooted learning problem in how these athletic programs affect the mind of the student, especially in their relation to student interest and social purpose. The problem has a complexity about it in that, when it comes to financial support of the total university program, the alumni are a major factor. The larger and more important question, however, is whether or not, because of the increasing power role of the athletic programs, there is a tendency to undermine the primary function of the state university, namely, leadership responsibility in the life of this Nation."

"There is no doubt in my mind, Lynn," said Ron Jervis, "that such is the case. The fundamental role of this university is in the realm of creative thought, the only source to which a free society can turn for realizing the intellectual and ethical components on which a civilized society can operate."

"Are you saying, Ron," asked Lynn, "that there has been a decay in the ethical underpinnings of our society, and that the growing trend in commercialized athletics has contributed to this trend, not only in the operations of the state university but in our culture? By ethical underpinnings, I assume that you refer not only to our personal well-being, but to a concern for the welfare of our fellow man."

"Yes Lynn, exactly so," replied Ron Jervis. "Today, we find ourselves in grave need for reviving the spirit and sense of purpose which made these United States the envy of the world. This spirit and sense of purpose will not be revived as long as our efforts and interest are directed toward high-powered athletic contests, cheap movies and meaningless television. Note the nature of the athletic contests. In an effort to defend these operations, we are told that they develop sportmanship, team spirit, loyalty, and a sense of personal responsibility. All of this defense is nothing more than a coverup of the detrimental intellectual and ethical effects of their operations. In these respects, the physical education program not only does a better job, but affects a great majority of the students; whereas the athletic program involves only a handful."

"Ron," said Lynn Edwards, "what bothers me most about these commercialized athletic programs is related to what you have called a coverup of the effects of their operations. Having been a high school coach for a period of seven years, I can tell you that commercialized athletics are not only affecting the quality of education in our universities, but they are also wrecking the educational efforts of the high school teacher. Sadly enough, this craze has even penetrated the Junior High School. In each case, the situation is so bad that the values and purposes for which the high school was established have been forgotten by the school adminstrators, if not by the teachers. Much of the discipline problem now plaguing these schools is related to these extracurricular activities. The boys and girls, especially the boys who are engaged in sport activities have come to think of themselves as BIG SHOTS. They have no interest in books, much less scholarship. Their sole interest is in playing ball, or in avoiding the classroom. Then, there is the hope of a university scholarship and the chance to make a million dollars as a professional. The athlete who is interested in the growth and development of the mind, in becoming a responsible leader in a free society, is by far the exception. Because of the public desire to be entertained, the money boys are directly involved in the promotion of these athletic programs. From time to time, they provide expensive gifts to promote school interest. In turn, competition is built up among the high schools in the state, all to the detriment of the culture and the community. Betting and gambling on the various athletic games are the order of the day. The ground gainers, the home-run hitters, and those who put the most balls in the basket get their pictures in the paper and their acts glorified. Community interest comes to be centered more and more on sport activities. Public values shift. Coaches of the winning teams receive fabulous salaries when compared with the teachers. Principals of the high schools are known to grant special privileges to the young athletes, privileges such as missing classes, being excused for bad conduct, and even being given passing grades when they should have been failed."

"From what you have said, Lynn," replied Ron Jervis, "I think that we have a partial answer as to what is happening to our public schools and why there is a need for their complete overhauling. Recent studies show that one out of every three students graduating from the high school is ill-educated, ill-employed, and ill-equipped to face the future, in or out of college. In these respects, the monolithic high school should be broken up for, if things continue as they now are, we will be promoting a culture of poverty for our young people. Twenty percent of these public school graduates are failing the basic working skills involved in reading and writing. We would be better off if compulsory schooling ended at the age sixteen and if regular classes were attended only one half of the school day, with work study programs of community service carried out on the other half. Above everything else, commercialized athletics should be abolished and replaced by physical education courses. The responsibility for keeping these programs under control rests primarily in the hands of the school administrators. It is most unfortunate that, in our present social crisis, there is such a poverty of leadership at the head of our public schools."

"Ron, in my judgment," said Lynn Edwards, "there are few school administrators who ever think about the ultimate goal of effective leadership in a free society. What I have reference to is the release of the creative potential of teachers so as to tap the real abilities of the students. Far too many school administrators think that once they have been appointed head of a school system, all they have to do is to placate the members of the school board. Few of them ever realize that they have been given the opportunity to provide the kind of leadership so necessary in our present-day cultural environment."

"What you have just said, Lynn," said Ron Jervis, "is especially true when you look at the problem of the relation of the public school to the community. Note that the situation is sure to get worse as the more intelligent and devoted teachers, because of low salaries and working conditions, leave the profession. This tendency is bound to lower the quality of teaching and contribute to a lower grade performance on the part of the students. As I see it, the most critical of all the issues with which we are confronted is that of the lack of a free mind. Robert Oppenheimer expresses the critical nature of our situation in his book *The Open Mind*. The predominance of anti-intellectualism in the American Culture is clearly indicated in the growing tendency to escape from our intellectual and ethical responsibilities. The squandering of our wealth in commercialized athletics, even at the secondary school level, will ultimately create, if it has not already done so, the same cultural conditions that led to the rise of Adolf Hitler in Nazi Germany. Synthetic barbarism is the inevitable product of a nation where there is little or no concern for the GENERAL WELFARE. What a contrast between the eighteenth century AGE OF ENLIGHTENMENT and the twentieth century AGE OF TERRORISM."

"Ron, when you turn to the college level of teaching," commented Lynn Edwards, "the situation is no different. The high quality of mind will continue to turn to the university in spite of the low salaries being paid to the professors, for it is a place of refuge from the marketplace. The fact, however, is that promotion to a full professorship is dependent upon the professor's research publications. As a result, the professor goes his own specialized way, and the student turns more and more to glorified entertainment, which is provided by the football, basketball, and baseball games. As for leadership, the residue is nothing more than a vacuum. At game time, business men, alumni, laborers, and hero worshippers pour into the football stadium, as they did into the Coliseum of Ancient Rome. Ron, from your knowledge of the every day life of Ancient Rome, I assume that you do not look upon this tendency in our state universities with any degree of satisfaction."

"Since I feel so deeply about the matter, Lynn, I would prefer not to get into the matter any further at this time. At a later date, and very soon if possible, I want to take up our discussion where we have just left off."

At home that evening, Ron Jervis turned to his wife to get her reaction to what he and Lynn Edwards had been saying about the cancerous effect of the commercialized athletic programs on the intellectual life of the University, and on the quality of the education efforts of the public schools.

"Helen," said Ron, "I was discussing with Professor Edwards the way in which commercialization of our athletic programs has affected the quality of the efforts of the state universities. It was his opinion that the effect of this commercialization was as detrimental at the high school level as it was at that of the college. Have you found this to be true at your school and in your teaching?"

"Ron," said Helen, "you know up to this time that I have refrained from talking to you about the problems with which I have been confronted in my classroom because I did not want you to think that I was giving vent to some of my personal gripes. But now that you have asked me about some of the problems with which we teachers are facing, I feel free to discuss the athletic issue with you. In the first place, the fact that my principal was a coach before he became an administrator has enhanced our difficulties as teachers, and especially when it comes to dealing with the boys who are on the athletic teams. Since most of the school principals in this state were former coaches, the problems which we teachers face here must be the same as elsewhere. This means that the scholarship interest of our principal is always secondary to his interest in sports. What I know, and what I hear from the other teachers, is the same story. Most of our principals have little interest in scholarship performance. What they want, and what they seek to get, is a chapionship athletic team. Since the salaries of these principlas are dependent upon the success of their athletic teams, they will go to any extreme to make sure that they are a winner. This being the case, you can imagine what we teachers have to put up with when it comes to our dealing with the troublesome athletes. His cultural deficiencies are made evident every time he speaks to the student body, as well as at our faculty meetings. In order to buy the necessary equipment for his athletes (he is not interested in any athletics for the girls), he is constantly cutting our morning classes for assemblies, where he can collect money from the students. If I try to discipline one of his boys for being late to class, he is always ready to intervene. He will not allow us to fail one of his athletes, for that might cause him to loose a game. Also, we are being pressured daily to let these boys out of class so that they can practice for an upcoming game. When I try to talk to these would-be athletes, they respond with an indifferent gesture, and with the comment, 'You talk to the coach.' Frankly, Ron, the situation could hardly be worse. No wonder so many of our older teachers are dropping out of teaching. The effect of such practices on the intellectual and moral fabric of our schools and Nation is appalling."

What Helen had said about the way in which commercialized athletics had penetrated the heart of the high school should be a source of concern to every responsible citizen. Because of such corruptive practice, it is not difficult to understand why college entrance examination scores are going down, and especially in the mathematics and the sciences. Of a truth, we are becoming an anti-intellectual fascist people. These college entrance examinations scores reflect not only a lack of depth in general knowledge but also a poverty of mind when it comes to being able to cope with problems which require even a minimum amount of rationality. This position is sustained by the fact that if it had not been for the formal education provided by the medieval university and by the eight colonial colleges, Western civilization could not have moved beyond the level of the illiterate sixteenth-century European.

Television, as a product of the scientific mind, must be held responsible for our declining capacity to deal rationally with our common problems. Please note that television does not require or encourage thinking in ninety per cent or more of the programs that are presented. All it says is just look and respond to your feelings. Along the same line, few of our people read anything in the newspapers except the headlines or the financial page. The reading of magazines, such as the *Atlantic Monthly* or the *Scientific Monthly*, is limited to an intellectually oriented few. Is it any wonder that our political system functions at the level of thirteen-year-olds? Such being true, you have the answer as to why our political system has failed when it comes to electing intelligent and responsible public officials. Along with the use of television as an advertising media, buying public office has become the common practice of our day.

"Helen," said Ron, "I got the surprise of my life today when I stopped at the gas station to put gas in the car. While I was waiting around, the mechanic on the job, in commenting on our commercialized athletic interests, said, 'Professor Jervis, we don't have a culture, only something borrowed from the different cultures around the world.' Maybe that is why we are so emotional about every thing?"

"Ron," replied Helen, "I had never thought of it in just that way, but your mechanic may have a point. There is nothing in our religion that gives expression to an American heritage. As to a melting pot, we have nothing but a vacuum and a witches' brew to drink from it. We talk of our Revolution, but we never followed through with anything but words."

"Helen," said Ron, "I think that I shall talk to one or more of the football players to see what they have to say about their life and just what they have in mind for the future. What do you think?"

"Ron," said Helen, "I think that you have a good idea, for it will give you the student's point of view on commercialized athletics. Why don't you talk to your daughter's boy friend? He, as you know, is not only tops as a football player, but is said to have a solid professional future ahead of him."

"That is an excellent suggestion," said Ron. "Since we know Steve Hamilton, it should not be difficult to discuss the issue of corrupt athletics with him. What about having him out for dinner some evening, say tomorrow, if possible? My understanding is that Betty has a date with him for eight o'clock. That should give us plenty of time for a discussion, if you schedule the dinner for the hour of six."

The arrangements for Steve Hamilton to have dinner with the Jervis family were left to Betty, who was pleased that her father would want to talk to him. Steve was equally pleased with the arrangements, and arrived at the Jervis home at the appointed time. Ron welcomed him at the door, and, after they were seated in the family room, Ron was first to speak.

"Steve," said Professor Jervis, "I want you to know that I, and I alone, had a personal motive in inviting you to have dinner with us. For some time, and increasingly so in recent months, I have been concerned about the effect of our athletic programs on the ethical and intellectual responsibilities of the state universities. In inviting you for dinner, I did so to get the student's point of view on the matter. You must have done some thinking on the problem, especially so since you have been directly involved in the success of the football team."

"Professor Jervis," responded Steve Hamilton, "I can only speak for myself. You must be aware that there is much controversy and difference of opinion among those of us who are on the athletic teams. There are those among us who think that our activities should be separated from the other departments of the University. When I ask them, however, what place we would have if we were separated from the university as a whole, they cannot give me an intelligent response. Higher education to me is a matter of dealing with those ideas which will help advance the quality of life in our society; whereas football and our other commercialized athletic activities are a matter of skill. As things now stand, everything is so corrupted that, were it not for the public interest, most of you professors would like to do away with the whole business. There was the time, when I was in high school, that I developed the Big Shot attitude, just as many do now. At that time, I gladly accepted the favors that came from our high school principal, the students, and people in the community. Now, I have come to see what it is all about, and have come to realize that most of this athletic business has little educational value. As a matter of fact, the principal of the school, while contributing to his personal glory and status with the school board, did us more harm than good. Entertaining the public is one thing, and education is another. That is why television is capable of doing the student more harm than good. In every instance, our values and our judgment is being distorted.

"The same procedure that prevailed in my high school prevails here, but in a category that is separate and apart from the regular university program. As I understand it, the Athletic Department finances itself through the charges made for attending the games. You know as well as I do why the football coach is paid a higher salary than the university President. Money talks. Actually, we are running a business, a very profitable business, and all under the guise of higher education. Our business, just as it was in the high school, is nothing more than commercialized entertainment. No one is fooling me on that score. As for myself, what I am doing is preparing myself so that I can land a position on one of the professional football teams at a salary in the hundreds of thousands of dollars. Why not? It may appear as greed to you, but the dollar is all that the American people believe in anyway."

"Where do you place your education in the picture that you have drawn for yourself, Steve?" asked Professor Jervis. "Don't you think that a university should be an educational institution rather than a business?"

"Professor Jervis," replied Steve Hamilton, "I finally understand what you are saying. I tend to agree with you, except that, since I did not create the situation, I can only try to fit into it, in terms of my best interests and needs. I see a chance here of making a hell of a lot of money, and I intend to do my best to make it. I am not about to turn down the chance of a lifetime."

"But what about your education?" asked Professor Jervis. "Are you not interested in the development of your mind, in your growth in knowledge, and the world around you, in the problems involved in the GENERAL WELFARE OF YOUR COUNTRY? You must be aware of the growth in unemployment by the peoples of the world. You must look forward to the possibility of marrying and having a family."

"I have thought about what you have said, Professor Jervis," replied Steve Hamilton, "and I am not indifferent about the future of my country. I know that, in the field of entertainment, we appeal to the emotions and not to the intellect. In the sense of monetary exploitation, we have a powerful force working against the cause of public education. In far too many of my classes, however, the emotional life of the student is given little or no consideration. My argument is that, if you neglect the feelings of the student, you neglect the growth of the mind. I know that the great majority of the athletes don't give a damn about the growth of the mind, and do not even read one book a year; but you know as well as I do that far too many professors don't give a damn about the welfare of this Nation. The fact that so many students would rather get an A on a course by cheating rather than a B which has been earned, has something to do with the environment in which we live."

"Steve," asked Professor Jervis, "do you know, as a matter of fact, that many of our students, as well as the athletes, are cheating their way through this University, and that it is quite popular to do so?"

"That is exactly what I am saying, Professor Jervis," replied Steve Hamilton. "As a matter of fact, what I am saying is common knowledge among the students. Why are they cheating? Well, in the absence of any ethical commitment to the GENERAL WELFARE in our culture, cheating has become a game and, because of such, it is very hard for a well-meaning student not to become involved."

"What you are saying, Steve," said Professor Jervis, "comes as a shock to me, although I have been aware of the fact that there has been a general breakdown in our ethical commitment to the Nation. But this business of cheating becoming a game, in which the student gambles for an A grade, is a new wrinkle. What you appear to be saying is that the basic activity of this University has resolved itself into a game. If such is the case, and I fear that you are correct, then we have A GROWING CANCER IN THE BODY POLITIC OF EVERY STATE UNIVERSITY IN OUR COUNTRY. Do you mind telling me, Steve, in what forms this cheating is taking place?"

"Well, Professor Jervis," said Steve, "I can tell you a number of the ways in which this is taking place, and especially as it is related to those of us who are athletes. Since money has become the worshipful God in our culture, much of the cheating is tied in with money payments by students to avoid failing. From time to time a student, in the wee hours of the night, gets into the professor's office and steals a copy of the upcoming examination. He makes copies of this examination and sells them to the other students in his class. A student will sit in on a large lecture class for another student for a given number of dollars. Students who work in the print shop, where many of the examinations are run off, have no difficulty in securing copies of a test. I know of a study where 80 of the medical students said that they had cheated on a course at one time or another, especially when the students thought that the course was irrelevant to their interests. Cases have turned up which show that students have been able to break into a computer room to change their grades. Ready-made research papers are available for any college course, and they are easy to get. Since high grade averages are required to get into the Graduate School, there is considerable pressure on the student to make high grades in all of his courses, regardless as to how he or she gets them."

"Steve," said Professor Jervis, "I have heard that those of you who are in athletics have a means of securing special course assignments which require little effort to secure a high grade. How true is this in our athletic program? I know from my teaching experience, that most of you athletes have difficulty in passing the traditional Arts and Sciences courses."

"Well, Professor Jervis," replied Steve, "I have, by personal choice, taken and continue to take the arts and science courses, but it is true that most of our athletes avoid the courses that require much reading and study. The courses that you refer to are in the Physical Education Department, and involve only a limited amount of physical activity, hitting a golf ball, jumping a rope, jumping a hurdle, running at a certain speed, or playing at tennis. I know of students getting a four-year degree who never read a single book during their four years of college."

By this time Betty had come into the room where her father

and Steve were talking. Noting that the hour was 7 p.m., Betty proceeded to inform them that dinner was ready and that her mother wanted them to move immediately before the dinner got cold. Since hungry men are always ready for a good meal, Ron and his guest moved forward, without further interruption, toward the dining room.

Over the past two months, Ron Jervis had noticed that his good friend Ricardo Martinez was no longer as mentally alert as he had known him to be over the years that he had known him. It was this observation that led him to go by Ricardo's office on the day following his discussion with Steve Hamilton. When he walked into Ricardo's office, he noticed that he was seated at his desk, with his head on his arms, as if he were asleep. As Ron approached him, he raised up and spoke in the manner of a sick man.

"Ron," said Ricardo, "I know that you were right last week when you suggested that I see my Doctor. There is something definitely wrong with my health. I should have gone to see him before now, but there is nothing more that I hate to do than to go see a doctor. This attitude goes back to the time before you came here. It was in 1945, when I was travelling for the Rosenwald Foundation. At that time I had exposed myself to the point of being hospitalized with a severe case of pneumonia. Since I had lost one lung in the early years of my life when I was a boxer, you can imagine the seriousness of my situation. Well, I did recover, but ever since then I have shunned seeing a doctor because the idea of my getting a major illness horrifies me. I just had to wait until the last minute before I could convince myself that I was really sick."

"Ricardo," replied Ron, "I am glad to see that you have finally made up your mind to go see your doctor. You are too important to all of us to lose you. I am sure that your good wife has been equally concerned about you. Modern medical science is not able to solve all of our medical problems, but I would much rather rely on a doctor's judgment than on my own in a case like yours."

"I know that you are correct, Ron," responded Ricardo, "and I now know that I should have gone to see my doctor before now. As for my good wife, she has been after me for some time about my health, and especially my beer drinking."

"Well, Ricardo," said Ron, "I am glad to see that you have made up your mind about taking care of yourself. I must be getting along now. I have a class coming up in a few minutes and I must be ready for that sleepy bunch of students. Do let me know about your condition when you get the word from your doctor."

The next morning when Ron stopped by his friend's office to hear about his health, he was informed that the doctor had put him in the hospital for a series of tests. At this point he picked up the phone and called his wife to see if anything had been reported to her. In talking to her, Ron learned that Ricardo's illness was more serious than he had anticipated. While the doctor was not one hundred per cent sure, he suspected that Ricardo was suffering from a case of the cirrhosis of the liver. That was the reason why he had ordered him into the hospital. The probable cause of the liver condition was due to his drinking large amounts of beer every evening instead of having an evening meal. The doctor had told Mrs. Martinez that if he had come to see him several months prior, he probably could have helped him avoid this illness; but now it was a gamble as to whether he would make it. He had determined to give Ricardo a series of blood transfusions to bring about a revitalization of his liver, but he had doubts that this would work.

On the following day, Ron found the time to visit his friend for, from what he had heard from Ricardo's wife, he was not too optimistic for him. When he entered Ricardo's hospital bedroom, he found his friend Lynn Edwards there. After shaking Lynn's hand, he sat down by Ricardo's bed for a brief chat.

"Well, old friend," said Ron Jervis, "what in the hell are you doing in a place like this? You should be on the firing line with me, whipping away at the power centers of Orthodox Christianity and the dogmatic coporate capitalists."

"Ron," replied Ricardo, "I had no idea when I visited my doctor this morning that he would put me in the hospital. I was hoping that he would give me a few pills and that would be the end of it. You can imagine how shocked I was when he told me that I was a victim of cirrhosis of the liver, and that I had to be placed in the hospital for immediate treatment. If the blood transfusions get my liver going again, I should be out of here by the end of the week. In the meantime, there are some things that I want you to do for me. I do not want my students to suffer because of my illness."

Ron Jervis assured Ricardo that his students would be informed of his illness, and that he should not worry about their interests being taken care of during his illness. Also, he would see to it that any necessary matters would be taken care of by him. After he and Lynn Edwards left, they stopped in the hall for a comment on his condition.

"Ron," said Lynn, "it does not look too good for our friend. I have talked to his doctor about his condition and he tells me that the odds are against him. The blood transfusions are not having the desired effect because of the bleeding from his veins. Also, he is not getting a positive response from the liver; and you know that no one can go on living without a functioning liver."

"I am sure that you are right, Lynn," said Ron, "but I had so much hope for him. I have known few people who have a greater will to live than Ricardo Martinez. Here he lies, at the point of death, and the best of medical science can do nothing for him. He has said to me quite often that he had no intention of retiring when he reached the age of seventy, for his work would be only partially completed. His work is his life. I cannot see him going on otherwise. What a tragedy that such a brilliant man could be so helpless."

Before the week had come to and end, Ricardo Martinez was dead. If there ever was an individual who demonstrated the spirit of democratic freedom, it was this man. He loved his people, and they loved him. This was symbolized by the fact that they insisted on having the new elementary school in their community named after him. At the time that he was Chairman of his Department he willingly sacrificed an increase in his salary for his right to speak up for his people. This was especially true in the way in which he defended their rights, both politically and economically. No university adminstrator escaped his wrath when he was convinced that he had done him wrong. The one major fault which bedeviled his friend was his tendency to substitute his feeling for his intelligence. In all respects, he was one from whom Ron Jervis had learned much. In his death, Ron had not only lost a companion and colleague, but the University, and the United States, had lost much with the silencing of his voice.

After Ricardo's death, Ron Jervis more and more found himself isolated from the affairs of his Department. Now he had become a minority of one, in a Department that was dominatated by a self-centered, incompetent, and power-motivated Chairman. This was reflected in his tendency to play up to the chairman of the Department of Curriculum and Instruction, in total disregard of the interests of the Department of the Cultural Foundation of Education. Also, he in no way indicated a desire to bring about an improvement in the quality of the secondary school, or the quality of university instruction for a free society. Instead, his tendency was to flirt with those of the Philosophy Department. While Ron Jervis did not find Professor Buckley supportive of his point of view, he did note that he was being ignored by the Chairman where his interests were concerned. As long as Ricardo and Ron could work together, it was possible to keep the Chairman from weakening the effectiveness of the Department but, now that Ricardo was gone, the situation changed drastically, and much for the worse. Because of such, Ron Jervis looked forward to his association with his friends in the college of the Arts and the Sciences. This was especially true in his relations with Bill Snyder. At this time, however, his first reaction was to sit down and write a long letter to Frank Ruffner, with whom he had kept in contact all these many years since leaving his former professorship. The letter, in part, read as follows:

"Dear Frank:
"It has been some time since I last wrote you about my reac-

tions as to what is going on here at this University. Unlike the situation which you continue to struggle under, I have no major problems with my Dean (there have been two changes at this level since I came here) or the President. Our President is a man to be admired, although I do not believe that he will be around very long because of his liberal and straightforward way of dealing with the faculty, and the Board of Regents.

"My main problem, as it has developed, is within my Department, where there is, at the present, no sense of unity or purpose. The situation for me has been made even more critical by the death of my good friend Ricardo Martinez. The two young men who have taken over the control of the Department are so power-drunk that they have little interest in anything but personal glory and advancement. What disturbs me most about their power-drunken grab is that they are willing to sacrifice any and every sense of responsibility, to their students, the university, or society in general, in order to achieve their personal ends. They have allied themselves with any force outside the Department that will help them in their common desire. As to the welfare and future of the Department, they could care less. Poor Professor Buckley, he really finds himself left out on the limb.

"Although I am now isolated from the power structure of my Department, I have made a number of good friends in the College of Arts and Sciences. It would be a source of genuine satisfaction to have you here to join in the discussions with us. The more I research the issue on the role of the state university in a free society, the more I am convinced that there has been a gross betrayal of the power structure of the state university by failing to provide an educated leadership for our governmental officials. The tragedy of it all is that our free society can not continue to survive the way our culture of violence is moving. Freedom was never meant to be something which could be handed out on a silver platter. It is more than disturbing to think that we have so abused our golden heritage, that we could believe that freedom consisted of nothing more than giving expression to our corruptive desires, of both body and mind.

"You will recall that on numerous occasions we talked about the place of commercialized athletics in the university program. It was your opinion, as well as mine, that most of the athletes had no interest in a college education, and that their sole interest was to be outstanding in a given sport. All of which raises the question as to whether or not the university would be more successful in its educative efforts if these programs were abandoned. Of recent date, I have become more and more convinced that these athletic games are far more detrimental to our higher education responsibility than we have ever realized. I think that this is true because entertainment has become the means by which our people seek an escape from the reality of their problems. Surely, our athletic games have become so highly commercialized that they serve only the purpose of a training ground for professional sports. Note how much money is poured into an average game. Does it not strike you as significant that the football coach is not only paid a higher salary than the president of the state university, but that he is much better known and appreciated by the people? Frankly, I have become convinced that our athletic programs have become a GROWING CANCER ON THE BODY POLITIC OF THE STATE UNIVERSITY. There is some agreement among those who are most concerned about the future of our country that the major problem facing us is an educational problem. This being so, if we must have these commercialized athletic programs, let us separate them from the university campus, and place them in the trade training schools where they logically belong.

"Take care of yourself, Frank, and let me hear from you as to how you are surviving these years of retirement.

Your Friend
Ron Jervis"

At home that evening, after mailing the letter to his friend Frank Ruffner, Helen handed Ron a copy of a current issue of a well-known national magazine.

"Ron," said Helen, "I think that, in the light of what you have been saying about commercialized athletics, you will find the lead article in this magazine interesting reading. It certainly opened my eyes as to what is going on in our universities."

Ron took the magazine with much interest, and, as he sat down in his reclining chair, he noted that the article to which Helen had referred had to do with a football player in one of the state colleges in California. As he read the article with particular interest, he observed that the young man had graduated without being able to either read or write. How in the world could he have gone through high school, much less through a state college, without the ability to read or write?

"My God, Helen," said Ron, "the situation is much worse than I ever thought it could be, and getting worse all the time. No wonder we are being looked upon by the peoples of other countries as a nation of semi-illiterates. Our greed for money is undoubtedly the cause of the abuses that are being perpetrated by our university athletic programs. It is gross hypocrisy to call these athletic grants scholarships when they are nothing more than handouts to buy high school graduates for their skill and performance on the field. It is now evident that it is not important to even be able to read and write. All of which is enough to make the founders of the state university wonder how we could have sunk so low in intellectual integrity. These abuses cover a wide range of corruptive acts, acts such as forged transcripts, credit for courses which the student never took, mail fraud and bribery violations, credit for summer courses which the student failed, and under the table payments for recruits. But where will it all end?"

"Ron," said Helen, "it will end when we become aware of how much harm this commercialization of our athletes is doing to countermand our efforts to provide a quality educational program at both the high school and college levels of instruction. Note how the football enterprise has become a half-billion-dollar-a-year college sports program. All of which supports your position that we have, in our athletic program, nothing more than a form of commercialized entertainment."

"Helen," replied Ron, "I think we can not leave out the fact that the success of big-time football, basketball and baseball is closely tied in with what goes on in our state universities, especially the ability of the university administration to raise money from the alumni. There is no doubt that the university athletic program has much in common with the overall entertainment business, involving as much as $30,000,000 in network television contracts. Does all of this not prove that college athletics have become big-time business? What is of even greater significance, however, is that this big-time business is involved in scandal, fraud, and wholesale corruption.

"Scandal, fraud, and wholesale corruption are bad enough when you think of our lack of concern for the GENERAL WELFARE; but, when all of this is tied in with the policy of an educational institution, whose historic responsibility is that of education for leadership in a free society, you lay the groundwork for the destruction of all that is true, good, and beautiful in our Nation. If we as a people were intellectually responsible, we would place the responsibility for what goes on in our television programs in the hands of a committee of professional educators, rather than in the hands of those who are interested only in the profit motive. Education should be the controlling factor, not only in the operation of our state universities, but in the operation of our television stations. This would eliminate those whose minds are obsessed with religious dogma, as well as those who would exploit the common good for the purpose of monetary wealth."

"Ron," said Helen, "when it comes to our athletic programs, the coach must assume much of the responsibility for these corruptive practices. His role is that of a power figure in a competitive enterprise, is it not?"

"Helen, you have put your finger on a crucial aspect of this problem," said Ron. "It is a well-known fact that the success of the coach depends more than anything else on his recruitment program. Yet here is where most of the corruption and scandal begins. The process, as of now, is known to involve much that is unethical. Is all of this recruitment carried out for the benefit of the student or the benefit of the coach and his team? The answer to this question is obvious on the face of it.

"If the rules were followed, as they are laid down for the

governance of recruitment, there would be little or no corruption in the administration of the athletic programs, but this is not what happens. While the funds which are provided by the University are called scholarships, you know that, as I have already said, they have nothing to do with the academic process. In many of the recruitments much more is involved than just the student and the coach. More often than not, there are the over-zealous alumni, who are ready to offer an automobile or an under-the-table payment. Trade scouts, not associated with a particular school, are always ready to provide a recruit for a given sum of money. Outstanding prospects, who have graduated from high school, frequently get offers of travel, scholarships for their girl friends, clothes, graduate school money, and even an apartment. Coaches become involved when they want a recruit for a particular position on the team. They have been known to go as far as to seek ways of getting students admitted to the university who are not academically qualified, even to the point of doctoring an academic transcript."

"Ron," said Helen, "I have noticed from my reading about the university athletic programs that girls are becoming more interested in commercialized sports. This is true for the public high school, but it is sure to contribute to a weakening of the academic record. Also, there will be a further breakdown of the educational responsibility of both the high school and the university. Since we, by our nature, are genetically feeling animals, the tendency toward commercialization in athletics will contribute immensely to our escapist cultural tendencies. I am aware of how much our cultural pattern follows that of the Romans. To grow in mind, to become really educated, involves self-discipline, of which we as a people do not seem to have very much. Along with a lack of self-discipline is our growing loss of respect for productive labor. How easy it is to escape into an emotional frenzy when all that we seek is to satisfy an emotional urge."

Ron Jervis slept well that night, tired from a full day of activity at the University. He was glad to be relieved of the fact that he would no longer have to concern himself about what went on in his Department. Why worry about something which you could do nothing about? Now it was clear that the state university, which was supposed to be devoted to the education of leaders for a free society, was being subverted by the cancerous growth of commercialized athletics. He would talk once again to his friend Bill Snyder and see what he thought could be done. This opportunity came the next day at the lunch hour when, after selecting his food, he saw Bill sitting alone at the table which they always occupied.

"Bill Synder," said Ron Jervis, "are you expecting someone, and if not, how about my having lunch with you?"

"Sit down, Ron," said Bill Snyder. "I know that you have something on your mind that you want to talk to me about. I, too, have something that I want to discuss with you, something that has come up in our Department during the past week but which concerns me a great deal. The matter involves two of Coach Adams's best athletes and just what action we should take in the light of their position on the football team."

"What a coincidence, Bill," replied Ron. "It is about the athletic program that I wanted to talk with you, especially on what the faculty should do to curtail the corruptive acts of our athletes which are having a devastating effect on the national standing of this University."

"Yes, Ron," said Bill, "the problem that has come up in our Department is an example of what you have in mind. The Student Conduct Committee has told us that we should recommend to the administration that the two students be expelled. Coach Adams tells us that if we do, it will destroy his hope for an outstanding team this year. Also, that if we do so act, we will gain the enmity of the two most influential members of the Board of Regents."

"Just what did these students do, Bill?" asked Ron. "They must have been extremely rash in their acts to have created such an uproar. It must have had something to do with cheating. Did it not?"

"There is no doubt that their conduct involved cheating," replied Bill, "for they were caught openhanded. There is more to it, however, than a single act. We know that since they entered the university, they have been paying very able students, not only to attend their class-room activities, but to take all quizzes and examinations in their Arts and Sciences courses. Because of the grades they were getting, we became suspicious that dirty work was involved. Last week, at the end of a quiz period, one of our professors called for the students' I.D. cards. Since the cards that were presented did not match the names on the registration sheet, the jig was up for the two boys. Later two students on the football team told the entire story to the Student Conduct Committee. In doing so, they not only confessed to their guilt in the English course, but told the entire story of how they were getting by on their other courses. Also, it came out how the other athletes were getting such high grades. Such means as stealing examination papers from the professors' office, bribing teaching assistants with money, and buying term papers were being used. The shocking part of it is that the students saw nothing wrong in what they were doing. Here we have a coach and his football team on the one hand, and the Board of Regents on the other. What a travesty that this University and its faculty should be subjected to this kind of demoralizing act, an act that threatens the very life of the Nation. What would you do, Ron Jervis, if you were in my position and were confronted with this problem?"

"Bill," said Ron, "I will answer just as Honest Abe Lincoln would have answered, 'Hew to the line and let the chips fall where they may.' This problem boils down to a question of values. If we cherish the concept of the free man and the free woman, above all the whims and threats of a football coach, we have no choice but to expel these two, and all the others who are known to have participated in these corruptive acts."

"Ron," replied Bill, "I agree with you, and will recommend to our faculty that we proceed accordingly. Now, what is it that you had on your mind and wanted to discuss with me? I am particularly interested in why you think that commercialized athletics has become a cancer in the body politic of the university."

Ron Jervis thought for sometime before responding to Bill Snyder's question. "Of recent date, Bill," he replied, "it has become quite evident to me that in looking at our athletic program, and the extent to which money, power, and corruption have taken over university policy, we are being confronted with a total change in what higher education is about, and what our future cultural outlook is to be. Instead of the university serving the GENERAL WELFARE of this Nation by providing the highest quality education for leadership in a free society, it has been captured by the desire to escape from the reality of our time. We have capitulated to the power of those whose minds are enslaved by a desire to accumulate wealth through corrupting entertainment. Today, we are confronted with monumental problems, both at home and abroad, which demand the highest possible constructive thinking, but what are we doing other than using our energy and resources in an emotional orgy on commercialized athletic games? We have joined the mob in the marketplace with the hew and cry of 'Eat, drink, and be merry, for tomorrow you will die.' The change to which I refer has been going on since World War I, but it has increasingly taken over our hearts and minds in the past decade. Since our minds are steeped in Medieval dogma, we find ourselves incapable of confronting the issues of mass unemployment, inflation, overpopulation, growing violence in our urban communities, and a breakdown in our family life. So, instead of having the needed creative, artistic, and scientific mind which is needed for quality living, we have resorted to a cheap form of entertainnmment, cheap in quality but expensive in dollars. By cheap, I refer to our anti- intellectual, sex-oriented, mechanized movies and T.V. programs. Look at our social institutions and see if they are not moving in a self-destructive direction. This cultural malaise indicates the extent to which we are misconceiving our heritage of freedom."

"Ron Jervis," said Bill, "you are not saying that you are against having a Department of Physical Education?"

"On the contrary, Bill," said Ron, "I am very much a supporter of physical education. A healthy body is fundamental to a healthy mind. There is a world of difference between a physical education program which is designed for all the students and a program of commercialized athletics which is operated solely for the glorification of the few. As you know, Bill, the only ones who profit from this commercialization are the coach, the alumni and a few athletes. As I see it, the university athletic program is nothing more than a training ground for professional athletes, nothing more than a money game."

"Ron," replied Bill Snyder, "you speak of our culture as moving in the direction of mass commercialized entertainment, and that this tendency is a result of a desire on the part of our people to retreat from the reality of our day. More specifically speaking, I refer to the problems which have been created by our urban industrialized society. How do T.V. and the movies fit into this situation?"

"Bill," responded Ron, "every serious-minded individual that I know who has commented on the role of T.V. and the movies in our culture has noted how these products of our age of technology are being used almost exclusively as a means of exploiting the human mind. In these presentations, money and vested interests work hand in hand against the possibility of contributing to the growth of the creative mind. A clearcut distinction must be made between commercialized entertainment and the educative process. Also, the way in which the T.V. programs are presented to us gives a picture of the emotional binge that now grips the heart of the Nation. To think of such as being educative is to indulge in the language of a schizophrenic. The purpose of education is not to entertain but to create, and, in doing so, help the individual develop the quality of his mind, along with any other talents that he or she may possess. As for entertainment, the opposite is the case. Here the intent is to play on the emotions, to cause the individual to lose an awareness of self, to become one of the crowd, or to retreat into a dream world of unreality. What is most important about this difference between education and entertainment is the way in which the individual is exploited by the entertainment process, even by dope and alcohol, as well as by big-time gambling and cultural degradation."

"Ron," said Bill Snyder, "now I begin to see why the commercialization of our athletic programs is viewed as a cancer on the body politic of the University. Wherever there is a choice in the minds of the great majority of our people between entertainment or education, entertainment will prevail. This is especially true when there are millions of dollars back of the entertainment activity, whether football or otherwise. When you add the televising of these athletic games to all of this activity, the curse of commercialization is multiplied. From a cultural standpoint, I see this thing in a broader light than just the gambler's money. Not only is the role of the university cast into a distorted corruptive pattern, but our entire free way of life is being ripped into shreds by the use of money as a power weapon."

"Exactly so, Bill," said Ron Jervis. "I am sure that you have noticed the way in which evangelists such as Billy Graham, Oral Roberts, and a host of others get our people to follow them. To see Oral Roberts perform on T.V., you would think that he had been trained in Hollywood. As a ham actor he is on a par with Ronald Reagan. See how he puts on a show — klieg lights and beautifully dressed young women side by side with their male escorts. No wonder gullible and innocent-minded people pour money by the millions into their coffers. While there is little evidence that gamblers have taken over the church pulpits, one can say that such Hollywood practices as those carried out by these evangelists have become one of the best forms of entertainment provided by T.V., especially as an escape from the realities of the everyday world. Even if their followers never get through the pearly gates, which are pictured so dramatically by these pulpit orators, they are left with that good feeling that comes after a refreshing shower.

"Having said all of this about these Christian evangelists, one should not forget what they owe to their illustrious ancestor, Aimie Simple Mcpherson. At the same time, one is left to wonder how much harm this emotional orgasm of the mouth is contributing to our escapist tendencies. In this respect, there is justification for Karl Marx's statement that 'religion is the opium of the people.' People are always willing to pay what the market demands in order to satisfy their emotional urges. What is most disturbing, however, is the fact that such conduct seems to be inherent in the nature of man. This being so, it is not difficult to understand why entertainment is preferable to education. Growth of the human mind seems to come only through human struggle, and such struggle runs in conflict with the organic desire for security and conformity. Creative art has never been an attribute of the great mass of humanity, only of the free-thinking individual.

"What is true today in the field of religion is equally true in the realm of politics. Unfortunately for our economic well-being, our political practices have become the Achilles heel of a free society. As I have said many times in our discussions, politics in our beloved country has never been an expression of the democratic way of life as conceived by Thomas Jefferson. There was in the minds of our Revolutionary Fathers the conviction that by giving the people the right to vote our Nation could avoid the violence, pitfalls, and chaos that in time had taken over other nations throughout the history of man. Unfortunately, this conviction was based upon the assumption that man was a rational animal. Since this assumption has been proven false, our problem is found to be tied in with man's organic emotional nature, which we know to be subject to many forms of exploitation. In politics, as in the field of religion, the real power rests not in the minds of the people, but in those who are able to control the emotions of the voting public.

"Through the use of T.V. and the expenditure of millions of dollars, it is possible for the power sources to elect any candidate who represents the interests of those who exercise the control. This was demonstrated in the elections of both Richard Nixon and Ronald Reagan to the Presidency of the United States. Also, the number of millionaires, elected to the Congress of the United States, and as governors of the fifty states, has increased significantly in the past twenty years. Buying office has become a common practice, for power rests not in the minds of the voters, but in the money that selects the candidate. Without having the ethical commitment and intellectual responsibility which Jefferson deemed fundamental in every candidate, the people are at the mercy of the monied few. Failures in our political life can be traced directly to the same sources as those which are found in commercialized athletics, and in evangelic religion, namely commercialized entertainment.

"In my childhood, I was led to believe that the Ringling Brothers-Barnum and Bailey Show was the greatest show on earth. I no longer hold to such an aberration. While such may have been true when I was a child, the claim can now be taken over by the professional football games, the crusade of Evangelist Billy Graham, or the national conventions of the political parties for the Presidency of the United States. The crocodile tears of the politician and the eternal damnation of the Ministers of God have been on the scene for many centuries, but so has the glorified gladiator, except that today he appears in the form of a muscle-bound commercialized athlete. What has made the difference in today's entertainment, however, is the T.V. and the sex-oriented movie."

"Ron Jervis," said Bill Snyder, "all that you say is very true, but it will be denied vociferiously by the defenders of the status quo. Big money has made the difference in all of these forms of mass entertainment. I do not assume that these forms of entertainment are bad in themselves. What is important, however, is the way in which these practices cast aside, and even belittle, the educational needs of the people. The tie-up between T.V. and the movies with the big money has led to an exploitation of the desires and felt needs of adolescent youth and the poorly educated adults, in both the Arts and the Sciences. Also, there is a connection between this entertainment binge and the mass amount of drug addiction which has invaded our junior and senior high schools. Rock music is an integral part of this invasion. Here are some examples of this emotional binge.

"What we have in rock music is an exploitation of the mind of the adolescent. Take a look at this music. Most, if not all of it, is anti-cultural, an appeal to the rebellious tendencies of our youth, tendencies such as negating parental authority. Also, we note in particular that there is a deliberate exploitation of the natural sex drives of young people. This commercialized exploitation of the sexual urges of the adolescent is at the heart of the gutter approach in all of this music. What is equally deplorable is the attack on the educational needs of youth, the use of bad English, and a glorification of ignorance.

"That all of this emphasis on sex is nothing new is indicated by this quotation which comes down to us from the past. 'You'll ruin me. Le me go now, baby, please do.' The difference, however, is that today we have T.V., the electronic amplifier, mod music, and big money."

"Bill," said Ron Jervis, "a lot of those who are promoting the sale of these junk records will classify us as Victorian moralists, but nothing could be farther from the truth. There are two things about this emotional binge that we are on which concern me very much. In the first place, what we have here in this sexual revolution is a pervasive anti-intellectualism, cultural degradation, and a retreat from the hopes and dreams of those who founded this country. What this trend represents is a trip back to the jungle, to an effort to find happiness in nothing more than physical freedom and sexual aberration. The rapid spread of massage parlors indicates the truth of the assumption that we have a retreat from the responsibility of an intellectually oriented and ethically humane society. Passing moral judgments against those who participate in what goes on in the massage parlors is not an intelligent substitute for an understanding of why we have such a play on the role of sex in our culture.

"In addition to the overwhelming evidence that there is a retreat from the reality of our times, there is the question as to whether or not we have something here that is far worse than primitive animalism. What I have reference to is a loss of respect for the human mind and the physical body. I have nothing but sorrow and pity for those who indulge in the orgy of dope and alcohol. The deaths, both mental and physical, as well as the many bodily injuries which come about from an overindulgence in alcoholic beverages, are not a part of what makes for a free society. In the final analysis, we are brought back to what is happening in our state universities. Are they providing the kind of leadership necessary for a society of free men and women? Have our state universities, in succumbing to the big-time commercialized athletic spree, become only another aspect of our increasingly decadent culture?"

"Ron," replied Bill Snyder, "I frankly do not like to admit it, but I greatly fear that, unless our present cultural trend is redirected, we are in for a period of social turmoil and economic decay. The road ahead looks very dim."

When Ron Jervis arrived at his home that afternoon he found a letter from his friend Frank Ruffner waiting for him. He was so overjoyed in receiving it that he sat down immediately for a reading. Since Helen was equally interested, she asked him to read the letter out loud. The letter went as follows:

"Dear Ron:

"It is always good to hear from you and to note how you are getting along in your teaching. I look forward to the time when I shall retire this coming June. Naturally, I am concerned about how I shall spend the future of my life, possibly in writing and traveling. You can understand my concern on this matter, for both of us have been so busy all of these years that to just sit on our asses is unthinkable. I do have a problem with walking and driving because of a bad case of arthritis. Walking with a cane has slowed me down but, as to mental activity, I am just as alert as I was when you were here. All of which brings me around to my continuing difficulties with Dean Hardbutt.

"After you left here, this bastard of a Dean turned on me more nastily than ever. Fortunately, Our President (the same man as when you were here) has always backed me up when the Dean gets nasty and tries to turn him against me. This has taken the sting out of much of what he has tried to do. What has burned him up, however, is the way my doctoral students have defended me every time he tries to run me down. Of recent date, my graduate students, knowing of my coming retirement, planned a dinner in my honor, at which time they had the President make a speech in my behalf, but, at the same time, failed to invite him. He continues to take dirty digs at you, at which time I point out how you have succeeded in your new position. Also, on each of these occasions, I express my opinion that you were the only real scholar on the College of Education Faculty at the time that you left. This really burns him up.

"The problem of commercialized athletics is as bad here as it is at your institution. We are surely on an entertainment binge in this country, and there seems to be little that we can do about it. I select my graduate students even though Dean Hardbutt objects, and I have no problem with them. It is a different matter when it comes to the undergraduates. I shudder at the thought that most of these students will be going out to teach in the public schools. Since they have been caught up in rock music, the drinking of hard liquor, and sex, they will be teaching more of what they really are than their subject matter. Gone is the dream and hope of those who saw the public school as a means of providing the leadership necessary for a free society. It is because I try to hold these young men and women to a reasonable standard of achievement that the Dean continues to bug me. Poor, power-driven helpless man, how he ever thought of becoming President of this University is an indication of how stupid he is.

"Now to come down to what I have in mind for my first venture after I retire. My new wife, whom you may not remember, but whom you met while she was a graduate student, wants a honeymoon which will take us through your city. At that time, if you and your wife are not away on one of your trips, we would like to stop over and have a visit with you. Also, I would like to meet some of your friends in the University. It would be my hope to discuss with them some of the problems that are so adversely affecting our public schools. One of the problems that increasingly concerns me is that of forced busing. I personally think that this issue presents the most critical challenge that the public schools have faced during this century.

"Keep us in mind, and let us know if you are going to be

around when we come through your city. I know that Helen was very fond of my first wife, just as was everyone else that knew her. Her loss was a great tragedy to me, and it was some time before I was able to get over her death. Fortunately, I was able to find a sweet and knowledgeable woman to take her place. I know that both of you will appreciate her just as much as my many friends do.

"Take care of yourself, Ron, and give our best regards to your dear wife. We hope to be seeing you soon, at which time I will be a free man in my own right."

"Your friend
"Frank Ruffner"

After laying down Frank Ruffner's letter, Ron thought for sometime before retiring for the evening. What a God's blessing it was for him that he was able to get out from under the tyranny of Hardbutt. Poor Frank, it must have been hell for him to have such a power-drunken man on his tail all the time. Things had not been perfect for him, but no position ever is perfect. What a contrast between his years here and those he had spent in his former position. Those years had not been wasted, however, for he had learned much about how a university is operated and had, inspite of the cussidness of some of his former colleagues, made many good friends. He well remembered his fine graduate students. Also, a number of things had happened here which were beyond his control, and for which he was not responsible. First, there was the death of his friend Ricardo Martinez. How well he remembered that it was he that was responsible for getting him to move. There was no doubt in his mind that the change was a wise one, not only because it removed him from the domineering character of Hardbutt, but because he had found his new environment much more open and less culturally restrictive. It was more than interesting to compare his new environment with that which prevailed in his previous position. The outlook of the two universities was reflected in the cultural differences between the two states. In the former community there was much of the carry over from the culture of the Old

South; whereas here there was much of the frontier spirit of the West, and that of the Mexican American. In the former university the rural communities so dominated the state legislature that to get support for the needs of the students and faculty it had to be expressed in terms of agricultural interests.

In his present position, Ron had found the State Legislature entirely under the control of those who were responsible for the state's industrial development. Since science and technology were paramount to industrial development, the University had received wide support in the fields of Chemistry, Physics, and Engineering. This practice had resulted in a tendency to diminish the significance of the Humanities, and this Ron Jervis deplored. In terms of human welfare, the exact opposite should have been the case. Since rural life was predominantly made up of Mexican - Americans, there was little of rural influence in the legislature. Poor Ricardo, he had fought so hard during his professional life to help correct the injustices that had been heaped upon his people. What concerned him most, as he thought of the recent developments affecting life on the university campus, was the way student life was being dominated by the growing influence of commercialized athletics. He knew that he and a significant number of the faculty were becoming increasingly unpopular with the students because of their outspoken criticism of the trend toward commercialized entertainment on the university campus.

There was no doubt that this trend was having a negative influence on the intellectual life of both the high school and the state university. He was not objecting to the kind of entertainment which served a positive purpose in taking the mind of the student off those things which disrupted the normal everyday activities on the campus. But worthy use of leisure time, as the great Aristotle held it to be, was not to be an escape from the realities of the world. Rather it was to be a pursuit of excellence and contribute to the growth of the mind of the individual. As for commercialized athletics, it had become increasingly evident that, not only was it an escape from reality, but, in addition, it was having a corruptive influence on the ethical character of the student as well as the body politic of the people. Such being the case, if the trend continued, how could a free society possibly survive?

It was with this thought in mind that Ron Jervis, at the hour of one a.m., finally made his way to bed. Although he made every possible effort not to awaken his wife, he was not successful in doing so. As he climbed into the bed, she opened her eyes, and sleepily commented with the words "What are you doing up at this hour?"

"Helen," said Ron, "now that you are awake, I cannot help but note the way in which the College of Education Faculty has been made to bear the brunt of the failure of the public school to provide a satisfactory education for the nation's welfare. Why can't the public see that the problem is rooted in our culture pattern, and especially in our high-powered commercialization of every aspect of our everyday life? I am very critical of the limitations of the so-called Education Courses, as you well know, but why do so many professors in the College of Arts and Sciences hold that public school teachers are incompetent because of their Education Courses, when more than eighty percent of the courses that are required in teacher certification are in the Arts and Sciences? You would think that, of all people, those who teach in the Arts and Sciences would seek for an answer in the culture and in their own failures, rather than to pass the buck on to someone else. What is missing, as I have said to you many times, is an ethical and intellectually responsible frame of reference, subject matter and the science of methodology would both be significant to achieve our common purpose."

"Ron," said Helen, "I am much too sleepy to understand what you are saying. Tell me again tomorrow and maybe I will know how to respond."

Following these comments, Helen drifted back to sleep and Ron, feeling much the same way, followed shortly thereafter.

CHAPTER VIII

EPILOGUE

Now that Ron Jervis and Bill Snyder have retired from the University, they are no longer forced to conform to university administrative policy, but are free to think and to act in accordance with their professional interests and personal needs. Although past the age of seventy years, Ron has no intention of retiring from his life interest, that of THE ROLE OF THE STATE UNIVERSITY IN A FREE SOCIETY. Now free from the required routine of teaching, he is still aware of the fact that university professors are as interchangeable as bricks.

How could a man like Bill Snyder, who had devoted more than forty years of his life to this University, be so easily ignored by the administration and by his colleagues? At no time since his retirement had they called him for an important meeting, or about making a contribution to the critical problems facing the institution. This practice of ignoring retired professors also was being experienced by Ron Jervis. Why did the administration fail to profit from or capitalize on the wealth of experience of those who were being retired after a lifetime of teaching? Surely the growth of mind which came from fifty years of teaching and research in four state universities had some educative significance. In the retirement of himself and Bill Snyder, there was a gross example of the waste of human experience.

As well as of simple mind, who engage in a belief that college professors are as interchangable as bricks, there are those of deeper insight who are devoted to the cause of human welfare. We now know that the evolution of the human race to a higher order of freedom and justice is a result of the advancement of knowledge and the development of an ethical sense of responsibility. This is the faith on which our Nation was founded, and whose living reality was to be sustained by the educative process. It is this faith that is being betrayed because of a conformity to dogma and a worship of material things.

On what grounds has such a harsh statement of betrayal of the faith on which this Nation was founded been made? At this point, Ron Jervis found it necessary to turn to the historical documents where the ideas to which our Revolutionary Fathers had committed themselves were recorded. By examining these documents he could reinforce the judgments by which he had lived and taught all of these years.

Just why was the American state university established? The major sources to which Ron returned were those which dealt with the University of North Carolina, the first of such institutions, founded in 1779. In the North Carolina Constitution of 1776, he found the clause which states that "all useful learning shall be duly encouraged in one or more universities." Governor Martin followed up this clause in 1784 by calling for "the continued development of a state university," but it was William R. Davie, an Englishman by birth and a devout Deist, who took the initiative in promoting the institution. At a meeting of the State Legislature in 1789, Davie introduced a bill calling for the establishment of a state university.

Davie's bill was passed by the legislature on December 11, 1789, with the provision in the Preamble of its Charter calling for a university which would fit the rising generation "for an honorable discharge of the social duties of life." The significance of the term "the social duties of life" should be doubly emphasized. All of the previous eight colonial colleges in the thirteen HAD BEEN MODELED AFTER THE MEDIEVAL EUROPEAN UNIVERSITY, and were controlled by Protestant denominations. Now the people were to have a university which was a child of the American Revolution, and an institution devoted to the education of the leaders of free-thinking governments, local, state, and national.

The provisions of Davie's bill called for forty trustees who were to handle all the funds and property of the university in special trust and confidence. These funds were to be paid over to the State Treasury, from which the university was to receive notes bearing six percent interest. The trustees were to meet in the following year to choose a President, a Secretary, and a Treasurer, and to select a meeting place for the next annual meeting. The trustees were given the power to hire and fire the President of the University, the professors, and the tutors, and to make all the rules for regulating and governing the institution. Hugh Williamson, Doctor of Medicine from the University of Edinburgh and friend of Benjamin Franklin and Thomas Jefferson, said of this Charter that it was passed for the purpose of promoting civic liberty, for "ignorance in the subjects and despotism in the rulers go hand in hand, and there never has been a nation which preserved the semblance of freedom WITHOUT BEING ENLIGHTENED BY THE WAYS OF SCIENCE."

On November 1, 1790, Davie addressed a letter to Governor Martin pleading for his assistance in establishing the state university in a country which was just forming its manners and government. Governor Martin in return appealed to the State Legislature saying that the university, which was to be ereacted for the cause of humanity, would do honor to the Southern states if it had the proper support by nurturing youth in TRUE RELIGION, SOUND POLICY AND SCIENCE,

AND MEN OF ABILITIES DRAWN FORTH TO FILL THE DIFFERENT DEPARTMENTS OF GOVERNMENT WITH REPUTATION. As a result of these efforts, a loan of $10,000 was granted by the legislature for the purpose of purchasing the land and the erection of the first building on the campus.

Following the purchase of a site on which to erect the buildings, the trustees, in arranging for a seal of the University, CHOSE THE FACE OF APOLLO, THE GOD OF INTELLECT, AND HIS EMBLEM THE RISING SUN as an expression of the dawn of a new concept of higher education in the Nation, "conceived in liberty and dedicated to the proposition that all men are created free and equal." In honor of the first civilized American, they named the main street of the new town Franklin Avenue.

On October 1, 1973, with the laying of the cornerstone of the first building, Dr. Samuel McCorkle, in giving the address of the day, spoke of science and learning as the great means of assuring the happiness of mankind, and then went on to say;

"Britons glory in the name of Newton....Americans glory in the name of Franklin....Knowledge is liberty and law. When the clouds of ignorance are dispelled by the radiance of knowledge, power trembles, but the authority of law remains inviolable."

Ron Jervis was delighted with the fact that the evidence he had been able to bring to light fully supported what he had been saying about the way in which those who had been given the responsibility of promoting the state university had, in time, engaged in an outright betrayal of those who had founded the institution. Now he was ready to present to his friend Bill Snyder the evidence that he had questioned him about. At this point he picked up his phone, called his friend, and arranged to have lunch with him on the following day.

When Ron Jervis presented to Bill Snyder the evidence on the origin of the state university, Bill's response wss one of genuine commendation. "You know, Ron," said Bill, "I never doubted your statement about the origin of the state university, but I must say that the evidence which you have presented is overwhelmingly conclusive. What do the records show as to the kind of curriculum Davie set forth to attain his objective?"

"That too, Bill," replied Ron, "he spelled out in some detail. Of the five professorships which were to be established, ONE was to be in Moral and Political Philosophy and History: ONE was to be in Natural Philosophy, Astronomy and Geography: ONE was to be in Mathematics; ONE was to be in the Philosophy of Medicine, Chemistry, Agriculture and Mechanics; and ONE in the languages. Science, English, and History, were to constitute the core of the curriculum. The Classics, although offered, were to be one of the electives."

"What amazes me, Ron," said Bill Snyder, "is the clearcut distinction which Davie made for the education of the leaders of our several governments, as contrasted with the Latin and Greek requirements for the education of the ministers of God. As I recall, Harvard did not give up these requirements until the latter part of the nineteenth century."

"That is true, Bill," said Ron. "What you note here is that the medieval liberal arts program, with its core in Latin and Greek languages, was designed to train the leaders of the Protestant faith; whereas Davie's program was definitely of the Age of Enlightenment. The way in which we seek security in religious dogma and satisfaction in material things is a clear indication of how we have turned away from the enlightenment sought by the founders of our Nation."

"Ron," commented Bill Snyder, "when you go to the very heart of these subject matters listed by Davie, what concepts concerning the nature of reality, and especially of man, were in conflict with the Protestant theologians?"

"The differences, Bill," said Ron, "are very clear. Let me outline some of these differences for you.

"1. Natural religion was to replace the supernatural medieval religion.

"2. Educational efforts in the state universities were to be closely identified with the present order of life, rather than life after death.

"3. Science was to become the divine force in everyday living, as understanding through knowledge took the place of divine worship in blind faith and ignorance.

"4. Happiness would come to mankind as creative free play in a world of reality took the place of the slave tradition in Christian dogma.

"5. Experimental philosophy was the only way to mitigate human suffering and multiply human enjoyments, for no restitution could be found in magic, miracles, and the Doctrine of Revelation.

"6. True religion would come with the advancement of science, not through pulpit oratory.

"7. Only those moral principles which were reasonable and natural should be retained.

"8. Science was the manifestation of the real power of God, not man's speculation about the nature of reality.

"9. Man was not evil by his nature, but a creature who had potentiality for the common good.

"10. The BIBLE, far from being the word of God, was only the writings of a limited number of Jewish scholars.

"11. Freedom of mind was fundamental to the development of the human race.

"12. People must have the freedom to worship God in their own way.

"13. Priests and ministers of God were only common men whose knowledge was limited by their everyday experience and formal education.

"14. The dignity and worth of man's life on this earth were to be glorified, not cheapened and reviled AS WAS HELD BY THE CHURCHMEN.

"15. Every individual had the right to a free public education in order to develop his or her talents."

"I see, Ron," said Bill, "that you are well versed in the nature of the conflict that has plagued our country these last two hundred years. How do you account for our having made so little progress in the field of human relations?"

"Bill," replied Ron, "when you stop to think on how the mind of the Western World has been steeped in Christian dogma, I think that you can understand why so little progress has been made on the dreams and hopes of our forefathers. The shame of it all is that the great ethical commitments which have come down to us from the Jewish Prophets have been so tied to religious dogma that they have been made worthless, or have been used to justify the wielding of acts of tyranny over the minds of millions of human beings. Please note that the Jewish people have suffered as much as Christians in that they too have been bound to their dogma of Zionism. If those who are tied to such dogmas could only realize that there is no hope of achieving their ethical commitments except through the rational scientific humanism of Franklin and Jefferson. It is at this point that the failure of the state university is so glaringly evident. Note how we have come to think of religious freedom as a right to be a slave to the dogma of a medieval religion. Note how all of these religious dogmas have led us to the brink of a Holy War with the communist U.S.S.R. rather than helping us to understand why Communism came to the Western world. It is significant to observe that our people want the products of science but negate the SCIENTIFIC MIND. Why? Because of the failure of the state university to provide us with a leadership that would replace the control which the ministers of God have held over the minds of our people since 1607."

"Ron," said Bill Snyder, "I have no difficulty in agreeing with your premise that the minds of our people are operating in the same pattern of religious dogma as that of the period before the American Revolution. In so agreeing, I am sure you will admit that many significant changes have taken place in our culture since that time. My problem is, just why have these changes not changed the general pattern of our thinking?"

"You raise an intriguing question, Bill," said Ron. "As I see it, individuals do not always profit from their experiences. Also, regardless of the fact that those of Christian faith have worthwhile personal motives, they are because of the nature of their indoctrinated minds, incapable of identifying themselves with that knowledge which is necessary for a solution of the problems that have come about as a result of the urbanization of our everyday life. The intellectual history of the Western world so indicates. The concept of the Man-God, as delineated in the BIBLE, had its origin in the intuitive nature of man, and should be so understood. You could say that those who wrote the biblical scrolls had a love for the creative art act, but the converse is true of our people today. Instead of a love for creative activity, our people want to be entertained at the lowest possible anti-art level. The truth of this statement is indicated in a poll taken of who is most admired by our people. The results not only placed Burt Reynolds at the head of the list but, of the first thirty-five named, all were either movie actors and actresses or professional athletes. Not a single scientist or member of our intellectually oriented professions was represented. Man can not continue to grow mentally without a deep religious sense, but the deification of this religious sense has negated the hope of a continued development of the human mind.

"Learning is never easy. It is almost impossible for the mind that has been molded into a rigid pattern to appreciate the joys of freedom to learn and to create. Statistical evidence is available to support this conclusion. Changes in the natural conditions around us, if they do not bring on a destruction of the self, do provide a gateway to human progress and the growth of the mind of man. Such were conditions in the Western world after the year 1000 A.D. which led to a concern for the second of the triad of human growth, that of the Man-Object relation. Creative-minded historians have pointed out, in such scholarly works as that of H.O. Taylor, THE MEDIEVAL MIND, how the fresco figures on the crown of the walls of the great cathedrals changed from gargoyle, mystical symbols to those representing the objects of nature. The crisis in this shift, from the mystical to the natural, laid the basis for the modern scientific approach to human life. This is indicated in the publication of the Copernican DE REVOLUTIONARIBUS ORBIUM COLESTIUM. Joining Copernicus in these new endeavors were men such as Galileo, Kepler, Harvey, Newton, and Priestley. The response of the dogmatists was bitter and violent. Bruno, the interpreter of Copernicus, was burned at the stake by order of the officials of the Catholic Church. Galileo was called before the Pope at

Rome and forced to recant on his telescopic findings. Servetus was burned to death with green wood by the order of John Calvin. Martin Luther called Copernicus a fool 'who wanted to turn the whole world of astronomy upside down.' Despite these manifestations of the power of the Christian dogmatists, the movement toward the development of the PHYSICAL SCIENCES has continued to our present day. It is worthwhile to note that it was this scientific movement which, during the course of the nineteenth century, made it possible for us to become the most powerful nation in the world."

"Ron," said Bill Snyder, "the analysis which you bring to bear on the significance of the MAN-GOD relation, as a frame of reference in our Western culture, with that of the MAN-OBJECT relation posits a real problem for the present-day university professor. On the one hand we have Christian dogma which, in spite of the development of the physical sciences, still holds sway over the great majority of the minds of the people of the Western world; and on the other hand, we have the dogma of the Communist which is an outgrowth of the MAN-OBJECT relation. It is this situation, what with the development of the neutron bomb, that provides the opportunity for a HOLY WAR and the wiping out of our Western civilization."

"Yes, Bill," replied Ron Jervis. "Our situation is indeed perilous. We have two theological dogmas competing with each other. Today Communism, in the U.S.S.R., is so devoted to the physical sciences that every schoolchild, from the primary grades through the secondary school, is required to make the physical sciences and mathematics the core of his program of studies. When a student graduates from the Soviet secondary school, he will have on his program at least two years of Calcalus.

"How do we propose to cope with this growing and powerful nation of more than 200,000,000 people? As things now stand, it would seem that we must engage in a destructive arms race. There is the alternative which was proposed by our Revolutionary Fathers, that which lays the basis for the third portion of our human triad, the Man-Man relation. The tragedy of our situation lies in what is going on in the world of Communism, that is, the deification of the Physical Sciences, just as the Christians deified the ethical premises found in the BIBLE. This deification of the Physical Sciences is most unfortunate for mankind because, in this deification process, we have a carryover of the dogma of the Medieval Mind from the physical sciences to the field of human relations. There is still the problem as to whether or not any of the social studies are worthy of the name of Science, studies such as Sociology, Economics, Psychology, Political Science, and Education. In saying this, I am in no sense discounting the significance of the social studies in our present-day culture. What is involved in the various social studies is an ethical commitment which ties these studies to a frame of reference that requires an understanding of their historical origin and development."

"Ron," said Bill, "how far would you go back for a justifiable analysis of our present culture pattern?"

"I would go back to the thinking of our Revolutionary Fathers," said Ron, "for it is in their thinking that we find the first real effort to develop a frame of reference that ties the three phases of our triad together. The thoughts expressed by these men had their roots in Greek Humanism as well as in the writings of various English and French authors. It was Francis Bacon who, in the NEW ATLANTIS (1627), pictured the great society in which the brotherhood of man was to be sustained by the achievements of science. Also, Jean-Jacques Rousseau held that the miseries of man were due to his departure from the demands of nature. One of Rousseau's deepest concerns was the way in which leaders of the Christian faith had enslaved the mind of man by the Doctrine of Revelation, by dogma, creeds, and miracles. As an advocate of Natural Religion, Rousseau was deeply concerned with the origins of society, for it was his conviction that there was need for many specific social reforms. It is to John Locke, however, that we must turn for an insight into the philosophical premises on which Jefferson rested his arguments for a free man in a free society.

"Just as Francis Bacon, in his classic THE GREAT IN-as have the leaders of the U.S.S.R., we have limited our thinking in the field of the sciences to a Cartesian Reductionism. By such, I mean that we have forgotten the mathematical premise that 'the whole is greater than the sum of its parts,' and have substituted a theory which reduces all theory to a particular thing. Although we have learned more and more about less and less, we have reached a point where we cannot see 'the woods for the trees!' "

"Ron Jervis," commented Bill Snyder, "I could not agree with you more. It is to Cartesian Reductionism that we owe most of the credit for doing away with the mysticism and fear of analysis which hampered our understanding of the natural world. Unfortunately, by applying this theory in our effort to understand the nature of man, we set aside the socio-cultural context in which man has evolved. By so doing, we eliminated the ethical and intellectual fame of reference which has evolved during the last two thousand years, a frame of reference not only fundamental to the democratic process, but to the humanizing of animal man. Our capitalistic free- enterprise economy, operating as it is today without any concern for the GENERAL WELFARE, is a major factor in the growth of violent crimes in our Nation."

"Bill," responded Ron, "the fact that our state universities have been partitioning off the arts and the sciences is a growing danger to our sense of unity as a people. With the growing power and influence of the Physical Sciences in our culture, as indicated by the development of the neutron bomb and the expansion of our industrial economy, there is little or no infusion of the spirit of the humanities which comes from a study of great literature and the arts. Likewise, those who delve into the arts are more often than not blind to the significance of the Sciences as a basis for human development. As a result, we have moved from a belief in the goodness and potentiality of our Nation to a fear of the growing power of communism as a way of life. Belief in the values of a knowledge of our heritage, and in the value of life on this earth, has given way to an erotic narcissism. Ignorance of history has become a marked characteristic of our people, while loss of faith in the role of Reason has been accompanied by a loss of faith in knowledge. Our affluence since World War II has only led to an impatient restlessness and boredom. Unless things can be turned around, and I doubt that they will be, the bond that has held our people together will snap, and we will find ourselves in the throes of a Fascist state seeking a Holy War with the people of the Soviet Union, the end result of which will be a destruction of all that we have held dear in our beloved country."

"Ron," said Bill, "there is another possibility as to what will happen to us when the bond of freedom snaps. I am of the opinion that, if we continue to ignore the GENERAL WELFARE of our Nation, there is the chance of another revolution, and this time it will be a class war between the rich and the poor. If such does come about, the intellectuals will be divided between the left and the right, the liberals and the conservatives. It is a dubious matter to speculate as to who will come out on top. The forces of the left will ally themselves with our country's revolutionary heritage and the rights of the people; while the forces of the right will speak of patriotism, loyalty, and devotion to the Nation. Property rights and institutional authority will be the established cry of the conservatives. Since there will be an absence of cultural depth and national unity, if such a situation does arise, the military will split between the two groups and bring about a state of anarchy. With the breakdown of law and order, there will come into reality more violence and crime. Normal means of transportation and communication will give way to hunger and the spread of disease. The dreams and hopes of our Revolutionary Fathers will be forgotten amid the destruction and the killing that will come upon us."

"Bill," said Ron, "there are those who will say that we have lost our marbles since our retirement and that it is our age that has led us to the vision of a gloomy future. But is that really so? I think not. So many changes have taken place in our Nation since World War II which lead in the direction of our pessimistic conclusions that no other logical conclusion seems possible. Up to now, we have done nothing to correct these destructive trends. Let me call your attention to some of them:

"1. By the end of World War I Great Britain was no longer a world power, and, while we had the wealth and the power to take Great Britain's place, we did not have the leadership to assume that responsibility. As egoistic idealists, our politicians are not even competent to serve at a quality level.

"2. By the end of World War I, Communism had its roots deep in the soil of the U.S.S.R.. As time passed, this revolutionary system became a major challenge to what we call the Free World. Two nations now find themselves in competition for world leadership, and there is only one throne.

"3. The decline of the power of the British Empire and the growth of the Soviet Union, accompanied by two world wars, have caused our national debt to rise from roughly one billion dollars to one trillion dollars in 1981. At the same time, and during the same period, the number of millionaires in the United States rose from 36,000 in 1940 to 600,000 in 1981.

"4. A drastic cultural, social, and economic change came about in the United States during the period from 1914 to 1981, as a result of the shift from an agrarian to an urbanized society. People are no longer a product of the soil, as was true in all of our early history, but of the marketplace, of urban slums, and of decaying cities. Accompanying this change has come a growth in unemployment, in crime, and a pattern of increasing violence. It can be said that money and fear are increasingly the marked characteristics of an insecure people.

"5. After World War I the United States was no longer beckoning the poor of the World to our shores, yet the poor of the World were on the increase. This has led to an increasing number of illegal aliens, upsetting the stability of the U.S. economy and adding to the burden of maintaining law and order.

"6. Science, which was viewed by the founders of our country as a means of doing away with poverty, war, disease, and hunger, has become the agent of death in the twentieth century. Now we must make up our mind as to what we want — PEACE OR WAR, for what we prepare for is what we will get.

"7. In our change from an agrarian to an urbanized society,

there has been a breakdown in the structure of family life. Since the family, throughout the history of man, has been the major social institution for the care of the young, this breakdown is fraught with serious consequences for the future. Our present cultural condition points to something deeper when we note that the average marriage today lasts only three months, that the number of divorces each year equals the number of marriages, and that there is a virtual explosion in the number of illegitimate births. The tragedy of it all is that the kids are not getting the love and affection necessary to grow up as responsible human beings.

"8. Paralleling the decay of the family as a prime factor in the evolution of culture has come a disturbing increase in major crimes such as murder, rape, armed robbery, and arson, especially among the young. As a result, there is an accompanying breakdown of law and order. Corruption has become rampant at all levels of government, as aggression and the lack of respect for human life take over. All of this gives clear evidence that our concept of freedom is without a meaning and value frame of reference — no respect for human life — no responsibility for the GENERAL WELFARE — do as one pleases — and believe as one pleases. Aggravating this growing chaos in our society is the unethical lawyer who cares more about winning his case and about money than he does about JUSTICE.

"9. One of the most marked aspects of our situation is a general retreat from the reality of our times. This retreat has taken on several forms, but in general falls into three categories: (1) Religious; (2) Dope Addition and the Consumption of Alcohol; and (3) Entertainment. In the field of religion, those who have retreated call themselves Born-Again Christians. Then there is the so-called Moral Majority that seeks to take over the control of government and force all people to conform to their will. Among the young, there is the tendency to join a Jesus Cult. Such an escape from reality is a tragedy both for the parent and the individual. In trying to escape from the control of their parents, these young people are being brainwashed by conniving adults who are more interested in power control than in personal welfare."

"Ron," said Bill Snyder, "I find myself very sympathetic with the young teenagers. In trying to grow up too fast many of them are trying to escape through drugs, suicide, crime, sex, or just running away from home. What I detect is a gross failure on the part of the public school in helping these young people to adjust to our culture chaos. Not only is this true for their Jesus Cult tendencies, but in the way they have turned to dope and alcohol. While alcoholic indulgence is as old as the American culture, this tendency to drug addition has come about since the Vietnam War. I get the feeling that this war was a direct result of a sense of failure in our way of life, and was an attempt to bring about a sense of unity among our people. This excessive use of alcohol cuts across all of our professions. There is, for example, the congressman whose effectiveness is being destroyed by drunk-drunkness, or the medical doctor who is not only destroying his own body but is no longer able to help his patient. Nowhere is the effect of an over indulgence in the use of alcohol among our young people more evident than on our highways. Here, they daily kill each other off, along with thousands of innocent people, by excessive speed and head-on collisions.

"Tied up in with this excessive indulgence in the use of alcohol and that of drugs, we have this running away from reality by seeking big-time entertainment. Those who exploit this weakness in our people are aware of the fact that people respond more to the emotional situation than to the desire for understanding. Big money and a television set are the means by which the mind is captured. Pulpit oratory for the man of God takes over here as the most outstanding historical means of brainwashing. Next to the religious dogmatist in historical priority, we have the egoistic politician. It was in the days of ancient Greece and Rome that the politician first gained ascendancy in Western culture. Note how realistically Shakespeare dealt with the role of Mark Antony at the occasion of the death of Julius Caesar. What American school boy has not heard of Patrick Henry's speech 'Give me liberty or give me death.' Here again we note how the use of television is influencing the election of the President of the United States.

"Today these historic means of pulpit and political oratory

are being exploited by the corporate financing of cheap anti-intellectual television programs. The destructive effects of these programs are impossible to measure, but you can rest assured that they are enormous. As a retreat from the reality of our day, they are both corruptive and deceptive. Ninety per cent of the time they are a waste of the human mind. Even though these programs are said to be successful much of the time, that success is measured in terms of corporate profits rather than cultural growth. At the same time it is important to note how these corporations are able to deduct their expenditures for such programs from their federal income tax. Sad, but true, for in the end these products are always sold at a higher price.

"That area of corporate financing of entertainment which has been most detrimental to the educative efforts of the public school is in the field of athletics. Here the negative attitude of the people toward the intellectual role in our culture is increasingly evident. Big money paid to and received by those involved in these programs, when placed side by side with the salaries of teachers and college professors, becomes the ultimate measure of value in our culture. Today, our state universities are recruiting many high school graduates, who are only borderline academically speaking, because of their physical brawn. They even hire Ph.D counselors to tutor their players.

"While big money so used is without doubt the most culturally detrimental factor of all the means used in financing our T.V. programs, there are negative effects that should be noted. Big-time gambling always accompanies these competitive games. Gambling and the excessive use of alcohol go along with the bribing of public officials and athletes. Today, it is not uncommon for the athlete to become a victim of the dope habit."

"Bill," said Ron Jervis, "I am becoming more and more convinced that the decay of the free-enterprise way of life is a marked characteristic of our present day culture pattern. In this respect, I see no relation between Adam Smith's concept of the free-enterprise system and what we have in our corporate economy. The thing that has changed the picture so drastically is the mechanization of our pattern of thinking and the power being exercised by corporate wealth. Adams Smith thought in terms of individuals, not in terms of groups. What would you say, Bill?"

"Ron," said Bill, "in the light of what you have just said, how could it be otherwise? Actually, there is little hope, in my judgment, that the trends in our culture can be modified into a more positive and humane direction. While organized labor is being held responsible for the high cost of our industrial products, I note that our corporation heads are receiving salaries ranging from $300,000 to $2,400,000 a year. As I see it, our economic problem is closely related to the fact that corporatism has grown up in this country since 1870 without any ethical or intellectual responsibility to the GENERAL WELFARE. The one aspect of our economy today that is not in trouble is in the luxury items, which indicates a failure to tax the wealthy in keeping with the needs of our people. All of which is enough to make Adam Smith turn over in his grave. The mechanical law of supply and demand can not work as its advocates say it should when it is being controlled and manipulated by those of wealth and power. Compare the way the automobile factories were closed down during the Depression of the 1930s with what happened to the farmer in the same period. Adam Smith was a friend of the laboring man of his day, not the supporter of a wealthy class. It was the accumulation of wealth in the hands of a few that caused Adam Smith to oppose the tie-up between wealth and government. Using the money of the federal government to bail out Lockheed and Chrysler when they were approaching a state of bankruptcy has little to do with the free-enterprise idea of economics. What we have in our country, with this gross abuse and false interpretation of free-enterprise capitalism, is an example of our lack of respect for the intellectual life.

"It is at the point of a lack of respect for social knowledge and a commitment to the GENERAL WELFARE that our free-enterprise system is breaking down. What we have developed is an invisible enterprise, estimated to represent, in corporate wealth, a power in excess of $150,000,000,000. This accumulated wealth is in excess of that of either the Chemical, Auto, Electric or Gas Utilities. What this invisible enterprise represents can be summed up in two words — ORGANIZED CRIME.

"The power of organized crime in the United States lies at the heart of the decay of free-enterprise capitalism. In organized crime we have a growing power which is free of government regulation and thus pays no taxes of any kind. What is so shocking about all of this exposure is that the government is so helpless in controlling the activities of such criminality.

"One example of what is going on in our country is illustrated in what the Pennsylvania Crime Commission found after its investigation of the activities of one man. Franklin Miller was running a numbers racket in Charter, Pennsylvania from which he grossed as much as $30,000 a day or roughly $10,000,000 a year. To create a front to cover his gambling operations, he began to use his profits in legitimate business enterprises, such as buying up rundown houses and renovating them. In addition, he bought four liquor bars, a fuel-oil distribution system, and an auction and salvage business. From all of these activities he was earning up to $140,000,000 a year until he was arrested for gambling and sentenced to prison for a period of only eleven months. As of the present, it is estimated that eighty-five percent of those who commit a crime go free."

"Bill," said Ron Jervis, "you would think that with all of these monumental problems facing us, we would have made some revolutionary changes to try to improve our daily operations, especially in our educational system in both the public school system and in our state universities. It is in our educational system, more than anywhere else, where creative intelligence could play a significant role. Yet such has not been the case, and I would guess that the reason lies in the Politics of Power. Sadly enough, our so-called 'Will of the People' is nothing more than what the vested interests in the Nation want it to be. In modern times, the nearest that we have come to a creative approach in our cultural life was in the Era of Franklin D. Roosevelt. Since that time, we have reverted back to a traditional way of reacting and thinking. McCarthyism has become the dominant way of our reacting and thinking about our critical social issues. Our anti-Communist way of responding to the issues which confront us is contributing to a growing loss of respect for our government. The climax of all this negativism came with WATERGATE during the Nixon administration. Loss of respect for an AUTHORITY FIGURE provides the background for NIHILISTIC TERRORISM. How else explain the attempted assassination of a President of the United States, the head of the ancient Christian Catholic Church, and the murder of the head of the Egyptian government, all in the year 1981? Power and personal gain continue to be the compelling motive in our public life."

"Ron," said Bill, "no man lives or grows up in a vacuum. As to the nature of self, there is the organic genetic base, but, along with the significance of the DNA, there is the cultural environment in which we develop a mind, as distinguished from brain. It is for this reason that what is going on in our Western civilization is so detrimental to the development of the self. As Adams Smith spelled it out in his THE THEORY OF MORAL SENTIMENTS, 'Bring a man into society, and he can see how others react toward him.' In the final analysis, individuals accumulate wealth to be approved by others. Capitalist man has a self, but it is a self which belongs to society. In our free urban culture today, the end result for the great majority of the people is the spreading of poverty, unemployment, and crime. We have nothing left which provides a sense of dignity and personal worth. In all of this decaying situation, our public schools, including our state universities, have little or nothing to offer."

As Ron Jervis made his way home that afternoon, he could not help but reflect on what was happening to the Nation that he loved so well. Was the United States of America headed in the same direction as the Roman Empire? The parallels of the two nations were disturbingly similar. It is a tragedy of major proportions when a beautiful ship like the Titanic goes down, but it is more than a tragedy when a great nation like the Roman Empire dies. There are those who believe that every nation is destined to die, just as a man dies; yet there is surely a creative way of renewing and giving a nation new birth. That way must be through creative intelligence, supported by an ethical commitment to one's fellowman. This our forefathers were deeply conscious of when they set forth the BILL OF RIGHTS OF THE CONSTITUTION OF THE UNITED STATES. They realized full well that a new power group which could compete with the organized power of the church dogmatists was vitally necessary. It was therefore the state universities that would provide the necessary leadership to overcome the blindness of Orthodox Christians. Was Christian dogma not the cause of the most violent wars in the history of Western civilization? Only by bringing into being leaders of government, with open minds, could the world be saved from the destructive forces of an atomic war, yet, because of our failure to follow the mandate of our Revolutionay Fathers, we face the possible annihilation of the human race.

At this point, Ron Jervis determined that he would make one final effort toward getting a constructive program started on the university campus. So, upon his arrival at home, he picked up his phone and called his friend.

"Bill," said Ron, "since our discussion at the lunch hour, I have been thinking about the possibility of one final course of action to get something started here on our campus. What would you think of our getting several faculty members together, men with whom we have been discussing the ROLE OF THE STATE UNIVERSITY IN A FREE SOCIETY, to see whether or not we can come to a consensus on a line of social action that should be taken by this University."

"Ron," replied his friend, "I would be happy to participate if you can get a sufficient number of people together, but I am not overly optimistic about the outcome. Don't forget that the great majority of our faculty are not only academically conservative, but do not think in the ethical and intellectual framework that we do."

"Well, Bill," said Ron, "it will at least be worth the effort. I will contact you when and if I get the fellows lined up for a time and place of our meeting."

After his talk with Bill, Ron got down to the business of lining up the people that he thought should be invited to the proposed meeting. After some hard thinking, he determined that he would invite the following men to a meeting, to be held on the Friday evening of the following week in the Faculty Lounge of the Student Union Building at 8 p.m.

Dr. Amos Spears, Professor of Biology,
Dr. Allan Sprague, Professor of Physics,
Dr. William Dean, Professor of Chemistry,
Dr. Hugh Drummond, Professor of Psychology,
Dr. Steve Ryan, Professor of Philosophy,
Dr. George Mangus, Professor of Sociology,
Dr. Robert Reynolds, Professor of Anthropology,
Dr. David Lucas, Professor of Political Science,
Dr. Loren Kaiser, Professor of Economics,
Dr. Harry Ackerman, Professor of American History,
Dr. Frank Ruffner, Professor of Secondary School Administration,
Dr. Larry Egan, Professor of Physical Education,
Dr. John French, Professor of Curriculum and Instruction,
Dr. William Snyder, Professor of English Literature.

All of these men were those with whom Ron Jervis, over a period of many years, had become good friends. While they were not in agreement on many of the issues affecting the welfare of the Nation, they had a mutual respect for each other's point of view. Ron's telephone call to each of these men proved to be very productive, for each man agreed to attend the meeting at the suggested time and place. Having secured permission to use the Faculty Lounge at the agreed time, Ron now set about to determine for himself what issues were to be considered. When the meeting did take place, Ron took the initiative in beginning the discussion.

"Gentlemen," said Professor Jervis, "as you know, Bill Snyder and I, over a period of many years, have been wrestling with the problem of the ROLE OF THE STATE UNIVERSITY IN A FREE SOCIETY. At different times we have called upon each of you for your suggestions and ideas. Of recent date, it seemed wise to get all of you together to try to form some kind of Hegelian Synthesis from our discussions. It is fair to assume that there is no significant difference between us on the origin of the state university, or as to why it was created. There are, however, understandable differences between us on whether or not there has been a betrayal by those who have been responsible for its operation. As for this occasion, we can at least identify our differences, and delineate our hopes, for the coming years. All of you have, at one time or another, expressed deep concern about our present situation, and the responsibility of the state university to the national welfare. As a beginning, Dr. Sprague, how do you view the scientific movement in relation to our growing crisis?"

"Professor Jervis," replied Professor Sprague, "it is only in recent years that I have been anything more than a subject matter specialist. I now find myself seeking to better understand the relation between the study of Physics and the American culture. This has led me to a search for the roots of the scientific movement in the Western World. What I have found is a blending of Babylonian Astrology with Aristotelian Philosophy at the time of the Italian Renaissance. It was this blending that provided a frame of reference for the development of the Physical Sciences, and especially that of Physics."

"Professor Sprague," asked Professor French, "in contrast with the origin of the scientific movement, what do you understand as to the nature of the prevailing belief of our people on the role of science in our culture?"

"Professor French," replied Professor Sprague, "the predominant thought of the people at the time of the Italian Renaissance was rooted in Christian theology, especially a belief in personal salvation based on faith against knowledge. This belief had its origin in the declining years of the Roman Empire and, while rooted in the legends of the Jewish people, was of a socio-revolutionary nature in its origins. A major change came about in the doctrine with the influence of Neo-Platonic thought, at which time the man Jesus was mystically converted into a Christ, and there was a shift to the doctrine of OTHERWORLDLINESS. In due time the Bishop of Rome became the head of the faith. With the support of the Nobility and the decline of the Roman Empire, the power of the Catholic Church became absolute. This is illustrated in the way in which Galileo, Servetus, Bruno, Copernicus, and Tycho Brahe were persecuted. It was the work of these, and other creative scientists, that laid the ground work for what Andrew D. While has characterized as the WARFARE BETWEEN SCIENCE AND THEOLOGY IN CHRISTENDOM."

"If I understand you correctly, Professor Sprague," said Professor Reynolds, "we have been trying to live in two Irreconcilable frames of reference, the one Otherworldly, as based on the Christian Dogma of personal salvation, the other naturalistic, as based on the theory of creative intelligence. Since Christian Dogma holds to the premise 'He that eateth of the fruit of the tree of knowledge shall be damned,' how do you explain the wholesale acceptance of the Physical Sciences by the American people?"

"That conclusion," commented Professor Jervis, "leads us to the cause of the Revolution of '76. I think that there should be no doubt that the leaders sought to create a new frame of reference by taking the ethical commitments found in the NEW TESTAMENT and placing them in a naturalistic frame of reference. Through creative intelligence operating through the open mind, men such as Benjamin Franklin, Thomas Jefferson, and Thomas Paine sought to bring into being a Nation where 'all men are created free and equal.' "

"Professor Ackerman," said Ron Jervis, "you state the case very well. In what you have said we find two reasons why they supported the establishment of a state university: (1) to lay the ground work for a new type of leadership, especially to fill the offices of government; (2) to provide a power force which could overcome the control which the Ministers of God had held over the people of the Western world for 1800 years. It is important to note that to achieve their purpose they promoted a significantly different program of studies for the university."

"Professor Jervis," commented Professor Dean, "I am now beginning to understand the relation between your cultural evolutionary theory and the study of the Physical Sciences. But where does the role of the College of Education fit into this picture?"

"I think that I can throw some light on your question, Professor Dean," said Professor Drummond. "In every teaching situation there is the problem of ends and means relations. As a psychologist, I am concerned with the quality of the means. What is involved here is the scientific method of teaching a given subject to a given individual. It is out of a need for the development of a scientific method of teaching that the College of Education came into being. I must add that, in any given teaching situation, there is a need for understanding the nature of the individual that is being taught. To me teaching involves, not only the matter of knowing a subject, but likewise knowing what makes an individual tick, and using the best possible method of getting your instruction across to the student."

"Professor Drummond," said Professor Ryan, "it is at this point that I find myself disagreeing most definitely with your so-called Education Professors. Man by his nature is a rational animal, and it was this conviction that went into the thinking of our Revolutionary Fathers. This being so, if a Professor knows his subject, all he has to do is to present his subject matter clearly and distinctly. When so done, the burden of the proof falls upon the student."

"Professor Ryan," replied Professor Jervis, "this is the place where you and I part company. All the evidence that I can get my hands on, in the field of the biological sciences and otherwise, clearly indicates that man is only potentially rational."

"Professor Ryan," spoke up Professor Spears, "I find myself in complete agreement with Professor Jervis. As a Biologist, I would hold that the human mind has developed over a period of many centuries from an unconscious to a conscious animal. There is no more justification for assuming that a man has a soul at birth than has a dog, a horse, or a cow. When born, the organism man is only another little animal, not a human being. Many of these deformed creatures never become human in any ethical or intellectual sense. Today, there is new evidence of what constitutes a human being, as compared with the thinking of an Aristotelian. With the new knowledge that has come about through the development of the physical and the biological sciences, and the social studies, we now know that the mind is an acquired socio-cultural entity and, in this sense, must be distinguished from the brain. Children who are born into great wealth suffer in mind growth because they are deprived of the challenge which comes only from a meaning and purpose in life. Aristotle's form-matter hypothesis is a great milestone in the evolution of thought, for it provides us with a realization of the significance of a meaning and value frame of reference, no meaning without form, and no value without purpose. Just as the Physical Sciences evolved from the Ptolemaic Theory to Copernicus, from the Copernican Theory to that of Sir Issaic Newton, and from the Newtonian Theory to that of Albert Einstein, so is it possible for us to move toward the development of a quality mind out of the religious, philosophical, and scientific background of our common heritage."

"Professor Spears," commented Professor Ryan, "I can appreciate what you have just said about our need for a quality mind, but you know as well as I do that it is the Orthodox Christian who blotted out the humanistic philosophical naturalism of the ancient Greek philosophers. That being so, how can you find anything of constructive value in the Christian tradition?"

"Professor Ryan," responded Professor Spears, "I think most if not all of those present will agree with you that Orthodox Christianity stands out as a major roadblock to the growth of a scientific mind in our Nation, but that does not support the assumption that a concept of reality, which has its roots in the intuitive nature of man, is not fundamental to the growth of a free mind. On the contrary, the very essence of creativity, which is an indelible ingredient of human progress, has its roots in what Albert Einstein referred to as 'a sense of oneness with the universe.' On the positive side, Christianity did supply the ethical component of the Jewish Prophets, of which the Greek naturalists were deficient. In this respect, intellectual dogmatism is just as vicious as religious dogmatism when it comes to the problem of human growth and cultural evolution. Actually, our allegiance to the free-enterprise economy is just as dogmatic as the Communist's allegiance to Marxism."

"Professor Spears," spoke up Professor Kaiser, "don't you think that you have overstated your case when you compare capitalistic dogmatism with Communistic dogmatism? At least we can say that we believe in freedom, which is certainly not true of the Communist."

"Not at all, Professor Kaiser," replied Professor Spears. "But since you do not agree with me, I wonder what our Political Scientist has to say in reply to your question."

"Professor Kaiser," responded Professor Lucas, "I agree with Professor Spears on the matter of dogmatic capitalism and dogmatic Communism. Keeping in mind Aristotle's form-matter hypothesis, I would say that freedom is not a monopoly of either the capitalist or the Communist, but a question of how it is defined in either of the two categories. Communists emphasize the significance of form to the GENERAL WELFARE, whereas capitalists are atomistically individualistic in their thinking. Freedom cannot be defined in a vacuum any more than GENERAL WELFARE can be limited to a frame of reference. We are constantly covering up the tyranny of wealth with our so-called allegiance to freedom, but freedom to what? Historically speaking, we know that accumulation of wealth has always been tied in with POWER, which, in turn, ends up by destroying the creative process which is the very essence of freedom. Note that, it was the opinion of Adam Smith that a free capitalistic system could not survive unless grounded in an ethical commitment to the GENERAL WELFARE, and with a sense of intellectual responsibility. Across the world of today we are being viewed as a Nation of cutthroats and thieves. Interestingly enough, both Franklin and Jefferson feared that such might be our ultimate fate."

It was visiting Professor Frank Ruffner, Ron Jervis's friend from out of the past, that now spoke up. "Gentlemen, I have enjoyed listening to you fellows discuss the vitally important subject THE ROLE OF THE STATE UNIVERSITY IN A FREE SOCIETY. As I see it, no way of life is any better than the individuals who make it. If ethical commitment and intellectual responsibility are fundamental to the constructive use of power in a free society, and I believe they are, then we in the field of public education have surely betrayed those who founded this Nation. There is the crucial question of how we got this way, before we can proceed to a resolution of our dilemma, that of reordering our pattern of thinking."

"I agree with Professor Ruffner," spoke up Professor Egan. "I am convinced that we need more understanding of how we got into our present crisis situation. To the concept of a nation of cutthroats and thieves, we could add that of a nation of beggars. We are a people of violence with little sense of the meaning and value of the evolution of the human mind. In the place of shared meanings, we have substituted a narcissistic individualism, thus creating a self that seeks only to satisfy its endless desires. Such desires have been cast in the realm of the sacred, but there are times when the suppression of these desires can be noble and inspiring. Note how a commercialized form of entertainment in this University has been substituted for the physical well-being and education of all of our students."

"Professor Egan, as a Professor of Sociology, I could not agree with you more," said Professor George Mangus. "The contradictions that are present in our thinking about self-fulfillment are driving us further and further apart. Because of such, we are faced with a period of bitter social conflict, a polarization of our people, with little sense of those values which are fundamental to the welfare of our Nation, especially those of unity and purpose. That we are a nation of violence is indicated by the fact that, in the Western world of 1980, we had 10,728 handgun deaths, whereas the nation closest to us, Israel, had only 58. On the international scene, the absence of a stable world leadership has opened the way for the freelance barbarian, when all that we have to offer is more deadly weapons of human destruction. The collapse of the control of religion, the family, and civil authority is indicated in the vigor with which our young people engage in aggressive destructive acts. The reason why this energy is not being directed toward creative acts in human development is traceable to the failure of our state universities to provide that quality of leadership which the occasion demands. We have turned our backs on our Heritage of Freedom, the foundation pillar on which this Nation was built."

"Gentlemen," responded Professor Synder, "let us see how much progress we have made in our discussion up to this point. I would say that there is general, if not unanimous, agreement in respect to (1) the lack of form in our culture, (2) the absence of a meaning and value frame of reference, which is necessary to provide the guidelines for a free society, (3) a schizophrenic difference between the quality of MIND demanded of those who are responsible for the development of the Physical Sciences and the Christian Orthodox mind of the majority of our people. (4) an atomistic capitalistic economy which fails to provide the needed sense of unity and purpose in our culture, (5) a narcissistic individualistic tendency which dictates the expression of our every desire, regardless of its negative or positive effect, (6) a neglect of the pattern of meaning and value laid down by our Revolutionary Fathers which integrated the religious, philosophical, and scientific achievements in Western civilization down to the nineteenth century. (7) the establishment of a state university which was to provide a new kind of leadership for our people, especially in the halls of government. Given these conclusions, why have we failed so miserably in carrying out the mandates of those who had such great faith and hopes for our future?"

"Professor Snyder," replied Professor Spears, "I believe that one reason for our failure lies in our limited understanding of man's nature. It is only during the past century that we have come to even a partial understanding of the origin and nature of man, of how his body functions and the nature of his Mind."

"Much is to be said for Professor Spears' thinking," said Professor Drummond. "There is a world of difference between the knowledge that is available to us and the use that we make of it. I would say that a second reason for our failure is the fact that we have never financed our public schools at a level that would provide for the quality of education that we seek. Paying teachers less than garbage collectors is no way to achieve a socially intelligent people. Education is our major problem. We need a reordering of our values by placing EDUCATION AT THE HEAD OF THE LIST."

"I can go along with what you have said about our educational need, Professor Drummond," said Professor Lucas. "I would want to clarify the issue, however, by adding a third reason as to why we have failed. This reason lies in the way in which our professions operate. During the past one hundred years or more, our professionals have assumed a role of leadership in our society, but how do they operate? While there are significant differences between them, all but one of them give full expression to the atomistic nature of our capitalistic society. Only the PROFESSION OF TEACHING can be said to identify with the concept of the GENERAL WELFARE. As to which operates in the most destructive way, I would say that it is the PROFESSION OF LAW. It is significant to note the differences between the lawyers of our day and those who have been identified with the founding of this Nation. There are exceptions to be sure, but the great majority of our lawyers are interested only in winning and making money. Ethics and intellectual responsibility be damned. The end result is a loss of faith in our government (since lawyers make up most of our government officials)."

"Professor Ruffner," inquired Professor Mangus, "in the light of your many years of directing the education of public school administrators, how do you account for the poverty level at which our public schools are operated when compared with the amount of money which is poured annually into the professions of Law and Medicine?"

"I think that you have the answer to your question, Professor Mangus, in what Professor Lucas has just said," responded Professor Ruffner. "The Professions of Law and

Medicine operate in an atomistic capitalistic economy, whereas the Profession of Teaching operates in our indifferent consideration for the GENERAL WELFARE. Because teachers operate under the banner of the GENERAL WELFARE, they are not permitted to strike as are the industrial workers. Doctors of Medicine differ from Lawyers in that they are honor bound to seek to save the life of the patient, whereas lawyers always seek to win as do politicians and athletes. Note that COMMERCIALIZED ENTERTAINMENT is one thing and EDUCATION is another. Commercialized entertainment involves excitement, feeling good, and a lack of effort by sitting back and looking on; whereas EDUCATION involves growth of mind, self-discipline, effort, and above all ethical commitment and intellectual responsibility to the GENERAL WELFARE. Much of the effect of COMMERCIALIZED ENTERTAINMENT is self-destructive, in that it induces a retreat from reality, and encourages an indulgence in the excessive use of alcohol, drugs, sex, and other forms of self-abuse, possibly criminal tendencies."

"Professor Jervis," interjected Professor Ackerman, "what you have just said leads me to a fourth reason as to why we have failed to promote a society of free men and women. That reason lies in the way we have intepreted the DEMOCRATIC WAY OF LIFE. By defining democracy as the rule of the majority, we have negated, not only the need for an ethical commitment to the common good, but the need for an intellectual responsibility to our fellow man. We have reduced our way of life to the lowest common denominator, that of cold unadulterated power. In this respect, our concept of DEMOCRACY has become nothing more than FASCISM. Note how the great mass of German people worshipped at the shrine of Adolf Hitler. It is important at this point to note how our culture changed during the course of the nineteenth century. Since the state university was born in the Southern states, its future was doomed as a free institution because of the power of the Southern planter and the drift toward the War Between the States over the issue of slavery. The state university movement spread, first to the states in the Northwest, and then to the West. In this spread, the cause of the founders was lost in the developing frontier. There is good reason to note that the first monument that was placed at Jefferson's grave is now on the campus of the University of Missouri, the first state university west of the Mississippi River. On this monument we read, 'Author of the Declaration of Independence, of the first Statute for Religious Freedom in Virginia, and Founder of the University of Virginia.'

"With the growth of Corporate Power Capitalism, the economy of the Nation shifted to the Northeast where it became a single power force until organized labor became a major source of opposition in 1937. Since the close of World War I, we as a people have been on the defensive with respect to our way of life. Confronted on the one hand by the rising power of the U.S.S.R. and on the other by a terrorist Fascism, at no time in our history has there been a greater need for facing up to the challenge presented by our Revolutionary Fathers. Unfortunately, that challenge calls for a quality of WORLD LEADERSHIP that we do not now possess. It is because of the lack of such leadership that we find ourselves floundering in many destructive ways, ways such as lining up with the nihilistic forces of the RIGHT all around the world, as if they were to be preferred to the Communistic forces of the LEFT. Such a policy is definitely a retreat from our heritage of freedom and a reliance upon Corporate wealth and power. What is needed above everything else, is to get our people to wake up to the explosive nature of the situation. If such is not done within the coming decade, our future as a free society will come to an inglorious end."

"Gentlemen," said Professor Jervis, "I think that Professor Ackerman has struck a true and resounding note for all of us, especially in terms of the direction which we must take. In so saying, let me add one final statement — to turn our backs on the SCIENTIFIC MOVEMENT would be truly self-destructive. The negative Fascist power forces are in the saddle today all over the world, with the most deadly weapons ever conceived by the mind of man. The fault lies not in the realm of science but in the minds of those who control the beliefs of the great masses of mankind. From the wisdom we have gained on the nature of man, we now know that we are emotional, subjective creatures, not mere machines, and that we live in and through our mental constructs of reality. The creative role in life always begins with the art form, and is sustained by the development of the human mind. When supported by the tested thought of the scientist, it becomes knowledge."

"Professor Jervis," replied Professor Dean, "I and my scientific associates fully concur in what you have just said about the need for support of the scientific mind by the people of the world. Unfortunately, that support is not apparent in our public schools. In general, there are few teachers, and even college professors, who have any conception of the scientific process of discovery, or of the great need for creative thought. What is needed is more rigorous education in such fundamentals as a precise use of English as well as the scientific knowledge which is used in our culture. There is something drastically deficient in our culture when only one student out of six takes any mathematics or science beyond the 10th grade. This being the case, important decisions are being made by those who have little or no knowledge of the role of science in our society. It is because of the shortcomings of our teaching that our people think that scientists work by the addition of one factor to another. As you have indicated, the scientist works much like the artist in that his discoveries are derived intuitively. It is by the intuitive process that new connections are perceived and the material reorganized in the mind. Above all, one must see through the contradictions that present themselves in order to arrive at a meaningful pattern of experience."

"I would like to add one final comment to our experience of this evening," spoke up Professor Ruffner. "I have known Professor Jervis over a period of most of his professional life, and I want to compliment him on our achievement of this evening. I know that most of you feel and think as I do, that, although no evolution will take place as a result of what has just been said, we have engaged in the process of creative thought, which is the foundation of human progress. By all means, let me thank each of you for the opportunity of attending this fruitful session of intellectual food and thought.

"From our discussion, it has been brought home to me how much we have betrayed those who founded the state university. Our history of the past one hundred and fifty years established the fact that we have failed to provide the leadership necessary for a free society. In so failing, we have not bridged the gap between the intellectual and the people which was supposed to come about through the public school program. As a result, our people have been, and are, increasingly frustrated in the realms of our economic and political life.

"We have an invisible university in our think tanks, seminars, conferences, and workshops, but this university has not provided our people with a meaningful image of our new age, a frame of reference in which they could identify the varied events which have come down upon them. Leadership is especially needed when it comes to faith in such spiritual resources as freedom, creativity, and scientific genius. But where do we find ourselves? At home, we see a coming collision between church and state. If we had followed through with the challenge of our Revolutionary Fathers, the minds of our people would have developed a faith in their heritage and in the knowledge that we have of man and his universe. Abroad, the poverty of our leadership is especially reflected in our failure to communicate on a constructive level with the leaders of the Soviet Union."

As Professor Ruffner concluded his remarks, Ron Jervis noted that the hour of midnight was coming up. Knowing that little could be accomplished at such a late hour, he called for the motion to adjourn. The motion made, and the vote for adjournment being unanimous, each of the men arose, and, as some of those present began an informal discussion with each other, Ron turned to his friend with the comment, "Thanks, Frank, it was good of you to respond to my invitation. We have traveled a long road together, and, although we have grown old in time, we shall continue our efforts to bring about the true purpose of THE ROLE OF THE STATE UNIVERSITY IN THE AMERICAN CULTURE."

ADDENDA

If Thomas Jefferson were alive today, he would be saying to us:

1. You have substituted an *Aristocracy of Wealth* for an *Aristocracy of Intellect and Talent*.

2. You are using your *High Schools and Universities* as mere training grounds for *Professional Athletes*.

3. You have so tied your *Ethics to Church Dogmas* that you are incapable of making *Independent Moral Judgments*.

4. You have become so *Anti-intellectual* in your non-thinking that you are rapidly becoming *Anti-scientific* in policy decisions affecting the *General Welfare*.

5. You are so addicted to the *Role of Power and Mechanization* in your everyday life that you no longer sympathize with the *Poor and Down Trodden*.

6. Your *Concept of Freedom as License* has destroyed its significance as a *Creative Force in Human Progress*.

7. You have reduced the *Free-Enterprise System* to nothing more than a means of gaining *Wealth at the Expense of Your Fellow Man*.

8. You have so warped and distorted your *Heritage of Freedom* that it has become a *Whipping Boy for Vested Interests.*

9. You are so much a victim of *Commercialized Athletics* that you no longer have any respect for *Creative Labor.*

10. Your ignorance of your *Historical Culture* has left you adrift in a *Sea of Cultural Chaos.*

11. Your *Narcissistic Individualism* has deprived you of the significance of the *Social Self.*